JESUS:
A MAN FOR OTHERS

HOW HE INTERACTED WITH THE PEOPLE WHO KNEW HIM

JESUS:
A MAN FOR OTHERS

HOW HE INTERACTED WITH THE
PEOPLE WHO KNEW HIM

By the author of
The Mystical Sense of the Gospels

James M. Somerville

Scranton: The University of Scranton Press

Library of Congress Cataloging-in-Publication Data

Somerville, James M.
  Jesus : a man for others : how he interacted with the people who knew him
/ by James M. Somerville.
    p. cm.
  Includes bibliographical references and index.
  ISBN 1-58966-067-6 -- ISBN 1-58966-059-5 (pbk.)
  1. Jesus Christ--Biography--Public life. 2. Jesus Christ--Friends and associates. 3. Bible. N.T. Gospels--Criticism, interpretation, etc. I. Title.
BT340.S66 2003
232.9--dc22   2003064540

Distribution:

The University of Scranton Press
445 Madison Avenue
Scranton, PA 18510
Phone 1-800-941-3081
Fax 1-800-941-8804

PRINTED IN THE UNITED STATES OF AMERICA

CONTENTS

Part Six: The Passion

Part Seven: Resurrection

PREFACE

I n the eyes of the evangelists and the first followers of the Way, Jesus was seen as a man for others. He revealed to them what God was like and what God—in the beginning—intended the human to be. Even before the divinity of Jesus was proclaimed in the Fourth Gospel, the aim of the earlier evangelists is to reveal to the world the words and deeds of a man who spoke and acted as the embodiment of God's *hesed*, God's loving kindness and unconditional love. Like us in all things, Jesus served, nevertheless, as the sign and sacrament of God: *sign* because his life and teaching pointed beyond himself to the transcendent God; *sacrament* because in his life and teaching he was the immanent visible manifestation in time of the eternal, unchanging, invisible God.

In the pages that follow I have tried to capture Jesus as a moving image of God's immanence and transcendence in his encounter with his contemporaries: relatives, friends, enemies, disciples, women, the rich and the poor, the deaf, the crippled, and the blind, some with names, and some without names. A studied effort has been made to incorporate in this meditation virtually all that is known or can be deduced about the men and women in Jesus' life, beginning with his conception in his mother's womb to the time of his death and resurrection. What results is a "Life of Jesus" spelled out in terms of his encounter with a wide variety of people.

A recurring theme calls to mind the reasons why the evangelists are at pains to lay blame for the death of Jesus on "the Jews" without distinction. A second theme is summed up in the Hebrew word, *teshuvah*: Jesus' appeal to the lost sheep of the House of Israel to return home to traditional Jewish practices and values in an increasingly Hellenized world.

Method

Jesus: A Man for Others comprises twenty-nine chapters. Several of them appeared as essays over the past fifteen years in *The Roll*, a quarterly review of philosophy, science, and religion. Most chapters begin with a straightforward approach to the text, what the Jewish tradition speaks of as *peshat*, the literal or plain sense. The same material is then reviewed from the point of view of the critical historian and the textual exegete. Finally, going beyond the literal and critical interpretations, attention is given, where appropriate, to what are called the allegorical (*remez*), the homiletic (*derash*), and the mystical (*sod*) senses of the four Gospels. What the reader needs to know is when to adhere to the literal sense and when not. No one can dispense entirely with the literal sense upon which the others depend. The plain sense has to be basic as a point of departure, though it should rarely serve as a terminal point of arrival. The evangelists do not hoist a flag to inform us when they are providing us with historical fact or a considerably evolved interpretation of a fact.

Therefore, in reading the Gospels it is imperative to scrutinize them carefully and view them critically. Familiar passages often contain obiter dicta and subtle hints that can serve as clues that provide important historical information that may be easily overlooked. We have to be on the watch for a "catch 22" buried in the fine print of the Greek text.

For example, one might fail to notice that in John's Gospel those responsible for the arrest of Jesus in the Garden of Gethsemane were not primarily the temple police sent by the High Priest Caiaphas—they were there in a subordinate role—but a band of Roman soldiers, a cohort or *speira*, headed by a *chiliarchos*, a Roman officer, a tribune, who can be in charge of as many as a thousand men. This has enormous implications for determining who was ultimately responsible for the arrest and execution of Jesus.

Again, one might not be curious about the identity of the so-called Beloved Disciple whose name the evangelist studiously refuses to divulge. But if that disciple was, in fact, the apostle John, as tradition would have it, why did the author or redactors of the Gospel withhold the name of such an important witness, one so close to Jesus? And how could an uneducated man like John, described as unlettered or even illiterate in the Acts of the Apostles (4:13), create the highly sophisticated literary and spiritual masterpiece represented by the Fourth Gospel?

There are many puzzles in the Gospels, koan-like sayings and events that challenge scriptural sleuths to try to get past the obvious sense of a text and find out what might lie behind it. What is the possible meaning of the strange story about the cure of the Gerasene demoniac and the drowning of an entire herd of swine in the Sea of

Galilee? Did Judas commit suicide or was he murdered by being cast down "head first" (prēnēs) from a high cliff (Acts 1:18) as David Flusser suggests? Did the Samaritan woman whom Jesus met at the Well of Jacob really have five husbands, going on six, or was that story an allegory about something else? How many ploys does Luke in his Gospel attribute to Pilate in the Roman governor's improbable attempt to save Jesus from the cross? Did Jesus go about claiming to be the Messiah and hold that he would soon return in power, coming with the clouds of heaven and seated at the right hand of God (Mt 26:64)? I do challenge the idea that Jesus was foolish enough to plan a kingly entry into Jerusalem and incite a riot in the temple by turning over the tables of the money changers, two actions equivalent to suicide because they invited lethal retaliation by both the Roman and the Temple authorities.

The evangelists were not eyewitnesses to the events in Jesus' life. Writing after the fall of Jerusalem and living in distant parts of the Roman Empire, their accounts often reflect the circumstances and needs of the early Church rather than the outlook of Jesus before his resurrection. In any case, their information came to them second- or third-hand. Particular words, phrases, stories, and events are often given conflicting interpretations by different New Testament writers, usually with the state of affairs of their own day in mind. The Gospel writers did not limit themselves to reporting the events in Jesus' life as brute fact. They often shaded the facts to further their individual apologetic goals. Thus, the later evangelists edit the earlier ones and rearrange the sequence of events. In the Fourth Gospel the author's reasons for doing this are partly aesthetic, partly mystical, and partly political. The scriptures may be divinely inspired but in their composition they are human documents.

It is important for the sake of our spiritual and literary health to be aware of the genre of literature we are dealing with. This applies to the Christian Scriptures as well as the Hebrew Bible. One cannot say it often enough: the evangelists are more interested in presenting their readers with moral and theological lessons than in history in the modern, professional sense of the word. If they came upon a rabbinic story that seemed to express very well the outlook of Jesus, they did not hesitate to put it into his mouth. Two parables found only in Luke's Gospel may be of this nature: The Parable of the Prodigal Son (Lk 15:11–32) and the story about the Rich Man and Lazarus (Lk 16:19–31).

The Gospels are promotional literature, propaganda in the best sense of the word, written to confirm the faith of believers and convert the nonbaptized. Their central figure, though truly human, is without blemish or flaw. He is master of every situation, especially in the Fourth Gospel. If he has any faults, we are not told about them.

Although Jesus was a mystic who believed in and taught about immortality and life after death, he was not simply an otherworldly dreamer. He was, rather, a man primarily engaged in a social mission to the poor and disenfranchised members of his nation, one whose advertised kingdom was very much *in* the world. So the Romans may not have been entirely wrong when they perceived Jesus' "Kingdom of God" as an alternative and a threat to their imperial sovereignty. For, like the generality of men in their day, they saw little distinction between religion and politics.

And, as a matter of fact, far from being a relatively harmless apocalyptic eschatologist who was warning his flock about judgment and a cataclysmic end of the world, Jesus was preparing for the long haul. His teaching incorporated a way of life that was destined to outlive the Roman occupation of Palestine and even the Roman Empire itself. Whether or not this meant that Jesus anticipated the establishment of a new world religion and what turned out to be "The Church"—that is, a community separate from Judaism—is a question that has been answered in the affirmative by many Christians and in the negative by a significant number of academic scholars. At the very least, Jesus hoped to create a community, or commonwealth, in which sharing one's resources offered a long-range alternative to the kind of oppression and corruption that was common to both the Roman and the Jewish elite.

My own theory, shared by many others, is that the Jesus movement, which began as a Jewish sect, along with the Essenes, the Zealots, the Pharisees, the Sadducees, and the disciples of John the Baptist, managed, like Pharisaic Judaism, to survive the war with Rome and the destruction of the temple. The two "survivors" then became rivals, both striving for legitimacy within the confines of the Roman Empire. This rivalry between Pharisaic, that is, Rabbinic, Judaism was read back into the Gospel accounts. It took the form of the adversarial relationship between Jesus and the Pharisees. Eventually, what began as a Jewish movement became Gentile Christianity, and, since the victors write the history, "The Jews"—especially the Pharisees in the

Synoptic Gospels—become the enemy and are represented as seeking to kill Jesus (Mt 12:14; Mk 3:6).

The fact remains, however, that Jesus was executed by the Romans on a charge of high treason. To counter this liability, the Gospels try to make it clear, at a time when Jews were in disfavor with Rome because of their rebellion, that blame for the death of Jesus lay not with the Romans who were unwilling accomplices but with the Jews. What resulted has been twenty centuries of Christian anti-Judaism. In the fifteenth century the agents of the Spanish Inquisition combined religious anti-Judaism with *racial* anti-Semitism based on blood. This culminated, as we know, in the Holocaust during the past century. James Carroll's *Constantine's Sword: The Church and the Jews. A History* provides an outstanding, absorbing account of Christian anti-Semitism.

The anti-Judaism of the Gospels—an outlook that Jesus did not share—is a theme that runs through many of the pages in this book. However, it should not be allowed to obscure what the Gospels do tell us about Jesus as a radiant, visible image of God.

To conclude this brief preface, let me say that my approach to Jesus is not that of the literalist nor does it embrace the reductionism of the more extreme forms of historical criticism. Having spent the past twenty years in the latter camp, I have come to realize that one can kill the oysters without harvesting any pearls. More important than either a literal reading of a text or a rigid critical analysis is the individual's personal experience of the divine that the text often illumines and certifies. This seems to me to hold whether one is meditating on the Hebrew Scriptures, the Christian New Testament, the Bhagavad Gita, the Dhammapada, the Tao Te Ching, or the Koran. Though the author of the Second Letter to Timothy was not thinking in such broad terms, I would embrace his general outlook when he declares: "All scripture is inspired by God and is useful for teaching, for reproof, for correction, and for training in righteousness, so that everyone who belongs to God may be proficient, equipped for every good work" (2 Tim 3:16–17).

As this study progresses, the main events of Jesus' career will be addressed, each in its proper place: his baptism, his healing ministry, the Eucharist, his betrayal, his passion, his death, and various theories about the nature of his resurrection and continued existence. Critics and reviewers, depending on where they are coming from, are bound to find some of my proposals unsettling. I hope so. We need constantly to keep revisiting and reconceiving Jesus in the light of contemporary attitudes, asking new questions, and challenging not only the evangelists but also the scholarly and religious orthodoxies.

It seems appropriate to begin this study with what we know or can surmise about Mary and Joseph, the parents of Jesus. After treating them in considerable detail, the next two chapters are concerned with a pair of men who played a role in the story of Jesus' birth and infancy: the wicked King Herod and John the Baptist, who in his mother's womb recognized that Jesus was the one who was to come after him in birth and ministry but was preferred before him (Lk 1:43–44: Jn 1:15, 27, 30).

PART ONE:

People in the Infancy Narratives

Chapter One

MARY, THE MOTHER OF JESUS

Maria Avatara

A side from the infancy narratives in the Gospels of Matthew and Luke, the mother of Jesus is mentioned only once in passing in the three Synoptic Gospels (Mt 12:47; Mk 3:32; Lk 8:19). She appears twice in John's Gospel, and Acts tell us that she was present with the disciples of Jesus in Jerusalem after his ascension into heaven (Acts 1:14). Even in Matthew's infancy account Mary never speaks. So we learn very little about her from Matthew. And while she is mentioned twice in John's Gospel, she speaks only once, when she calls Jesus' attention to the fact that the wine supply at the wedding in Cana has given out. This single instance gives us some insight into Mary's character: she feels compassion for the embarrassed young couple whose wedding celebration will be spoiled at the end when it is discovered that there is no more wine. But when Mary stands at the foot of the cross, she says nothing according to the account in the Fourth Gospel (Jn 2:1–12; 19:25–27).

So, if we want to learn something about Mary as a distinct human being with certain kinds of personal traits, we have to turn to Luke's infancy story. Mary, a girl in her teens, appears to be prudent: she asks the angel the right questions. Also she appears to be charitable: she undertakes a long trip to be with her relative Elizabeth on the occasion of the birth of John the Baptist (Lk 1:39). It is then that Mary speaks her Magnificat, a canticle of thanksgiving for the benefits she has received, though scholars usually attribute the final form of the prayer to Luke, who adapts the wording from the prayer of Hannah in the First Book of Samuel (1 Sam 2:1–10).

With so little written about her, it turns out that we really do not know very much about Mary.[1] Yet from a devotional point of view and from subsequent theological elaborations, she has grown in stature in the minds and hearts of her devotees and in the liturgies of Catholic and Orthodox Christian Churches. Majestic basilicas have been built in her name. There are busy shrines in various countries where she is

1

honored and where people say they are cured of their diseases. Thousands of books have been written about her in scores of languages. The Rosary pays homage to her, and the Litany of Loretto lists her titles.

How can it be that Mary looms so large in the lives of millions upon millions of people when we know so little about her from the scriptures? In the following pages an attempt is made to trace the logic of Marian devotion as it has evolved and grown over the centuries. This attempt is undertaken from the historian's point of view, taking into consideration the human and emotional factors involved. The method seeks to explain how and why Marian devotion has achieved such importance in the Church.

Mary in the New Testament

The New Testament is not entirely silent about Mary's privileges. The angel of the Annunciation declares that Mary is "full of grace, or highly favored," (kecharitōmenē) implying that even though the redeemer has not yet come, she has already been pleasing to God (Lk 1:28). Also in the Book of Revelation the figure of "a woman clothed with the Sun," while it is meant to symbolize the true Israel, could also be read in an accommodated sense as referring to the person of Mary. For the text goes on to say, "And she [the woman] gave birth to a son, a male child, who is to rule all the nations with a rod of iron. But her child was snatched away and taken up to God and to his throne" (Rev 12:5). The male child who is to rule all the nations and who was taken up (ascended) to God is ostensibly Jesus, and the one who gave him birth would be his mother Mary. In Christian art, Mary is sometimes represented as the "Woman Clothed with the Sun." The moon is under her feet, and she is crowned by the twelve stars that represent the twelve apostles, or the twelve tribes of Israel. "Being clothed with the sun" is to bask in the glory, kavod, of her child. So, "the Woman," viewed as a community, stands for the new Israel, but taken as an individual, she has been interpreted to represent the mother of Jesus, clothed with the light reflected from her Son's glory.

John Henry Newman was a firm believer in the development of doctrine and theological insight. Certainly the divinity of Jesus becomes more and more explicit with each succeeding gospel writer, until we come to the Fourth Gospel, where there can be no misunderstanding about the intention of the author. A similar but considerably longer development has taken place in Mary's regard. Building on the few references to her in the gospels, she has grown to cosmic proportions in the eyes of those devoted to her. As with the words of the gospels, the wording of the United States Constitution has not changed since it was framed in the eighteenth century, beyond the addition of the Bill of Rights and the Amendments. But the Supreme Court's interpretation of the First, Second, and Fifth Amendments has evolved considerably over a period of two hundred years or more. The Catholic Church's view of Mary has undergone a similar evolution. Her original prerogative of being free from personal sins—because the early Church Fathers could not imagine that the Redeemer would be born of a sinner—evolved into her being preserved from the stain of original sin.

St. Augustine thought that all humankind had in some mysterious way sinned "in Adam," and that the contagion of Adam's sin had been passed on to all his descendents in virtue of the concupiscence connected with the act of generation.[2] Among other things, Augustine's position was based on a misinterpretation of the two Greek words, $\varepsilon\varphi\ \acute{\omega}$, in Paul's Letter to the Romans (Rom 5:12). He interpreted the text as declaring that sin and death come into the world and spread in virtue of the sin of one man, Adam, *in whom* all sin. The Douay Version perpetuates this error. The passage is obscure, but what Paul actually means is that death spreads abroad *because* all have sinned after the example of Adam. That is, human beings actively and consciously commit personal sins when they are old enough to distinguish between right and wrong.

Augustine's quasi-mystical interpretation has prevailed in the West. It imputes some kind of inherited sin and guilt passively received, even by the unborn, and prior to a person's opportunity to commit personal sin. Had anyone asked Peter or Paul whether he thought that Mary could be, or should be, or actually was preserved free from the guilt of Adam's sin from the moment of her conception in her mother's womb, he would have been puzzled. How could anyone, before he or she was born, be guilty of someone else's sin? Both Jeremiah and Ezekiel declare that God does not visit punishment for the sins of parents upon their children (Jer 31:29–30; Ezek 18:2–3). How then could Adam's sin have tainted the souls of others who did not even exist when he is reputed to have sinned hundreds of generations earlier? More to the point is the question of whether Adam and Eve are historic persons who, after committing the primordial sin whose guilt all have inherited, went on to generate three male children (no girls as potential brides are mentioned) and become the ancestors of all human beings living on the planet today. Could Mary have been conceived and born free from the inherited sin of two mythical ancestors who never existed?

Setting aside that particular koan, what the Myth of Eden is trying to tell us in storybook form is that there is an evil inclination in human beings, both male and female. And what the doctrine of the Immaculate Conception of Mary must mean is that she, like Jesus, did not inherit the evil inclination that is the common property of everyone else. Theologians and mystics offer arguments based on scripture, tradition, and reason in support of Mary's privileges, including her bodily assumption into heaven. In the final analysis, however, we are dealing here with matters of faith.

The Role of the Feminine in Devotional Practice

From the psychological point of view, many people would welcome a feminine religious icon to supplement their image of God, Father and Son, as male. Mary has filled that role for Christians down the ages. Short of granting her divine honors and within the limits set by the Church, men and women have been able to release their psychic energies by according to Mary a reverence greater than that paid to the saints and inferior to that paid to God. It is called *hyperdulia*. People in the Hindu tradition have not been so chary. Their avatars come in male and female pairs, as Rama and Sita, Krishna and Radha, and, in our own day, Sri Ramakrishna and his wife, Sarada Devi.[3]

A legitimate question to ask is whether the fullness of God can be adequately expressed by any finite symbol, even by an incarnation that also includes the female. In the patriarchal world of ancient Jewish messianism, it would not have occurred to the priests and prophets to think of the Messiah as having a female consort. Besides, any kind of divine incarnation was, and still is, all but inconceivable for Orthodox Jews for whom YHWH is one without a second, even though there is evidence that originally the Hebrew God had his *Asherah*, (female consort).[4]

Even for early Christians Mary, as a woman, would hardly be regarded as anything more than an instrument used by God to bring the future redeemer into the world. Nonetheless, short of being a divine avatar, Mary has functioned as a kind of available divinity. She is one to whom prayers are addressed, and while she does not die physically for sinners, the aged Simeon, holding the infant Jesus in his arms, announced to Mary, "And your own soul a sword shall pierce" (Lk 2:35). Luke's compassion is evident here because he wants to communicate that Mary dies inwardly when, as in John's later Gospel, the centurion's spear pierces the side of her Son on the cross (Jn 19:34).

As indicated above, there is a kind of elegant, holy logic connected with the mystery of Mary. Hers is the story of the emergence into daylight of a rather shadowy and peripheral figure in the Bible whose true dignity is revealed only gradually. She is represented as thinking of herself as but a servant girl, even the slave, *hē doulē*, of the Lord (Lk 1:38). In her Magnificat she praises God for having blessed her in spite of her abject lowliness (*tapeinosis*). By contrast, the Litany of Loretto hails Mary as "Queen of Angels," while at the Cathedral of Chartres in France and at Guadalupe in Mexico, the cult of Mary has replaced devotion to an earlier pagan goddess. There was a smooth transfer of allegiance without missing a beat. The shrines at Lourdes, Fatima, and Czestochowa in Poland owe their existence to her, and the Cathedral of Notre Dame is at the very heart of Paris.

Feminists continue to remind us that Christianity has for too long been dominated by the image of a male God who is often seen as a severe father figure, even a God of wrath and vengeance, one easier to fear than to love. Mary, the compassionate mother of Jesus, neutralizes the Jovine figure of an austere and exacting judge, replacing it with the image of a mother who has access to the tender and merciful side of God. In contrast, the Christ in Michelangelo's Last Judgment scene in the Sistine Chapel, with powerful condemning arm raised, sends sinners with contorted faces tumbling into the pit of Hell.

The Fourth Gospel

The author of the Fourth Gospel introduces Mary twice, once at the start of Jesus' public ministry, when he changes water into wine, and again at the end of his earthly life, when he dies on the cross in the presence of his mother, Mary. The clue to this deliberate positioning can be found in the fact that in both passages Jesus addresses his mother as "Woman," (*γύναι*), the vocative case, Anglicized as *gynai*, from which is derived the medical term "gynecology" (Jn 2:4; 19:26)). Adam also says of Eve: "She shall be called *gynē*" (Gen 2:23). It was largely on the basis of these texts that the early Fathers of the Church called Mary "the second Eve" or Eve's antitype. In her obedience to God's will she reversed Eve's disobedience, *mutans Hevae nomen*. In a Latin version of the greeting of the angel of the Annunciation, God says to Mary, "*Ave!*" or "Hail!" By a curious coincidence Ave is Eva's name spelled backwards, thus reversing Eva's name.[5]

When Mary at Cana implicitly asks Jesus to relieve the embarrassment of the young bride and groom after the wine has run out, Jesus turns to Mary and asks, "Woman, how does this concern me and you?" This is often interpreted as a rebuke, as though Jesus is saying, "What is there between you and me?" or "What have we in common?" or "You stay out of my business." But Jesus not only does what Mary asks, but he also overdoes it. Toward the end of a long marriage feast, he provides between fifteen and twenty-five gallons of very good wine.[6] Additionally, calling Mary "Woman" should not be taken as a belittling insult; it expresses her dignity as standing for half the human race, for all of womankind. Without passing judgment on later Marian developments, I think that the intention of the author of the Fourth Gospel is to envision Mary as a kind of universal feminine archetype who also embodies the ideal of spiritual motherhood.

At Cana Jesus says that his "hour" has not yet come. John, wants us to understand that Jesus' and Mary's hour comes when Mary, at least in spirit, stands at the foot of the cross and agonizes with her son. There, Jesus once again addresses his mother as "Woman." Referring to the Beloved Disciple who is present, he says to his mother, "Woman, here is your son." Then, turning to the Beloved Disciple, Jesus says, "Here is your mother." And the evangelist adds that from that "hour" the Beloved Disciple adopts her as his own mother.[7] By becoming mother of the Beloved Disciple, who stands for all the faithful, Mary, like Eve, whose name means Life (*Zoe*), thus becomes a source of Life for all who live in the Spirit through the grace of Christ. Mary, then, has inherited Eve's title on a purely spiritual level. She is the one whose sinless and immortal son, according to Genesis, would be victorious over the lying serpent of sin and death by striking it at its head where it is most vulnerable (Gen 3:15).

No doubt, a good bit of this exegesis, based as it is on the mythic story of the Garden of Eden, will seem strained to some. But much of it is backed by a long Catholic tradition that has learned how to live with myth and translate story into doctrine. It might serve as a good example of Christian *midrash*. The author of the Fourth Gospel is trying to tell us something he regarded as important in highly symbolic language. Or why would it have introduced the two episodes at all? The trajectory from Cana to Calvary with Mary, "The Woman," at the beginning and the end, would be pointless, unless John believed that in pairing the two episodes he was calling attention to something he thought was mystically important. Nothing is in John's Gospel by chance.

Protestants complain that Catholics glorify Mary too much. Catholics think Protestants honor her too little.[8] Setting that aside, I have tried to account for the fact that Mary has become such an important figure in the lives of so many. Independent of any supernatural influence, Mary answers to a deep longing in the human heart, which has elevated her to the left hand of God—with Jesus at his right hand—even though so little is said about her in the scriptures.[9]

Excursus on Catholic Dogmatic Proclamations

Aside from Jesus, Mary is the only gospel personality on whose behalf the Church has promulgated important dogmatic statements, one whose career in time, therefore, has not ended with her death. So it would be remiss not to devote a few paragraphs to a consideration of her continued relevance for many. While the Vatican has consistently refused to accord to Mary the title of Co-Redemptrix, as some Marian enthusiasts have wished, Rome has honored her with two fairly recent dogmatic declarations that grant her extraordinary privileges. Her Immaculate Conception has been mentioned briefly in the body of this chapter. On December 8, 1854, Pope Pius IX defined as a doctrine of faith that Mary was conceived free from the stain of original sin. The Bull *Ineffabilis Deus* declares that Mary shares with her son exemption from inheriting the sin of Adam. I have tried to translate this into more meaningful contemporary language. Then, in 1950, Pope Pius XII defined as a dogma of faith the bodily Assumption of Mary into heaven at the end of her earthly life. The Bull *Munificentissimus Deus* leaves open the question of whether Mary was assumed into heaven before or after her death.[10] Since her son died, it would seem appropriate that Mary would follow a similar course.

The Immaculate Conception of Mary in her mother's womb (not to be confused with her virginal conception of Jesus) and her Assumption into heaven parallel the privileges enjoyed by Jesus. He is conceived without inheriting the blight of original sin and at the end of his earthly life he is "carried up to heaven" (Lk 24:51). How does the Catholic Church know so much about Mary? Bruce J. Malina has one possible answer. For the Fathers of the Church and the framers of dogma, one argues from what was fitting to what must have happened to what did happen.[11] It was fitting that the mother of the savior, who was God Incarnate, be without sin or the inclination to sin, and that her body not be allowed to molder in the grave. Therefore, God must have preserved her from sin and taken her bodily to heaven. Therefore, he did.

But scripture does not say that Mary is without sin, and no mention is made of her Assumption into heaven. Can one legitimately argue from the "ought" to the "is," from what was fitting to what actually took place? What is the alternative? Doctrinal questions such as these are answered in the language of faith, though believers try to make their beliefs as logical and reasonable as the matter allows.

What should we believe, assuming that belief is the only access we have to some doctrines? Must one adhere to scripture, *sola scriptura*, as the only source of divine revelation? No, replies the Catholic Magisterium. Although there are only those few scripture texts, they are not our sole source of revelation about Mary. Catholics hold that tradition as well as scripture constitutes a valid source of divine revelation. The Holy Spirit is believed to be with the Church, actively guiding her in her understanding of the mysteries of faith. Therefore, it is argued, the public proclamation of the two privileges of Mary, her Immaculate Conception and Assumption, reveal explicitly what was implicit in the Church's understanding of Mary from earliest times. As an embryo develops and reveals what is latent in the egg, so, over the course of time and with the development of doctrine, what is latent in the original revelation comes to light in the fullness of time. The Bull *Munificentissimus Deus* (1950) does not stress scriptural sources for Mary's privileges, although Pius XII declares, "The truth of this dogma [the Assumption] is based on Sacred Scripture and is deeply rooted in the hearts of the faithful. It is sanctioned by the worship of the Church from most ancient times. It is completely consonant with other revealed truths."[12]

The Catholic Church does not say that Mary is a divine incarnation or even some kind of lesser avatar, but because God created the human species as both male and female, and because both male and female sinned in the Garden of Eden, it has seemed appropriate that the work of redemption be shared by a man and a woman. Although the Church's outlook on women in theory and practice has been anything but equal in the past, supporters of Marian devotion feel confident that a new day is dawning. Revelation, they maintain, is not a dead letter, nor should Christianity be strictly a religion of the Book. It must be seen as a living organism of truth. The Divine Spirit constantly brings to our attention old truths that only seem to be new: "Therefore, every scribe who has been trained for the kingdom of heaven is like the master of a household who brings out of his treasure what is new and what is old" (Mt 13:52).

If belief in the divinity of Christ grew gradually after his death, may not a more developed understanding of Mary's privileges also evolve? Such is the logic that supports Marian devotion. It is sometimes based on superstition and emotion and, sometimes carefully thought out by trained theologians. Either way, there is a logic in Marian devotion that over the years has guided those who believe it proper to magnify Mary, whose Magnificat sought only to magnify God.

Two Positions: Protestant and Catholic

The Protestant response over the past four and a half centuries has been consistent. Granted that the mother of Jesus is entitled to the respect of all Christians, the excessive exaltation of Mary by Catholics is "unbiblical." As with so many accretions that have built up over the centuries, the reformers sought to clean house, and in doing so set in motion an early effort to get back to the historical Jesus. If Mary were all of the things Catholics claim for her, the Bible would have said so. St. Paul mentions the mother of Jesus but once, and even then only indirectly when he says that Jesus "was born of woman" (Gal 4:4). He apparently knew nothing about Mary's Immaculate Conception and Assumption into heaven. If she had been conceived without sin and assumed into heaven like her Son, Paul or some other New Testament writer would have at least mentioned such extraordinary privileges. As for the Assumption, had Mary been taken bodily into heaven, others should have observed it. But how could anyone detect that an embryo had been conceived free from the blight of original sin? Is not the Catholic position a combination of myth, mystery, and mysticism?

"Yes, all of that" is one possible Catholic reply to which Marianists would want to add, "experience." Those devoted to Mary claim to have frequently felt the effects of her living presence in their lives. Unsophisticated children have been visited by Mary in various parts of the world. Cures that cannot be explained by the most advanced medical wisdom take place at her shrines. Is God not telling us in so many different ways that Mary belongs alongside Jesus as the essential feminine aspect of all for which he stands? Apparently the members of the Johannine community adopted Mary as their spiritual mother, an idea the Fourth Gospel introduces when it describes Jesus as telling the Beloved Disciple to regard Mary as his mother, something Christians do when they pray the Rosary or recite the prayer that dates from the time of St. Bernard of Clairvaux: "Remember, O most compassionate Virgin Mary, that never was it known that anyone who fled to thy protection or sought thy intercession was left unaided."

Anyone approaching the Christian Mysteries from the historian's point of view does so primarily as a reporter, not as an advocate of one side or the other. The aim of this chapter has been to represent various positions fairly. The Protestant position is clear: Jesus is the Unique Mediator between God and the people of God. Any attempt to elevate Mary, or anyone else, to an equal share in that role is unacceptable. If Catholics are unwilling to call Mary "Co-Redemptrix" in so many words, by their devotional practice and by reason of the Church's dogmatic pronouncements, the mother of Jesus functions for all practical purposes as a mediator. Indeed, she is even called "Mediatrix of All Graces."

The Catholic position is clear, too. Mary can have only an ancillary role in the work of redemption. Luke has her define this role herself when in response to the message of the angel of the annunciation, she replies, "*Ecce ancilla Domini* (Behold the servant girl of the Lord). (Lk 1:38). Given the fact that Mary was the mother of Jesus, the first to believe, and a loyal and self-effacing disciple, should not even a nominal Christian, whether Catholic, Protestant, or among the un-churched, at least feel comfortable in honoring her as a highly privileged person, and as preeminent among the saints?

Notes

[1] Apocryphal gospels and pseudepigrapha deal with legends about the childhood of Mary and Jesus. Few, such as the *Protoevangelium Jacobi*, have any historical value.

[2] In Augustine's interpretation of St. Paul on the propagation of original sin, see Elaine Pagels, *Adam, Eve, and the Serpent* (New York: Vintage Books/Random House, 1988), 109–126.

3 The relation between Hindu avatars is complementary and spousal, between husband and wife or suitor and the beloved. Mary's relation to Jesus is asymmetrical. It is between mother and son. Mary is sometimes conceived as living within the Holy Trinity, as daughter of the Father, mother of the Son, and spouse of the Holy Spirit.

4 On the history of the female consort of the Hebrew God, see Raphael Patai *The Hebrew Goddess* (New York: Avon Books, 1967,and 1978), and Susan Niditch, *Ancient Israelite Religion* (New York: Oxford University, Press, 1997).

5 *Mutans Hevae Nomen* is from the hymn, "Ave, Maris Stella." It is in Second Vespers of the Common of Feasts of the Blessed Virgin Mary. The full stanza reads, "You who received 'Ave' from Gabriel's lips, establish us in peace, reversing the name 'Eva.'"

6 How much water was changed into wine at the marriage feast of Cana? Raymond E. Brown says fifteen to eighteen gallons. But then adds: "The jars hold two or three measures; a measure is about eight gallons." Three measures of eight gallons, even smaller Hebrew gallons, would add up to about eighteen gallons in each jar for a total of 108 gallons! Brown must have meant something like three or four gallons in each jar to arrive at a total of fifteen to eighteen gallons. See *The Gospel according to John* (Garden City, NY: Doubleday/Anchor, 1966), I, 100.

7 The New RSV has "took her [Mary] to his own home," as a translation of Jn 19:27. The Greek *elaben auten eis ta idia*, could mean adopted here as his own mother, as Jesus had requested on the cross.

8 A balanced account from a contemporary Protestant point of view by Daniel L. Implore, "Mary: A Reformed Perspective," was featured recently in *Theology Today* 56 (October 2000), 236–359.

9 The brothers James and John seek places of honor at the right and left hand of Jesus when he comes into his kingdom (Mt 20:21–23). It has probably occurred to some of those devoted to Mary that one of those positions might have been reserved for her.

10 The English text of the two papal bulls will be found in *The Church Teaches: Documents of the Church in English*, by the Jesuit Fathers of St. Mary's College in Kansas (Rockford, IL: Tan Books, 1972), 207, 212–213.

11 Bruce J. Malina, *The Social World of Jesus and the Gospels* (London and New York: Routledge, 1996), 102.

12 The text of Paul XII's statement is on page 213 in *The Church Teaches*. The original text is in Densinger, Enchiridion Symbolorum 2333.

Chapter Two

JOSEPH THE HUSBAND OF MARY

The Silent Sleeper

I n Matthew's Gospel, Joseph, the foster-father of Jesus, is called a righteous man (*dikaios*; Heb. *tzaddik*), which in the context means that he is careful to observe all the prescriptions of the Torah. Learning that his fiance, Mary, is found to be with child before they have come together, Joseph has every right to expose her publicly. In that case both she and her presumed partner, if he could be found, are to be stoned to death in accordance with the Law of Moses: "If there is a young woman, a virgin already engaged to be married, and a man meets her in the town and lies with her, you shall bring both of them to the gate of that town and stone them to death" (Deut 22:23; Lev 20:10).

Even had Mary been the victim of rape at the hands of a Roman soldier or one of Herod's militiamen, Joseph would not have been obliged to receive her into his home and adopt any offspring she might bear as his own child. Matthew tells us that Joseph chooses not to expose Mary publicly but to break off their engagement and "dismiss her quietly." Then he learns in a dream that "the child conceived in her is from the Holy Spirit" (Mt 1:20). So Joseph took her to be his wife and had no relations with her until her son was born.

Matthew, searching the scriptures, chooses a text from the prophecy of Isaiah to show that Mary's virginal conception had been foreseen and planned by God: "Behold! A virgin [*parthenos*] is with child and shall bear a son, and they shall name him Emmanuel" (Isa 7:14). It was all but inevitable that the enemies of the Christian faith would make capital over Matthew's story and spread the rumor that Jesus was a *mamser*, born out of wedlock or in questionable circumstances. Thus we find Celsus, a pagan writer of the second century, claiming that Mary had indeed had relations with a Roman soldier named Panthera.[1] The charge was specious, because by exchanging the positions of the 'n' and the 'r' in the stem word 'panther' it becomes 'parthen,' the word *parthenos* minus the ending.

13

Coincidentally, I discovered that the Greek word *leopardos* (leopard), which is a species of panther (*panthera pardus*), can mean soldier. Ignatius of Antioch, on his way to his martyrdom in Rome, writes of his being, "*dedemenos deka leopardois, ho estin stratiōtikon tagma*." He says that he is "bound to ten leopards; that is, a company of soldiers."[2] Among the Greeks a leopard or a panther was apparently a nickname for a soldier. Ian Wilson calls our attention to the tombstone of a Roman archer found in Bingerbrück in Germany. The carving on the tombstone reads, "Tiberius Julius Abdes Panthera." "Panthera" may not be the man's last name. We may simply be informed that T. J. Abdes was a *panther* (soldier).[3]

The evangelist Luke was aware of the tradition about the virginal conception of Jesus, but he carefully eliminated any reference to Joseph's distress over Mary being found with child before they were formally married. It was all too easy, as we learn from the wording of Matthew's text, to accuse Mary of marital infidelity before Joseph took her into his home. Even Matthew rectifies a statement in Mark's Gospel. Mark writes: "Is not this the carpenter, the son of Mary?" (Mk 6:3). Because this question could be interpreted to mean that Jesus' father was unknown, Matthew writes: "Is this not the carpenter's son? Is not his mother called Mary?" (Mt 13:55).

There is no indication in Luke's account that Joseph ever considered divorcing Mary or sending her away. If we had only Luke's Gospel, it could be argued that the question of a virginal conception might never have arisen. The angel of the annunciation tells Mary, "You will conceive and bear in your womb a son." This statement parallels the message the angel imparted to Zechariah, the husband of Mary's relative Elizabeth. There the angel says, "Do not be afraid . . . your wife Elizabeth will bear you a son and you will name him John" (Lk 1:13). Both messages, that to Mary and that to Zechariah, refer to the future. Still, Mary is puzzled by the angel's announcement that she will become pregnant, because she is at that moment an unmarried young virgin. But this text does not imply that Mary was to conceive a child before she was formally married. Luke is not denying the virginal conception, but he is introducing damage control in a matter that is easily open to malicious and snide gossip. Historians of antiquity know that classical literature is replete with stories about women conceiving without benefit of a human male partner. The woman is characteristically inseminated by a god. Alexander the Great's mother assured him that he was sired by Zeus.[4] In order to check on her tale,

Alexander marched a division of his army into the Egyptian desert to consult an oracle concerning his status as a divine offspring. Needless to say, with an army camped around the seer, it turned out that Alexander's mother had told the truth.

What is different about the conception of Jesus is that there is no intimation of sexual intercourse or insemination. In Luke's account of Mary's conception the angel informs her, "The Holy Spirit will come upon you, and the power of the Most High will overshadow you; therefore the child to be born will be holy; he will be called Son of God" (Lk 1:35). Could the conception of Jesus be an instance of parthenogenesis stimulated by the Spirit? Biologically this presents difficulties.[5] In any case, the conception of Jesus would have been quite unlike that of any other man mentioned in the Hebrew Scriptures. Samson's mother conceived unexpectedly, although she had been barren for many years (Judg 13:2 and 24). Other barren women, such as Sarah, Rebecca, Rachel, Hannah, and Elizabeth, conceived after they had given up hope of bearing a child. But when they did conceive it was after the usual manner, in contrast to Mary. No male, human or divine, had any share in her conceiving. So what is reported of her is unique.

Joseph's Forebears

Joseph, Mary's husband, was said to be of the House of David and, therefore, of royal descent. Both Matthew and Luke provide us with the names of Joseph's immediate forebears, eventually leading back to King David—to Adam in Luke's Gospel. However, the names of Joseph's five most recent ancestors differ in the two genealogical lists. For Matthew, these five names are Jacob, Mattan, Eleazar, Eliud, and Achim (Mt 1:14–15). For Luke, they are Heli, Mattat, Levi, Melchi, and Jannae (Lk 3:23–24). Is there any way to reconcile the two lists? It is possible that Matthew traces the ancestors of Joseph from David's son Solomon, while Luke traces them from his son Nathan. At least Matthew's second name "Mattan" resembles Luke's second name "Mattat."

Another puzzle concerns the problem of how Jesus could be a lineal descendent of King David because, according to Matthew, Joseph was not his father. Again, we can look for possible solutions. Inasmuch as Joseph was Jesus' presumed father and guardian, Jesus would have been legally of Davidic descent. If this lineage could be verified in Jewish law, perhaps Mary was of the House of David. After all, Jewish marriages usually took place between members of the same tribe.[6] If that is the case, why do the evangelists link Jesus to David through Joseph rather than through Mary?

The brothers and sisters of Jesus (Mk 6:3) present another problem. Both Matthew and Luke call Jesus Mary's firstborn son (Mt 1:25; Lk 2:7). Were the other six or more brothers and sisters of Jesus her children? If they were, and if Jesus was her firstborn, then he would have been the oldest in a family of at least seven children, and Mary would have borne at least six more children after Jesus.[7] However, since the Church has always insisted on Mary's perpetual virginity, calling Jesus her firstborn could simply mean that he had the right of primogeniture in relation to any other children that his mother might bear, whether she bore them or not.

But if Mary did not bear to Joseph other children after Jesus, who bore these other siblings of Jesus? A desperate solution is to hold that these "brothers and sisters" were really cousins. But there are nouns in Greek and Aramaic for cousin, so there would be no point in calling the relatives of Jesus brothers and sisters, if they were only cousins. Another proposal, dating from the second century, holds that Joseph was married twice and had children by a former wife.[8] Then, the siblings of Jesus would have been his stepbrothers and stepsisters, and Mary would have been their stepmother. While a Jewish man might have two wives simultaneously—King David had several—there is no indication in the Gospels that would lead one to believe that Joseph had more than one wife at the same time.

None of these problems arise in Mark, John, the Letters of Paul, or in any other part of the New Testament, since they do not speak of the circumstances surrounding the birth of Jesus. Paul, as already indicated, is satisfied with saying that Jesus was "born of woman" like any other Jewish infant (Gal 4:4).

Perhaps the simplest solution to these difficulties is to admit that the evangelists did not know very much about the early years of Jesus. But they felt it important to introduce some material about his conception and birth. They made use of bits and scraps of rumors gleaned from the fluctuating oral tradition, then fleshed them out with appropriate details. As with any hero among the ancients, the circumstances associated with the birth of Jesus should be auspicious and foreshadow his future greatness. In any case, we are on fairly solid ground when there is question of the names of Jesus' parents. The Synoptic

Gospels, including Mark (Mk 6:3), all call Jesus' mother Mary, and she is "Mary" in Acts (1:14). Oddly enough, she is not mentioned by name in the Fourth Gospel but is simply called "the mother of Jesus" (Jn 2:1, 2:12, 19:25). Joseph, for his part, is called the father of Jesus in Matthew, Luke, and John (Jn 6:42), although he is not mentioned at all in Mark's Gospel. We may safely conclude, nevertheless, that a couple named Joseph and Mary were the parents of Jesus.

Joseph the Dreamer

Joseph is told in a dream not to put away Mary, who is found to be with child, but to take her into his own home because "the child conceived in her is from the Holy Spirit" (Mt 1:20). In one dream after another, Joseph is told what his next step should be. Matthew suggests that Joseph was a prayerful man and that his dreams were conveyed to him in a kind of mystical sleep. In other words, Joseph was a mystic. Evidently, he was a man of few words. Although present at the birth of Jesus and at his presentation in the Temple, he never speaks a word. Even Zechariah, the husband of Elizabeth, not to mention Mary and the aged Simeon, broke out in canticles of praise of God, for example, in the *Benedictus*, the *Magnificat*, and the *Nunc Dimittis*. However, Joseph does not give utterance. When the adolescent boy Jesus is lost for three days and is found in the Temple at last, it is Mary who asks Jesus why he has treated her and Joseph in this way by not telling them where he has been. Joseph says nothing, although one would expect that the boy's father be the one to demand an explanation.

So we are given the impression that Joseph was a very interior man. He was probably not an aggressive businessman, which could have resulted either in his winning him many friends who trusted him or in his being taken advantage of by men of lesser integrity. He is supposed to have been an artisan of some kind, a *tekton,* which could mean a woodworker, carpenter, joiner, cabinetmaker, and even a mason. In any case, the services of a man of his craft would have been greatly in demand when Herod Antipas was rebuilding the city of Sepphoris, which had been burned to the ground by Quintilius Varus, governor of Syria, after the death of Herod the Great.[9] The town was visible from Nazareth and less than a ninety minute brisk walk from Joseph's home.

We are not guessing when we maintain that virtually every carpenter, mosaic artist, and stonemason in the area would have been hired or conscripted by Antipas to work on the new city. Could Joseph have refused on the basis that some of the structures being erected were to house statues and mosaics of pagan gods, that there was to be a theater and even a gymnasium in the city?[10] We cannot settle this question, but what is less questionable are that Joseph and his son Jesus must have been familiar with the city and that Jesus must have known what Varus did during the Galilean insurrection, led by Judas, son of Ezekias. He not only burned the city down but also enslaved most of its inhabitants, while his soldiers raped the local women before the Romans moved south and crucified two thousand men around the city of Jerusalem. All of this took place shortly after the time when Jesus was born. Such events leave an indelible memory, and they did not endear the Romans to the people of Nazareth. We must never forget that Jesus was brought up in surroundings where dreadful events occured from the time of his birth or shortly thereafter. If he did not witness them, his friends and relatives likely remembered and talked about them in his presence.

Were Joseph and Jesus illiterate? Some have thought so. But Joseph, were he to engage in any kind of business transaction, would at least have known how to add and subtract. As for Jesus, it is hard to believe that he was illiterate. There were teachers of young boys in the synagogues of Palestine, and since Jesus was an unusually bright child, it is hardly likely that he failed to master the twenty-two letters of the Hebrew alphabet so that he could read the scriptures. He quotes them often enough. The fact that he did not write anything kept throughout history may have been deliberate. Putting one's inmost thoughts into writing can petrify them and turn them into "scripture," which small minds can wrest to their own destruction (2 Pet 3:16). Maybe that is the reason why Buddha, Socrates, and Ramakrishna did not put their thoughts into writing.[11] Plato refused to commit his inmost personal thoughts to parchment, lest philosophical fundamentalists imprison his living thought in a box and not allow it to evolve and grow.[12]

Who Is My Father?

Iconographers traditionally represent Joseph as an elderly, balding man.[13] If he had been married before he took Mary into his home and had fathered six or more children, he could well have been twice Mary's age. In any case, we hear no more about him after he and Mary find the truant Child Jesus in the Temple listening to the discussions of the rabbis and asking them questions. Still, Matthew's Gospel presents us with a problem. If Joseph's first wife had died, perhaps in childbirth, and if he took Mary and the child Jesus to Egypt for several months or years, who took care of his several children, some of whom were but infants, while he was several hundred miles away? Then turning to Luke's account, if Joseph had all these children, why did he take only Mary, his pregnant wife, on the difficult journey from Nazareth to Bethlehem when she was about to give birth?

Luke says that he did this because of the census, which we now know took place in 6 CE, when Jesus would have been at least ten years old.[14] This suggestion questions the accuracy of Luke's account, for it is he who introduces the idea of having Joseph and Mary go to Bethlehem to register there for the census. But those who had to register for a Roman census did so in the place where they earned their living, not in the family seat. Does Luke's account make Matthew's more likely? In Matthew's account Joseph and Mary did not have to travel to Bethlehem for the birth of Jesus because they had a house and already lived there (Mt 2:11). In Luke's defense, we should not forget that the dating of Jesus' birth as having taken place some time before the death of Herod in 4 BCE has Matthew as its sole warranty in an account which many scholars regard as historically questionable. But if Luke is right, then Jesus must have begun his public life at the age of twenty-four years, not thirty, as is commonly believed.

Because the infancy accounts present us with such conundrums, there is always the nonscriptural solution: All Joseph's children were also Mary's. Or, treating Bethlehem, the census, and the flight into Egypt as pious midrash, pick up again the theory that Joseph was twice married and that Mary was his second wife who, after his death, became the materfamilias of a large household, featuring seven or more children, among whom Jesus was the youngest.

A Troubled Household

What follows is largely guesswork, but it is based on an analysis of the texts we have and what they may imply. Because Jesus and his young mother were newcomers to the family of Joseph, one or more of whose daughters may have been no more than a few years older that Mary, not all may have been pleasant for Jesus and his mother. Typically, a stepmother and her young son do not fit easily into an already established household. We have evidence that the relations between Jesus and his brothers were not always cordial. When, later in life, Jesus returned to his own native village of Nazareth, he was poorly received. Jesus includes his "own kin" and members of his own house among those who are unfriendly (Mk 6:4). Earlier, Mark says that when Jesus is tossed about by an unruly crowd, "his family" hears that he has gone out of his mind and so they go out to "restrain him" (Mk 3:20–21).[15] John in his Gospel reports that on one occasion his brothers keep badgering him to show himself to the world and do something spectacular in Jerusalem to win attention. Jesus finds their attitude unacceptable and he tells them "My time has not yet come, but your time is always here." Or, again, "The world cannot hate you." And the evangelist concludes by adding, "For not even his brothers believed in him" (Jn 7:5–7).

We would certainly be justified in holding that these uneasy relations between Jesus and his family members had a long history. The tension might have arisen because he was a stepbrother or, possibly, the youngest and Joseph's favorite—think of the patriarch Joseph and his relations with his brothers. Or the familial hostility may have arisen simply because Jesus was "different," his interests were not the same as theirs. As a man concerned for the welfare of others, he was far more socially involved, more spiritually alive, and less apt to be satisfied with pat, traditional answers to religious and political questions. He had memorized the scriptures and took a keen interest in the lives and problems of the impoverished people around him. Only one of his brothers, the one named James, may have looked with favor on his religious interest, although he would turn out to be far more conservative than Jesus. This James later became a pillar of the Church and the first bishop of Jerusalem. He was known as James the Just. Josephus refers to him as "the brother of Jesus, who was called Christ."[16]

James may have been the oldest of Joseph's sons, with Jesus as the youngest. By law, Jesus would have ranked last, with no title to inherit Joseph's property or business. This rank placed less responsibility on Jesus and gave him the freedom to study and, perhaps, to travel a little. After Joseph died, Jesus and his mother would grow even closer together. We have no way of gauging the exact nature of the relationship between Jesus and Joseph. It may have been idyllic, but when Joseph and Mary found the boy Jesus in the Temple, Jesus reminded them, with his foster-father standing before him, that his vocation was to be "in my Father's house," or, in another translation, "in the things that concern my [heavenly] Father" (Lk 2:49).

In his adult life, Jesus is credited with having said, "Call no one your father on earth, for you have one Father—the one in heaven" (Mt 23:9). This statement was not meant as a put down or a rejection of Joseph. Similarly, Jesus was not rejecting his own mother when he told an audience that his true kinfolk were those who hear the word of God and do it (Lk 8:21). Mary and Joseph would certainly have qualified as kin to Jesus on the spiritual as well as on the human level. But transcending all human parenthood was God as Father "from whom every fatherhood in heaven and on earth takes its name (Eph 3:14). It was in an almost Platonic sense, then, that Jesus sees in his heavenly "Father of lights" (Jas 1:17) the archetype of the ideal human father.

Granted that Jesus thought of God as his Father par excellence, was the sentiment reciprocated? Did God regard Jesus as Son? Surely the local villagers in Nazareth must have known that he was conceived before his parents were actually married. Could the irregularity of his conception and birth be one of the reasons why he never married? If there ever was this kind of problem for Jesus, it was resolved at the time of baptism. Just as Jesus is coming up out of the water after his baptism by John the Baptist, he hears the voice telling him that he is God's "Beloved Son," and that his heavenly Father is well pleased with him (Mk 1:11). For Jesus, that assurance was all that mattered. If he had experienced any doubt or insecurity about his birth or about his relationship with God, it would have dissolved in his baptism.

Meditating on this rare experience of the Fatherhood of the invisible God, Jesus must have reflected often on Joseph, his visible father, or foster-father. Matthew says that Joseph was a just and righteous man. That sounds rather flat and prosaic, but the implications are far from ordinary. Joseph was the man who kept a low profile in the gospels. He was seen but not heard. Jesus regarded him as a great saint, and he derived his lofty image of God as Father by extrapolating from his experience of Joseph, the husband of Mary.

Notes

[1] Origen quotes Celsus as having said, "Mary was turned out by her husband, a carpenter by profession, after she had been convicted of unfaithfulness. Cast off by her spouse, and wandering about in disgrace, she then in obscurity gave birth to Jesus by a certain soldier Panthera." Cited by Origen in Contra Celsus in Refutation. Quoted by Ian Wilson in *Jesus: The Evidence* (San Francisco: Harper & Row, 1984), 189.

2 "Ignatius to the Romans," in *Apostolic Fathers*, Vol I. Translated by Kirsopp Lake (Harvard University Press, 1985), 232.

3 Ian Wilson, *Jesus: The Evidence*, 65.

4 E.P. Sanders, *The Historical Figure of Jesus* (New York: Allen Land, Penguin, 1993), 243, cites Robert Lane Fox's *Alexander the Great* for the story about Alexander's hybrid origin. "His mother was hit by a thunderbolt before she and Philip of Macedon consummated their marriage." Since the thunderbolt was identified with Zeus, Alexander was clearly son of a god.

5 In the higher mammals parthenogenesis, if it were possible, would normally produce an offspring of the same sex as the mother.

6 In the Gospel of the Birth of Mary not to be confused with the Gospel of Mary [Magdalene] we are told that Mary was "sprung from the royal race and family of David." See *The Lost Books of the Bible*, translated by Jeremiah Jones with a foreword by Solomon J. Schepps (Avenel, NY: Gramercy Books, 1979), 17. Several medieval writers hold that Mary was of the House of Levi and, therefore, of a priestly line.

7 Had Mary borne six children before the birth of Jesus, and assuming that she was married at the age of sixteen or seventeen, she would have been near thirty years of age when Jesus was born and near sixty years of age when he died on the cross. One does not get the impression that Mary was, by ancient standards, an old woman when Jesus died.

8 According to the *Protoevangelium Jacobi* VII, Joseph was a widower and an old man when he was induced to marry the young Mary. He said that people would laugh at an old man wedded to such a young girl. Josephus, in *The Antiquities of the Jews* 17,1,2, says, "It is an ancient practice for us [Jews] to have many wives at the same time." Could it be that Mary was one of at least two wives of Joseph? In this case, "the brothers and sisters" of Jesus (Mt 13:55–56) would be the children of Joseph's other unnamed wife. I am not aware of this having been mentioned elsewhere. The *Protoevangelium* will be found in *The Lost Books of the Bible*, 28–29; see note 6 above.

9 For the burning of Sepphoris, see Josephus, *The Antiquities of the Jews* 17,10,9, in *The Works of Josephus, Complete and Unabridged*. Translation by William Whiston (Peabody, MA: Hendrickson Publishers, 1995), 471a.

10 Josephus called Sepphoris "The ornament of Galilee." See Richard A. Horsley & Neil Asher Silberman, *The Message and the Kingdom: How Jesus and Paul Ignited a Revolution that Transformed the Ancient World* (New York: Grosset/Putnam, 1997), 24. An astonishing, almost breathtakingly beautiful head of a woman in mosaic was uncovered in Sepphoris by archeologists. The best mosaics today could hardly improve on it. J.R. Porter offers readers a half-page color reproduction of the mosaic, *Jesus Christ: The Jesus of History, The Christ of Faith* (New York: Oxford University Press, 1999), 23.

11 It is probable that Mohammed did not write any part of the Koran in his own hand. He was told by the angel Gabriel to "recite," and scribes wrote down what he said in a kind of trance state.

12 Plato in his Seventh Letter wrote, "Hence no intelligent man will ever be so bold as to put into language those things which his reason has contemplated, especially not into a form that is inalterable, which must be the case with what is expressed in writ

ten symbols" Edith Hamilton and Huntington Cairns, eds. *Plato: Collected Works.* (New York: Pantheon/Random House, 1964), 1590.

[13] See note 8 above.

[14] Josephus refers to the tax under Quirinius (Cyrenius) in *Antiquities* 18,1,1.

[15] James D.G. Dunn, following Schweitzer, does not think that Jesus was in any sense mad or insane. Mark uses the word *exestē*, related to "ecstasy," to indicate that Jesus may have gone into some kind of trance or altered state. The Scribes who came from Jerusalem said that he was possessed and had a demon. The Gospel of Mark says that he had to be restrained or overpowered (the infinitive, *kratesai*, from the verb *krateō*, implies the use of force). See Dunn. *Jesus and the Spirit: A Study of the Religious and Charismatic Experience of Jesus and the First Christians as Reflected in the New Testament* (Grand Rapids, MI: William B. Eerdmans Publishing Company, 1997; original 1975), 86–87.

[16] Eusebius. *History of the Church from Christ to Constantine* (New York: Dorset Press, 1984), devotes five pages to James and his execution, 99–103; *Antiquities* 20,9,1. In this and other similar material, he borrows from Josephus.

Chapter Three

HEROD THE GREAT

"It's safer to be Herod's pig than his wife"

Herod, called "The Great," according to Matthew's Gospel, has ordered the slaughter of all the male infants under two years of age in Bethlehem (Mt 2:16). The Magi, traveling from the East, announced that they have come to pay homage to the newborn King of the Jews. Upon being told that the prophecy of Micah has indicated that the future king would be born in Bethlehem (Mic 5:2), Herod orders the massacre of the infants. Although near death himself, he does not want anyone not of his blood to rule in Israel. Meanwhile, Joseph and Mary with the infant Jesus flee into Egypt after Joseph is warned in a dream about the danger to the child.

While scripture scholars question the historicity of the massacre of the male infants and the visit of the Magi, the Herod we know from history was quite capable of such a deed.[1] Superstitious, suspicious, and always afraid of plots to assassinate him, he killed off everyone who had any chance of challenging his rule. The rumor, whether true or false, of the birth of a future king not of his family, was enough to cause Herod to take steps to eliminate him.

Herod's Rise to Power

After the Maccabean Revolt, the Jews became politically independent under the rule of the Hasmonean family. Alexander Janneus appointed Herod's grandfather Antipater I to be governor of Idumea, a large territory south of Judea and west of the Dead Sea. After the death of Alexander, Antipater II was lucky enough to have supported Alexander's oldest son Hyrcanus II as king and high priest, a choice later approved by Pompey and Julius Caesar. Eventually, Antipater II, Herod's father, was granted Roman citizenship and made procurator of Judea. He appointed his son Herod as governor of Galilee. Later, Herod, having married Mariamne, a member of the priestly Hasmonean family, to legitimate and improve his political position,

25

captured Jerusalem and became de facto king of the whole of Palestine.[2]

Court intrigues, however, made Herod's hold on the throne precarious. He became increasingly wary, and to eliminate all possible opposition, he murdered his wife Mariamne, had his mother-in-law's son Aristobulus drowned, and killed his brother-in-law Costobarus. Finally, he had Mariamne's two sons, Alexander and Aristobulus, strangled. In this way he was able to eliminate all male relatives of Hyrcanus II, any one of whom might have been in a position to challenge his hold on the throne.

Herod had ten wives, five of whose children had a part to play in the drama of succession. There was Doris, mother of a younger Antipater. Five days before his own death, Herod had Antipater killed. Mariamne was Herod's second wife. As indicated above, he killed her, and in 7 BCE had her two aforementioned sons destroyed. A third wife was another Miriamne whose son Philip seemed to have passed most of his life safely in Rome. Wife number four was Malthrace, a Samaritan, the mother of Archelaus and Herod Antipas, both of whom play a role in the Gospels. The fifth wife, for whom we have some information, was Cleopatra of Jerusalem. Her son Philip became tetrarch of a territory northeast of the northern section of the Jordan River, including Golonitis within which are the modern Golon Heights and the city that Philip built and named Caesarea Philippi. It is near here that Peter makes his confession when he declares that Jesus is the Messiah and the Son of God (Mt 16:16).

Herod made six wills, changing the names of the heirs to his throne that number of times. In the fifth will Herod Antipas was made sole heir. But just five days before his death Herod changed that will and made another. In it, Archelaus was to become ethnarch of Judea, while Herod Antipas received the lesser title of tetrarch and was given rule over two separate territories, Perea and Galilee. Naturally, Antipas resented Herod's final will that forced him to share rule with Archelaus who, in the bargain, inherited Jerusalem and Judea, along with Idumea and Samaria. Pressing his case before the Emperor Augustus, Antipas lost and had to be satisfied with Perea and the Galilee.[3]

In monarchies where kings have absolute power, there is often a dispute over who is to succeed to the throne. After the War of the Roses, Henry VIII in England felt it imperative to produce a male heir to succeed him. In spite of six successive marriages, his only male heir was the sickly Edward VI, son of Jane Seymour who died in child-birth. Edward died at the age of sixteen, a child monarch after a reign of only six years. One can understand, then, Herod's anxiety to keep his male heirs in power. His only problem was to determine which of his many sons should be rewarded with the prize. His preference shift-ed from month to month, with his final choice made during the very last week of his life. And as it turned out, it was not a very good choice in the case of Archelaus. He soon proved to be an impetuous and bloody ruler whose violence and murderous inclinations forced Rome to depose him and exile him to Gaul.

Herod and the Gospel According to Matthew

Matthew's Gospel mentions Herod the Great. There is an appro-priate symbolism in the Matthean story of Gentile magicians, or learned wise men, seeking out the newborn king of the Jews. They represent the influx of the Gentiles into the Christian community at the time when the First Gospel was composed, about seventy years after the birth of Jesus, which Matthew sets at some time before the death of Herod in 4 BCE.[4] Matthew says that Jesus is persecuted by a power-ful Jewish monarch and visited by the educated Magi. This account contrasts sharply with Luke's infancy narrative. In the latter case, sim-ple, illiterate, peasant shepherds are told by angels where to find the newborn savior. He will not be found in a house, as in Matthew (Mt 2:11), but in a barn or cave where his crib is a manger, or trough for feeding animals (Lk 2:7).

Actually, the two accounts are to some degree complementary. True seekers find God either by using their God-given intelligence or by faith and the unexpected gift of God. The Magi were later described as "three kings," and again we have the contrast: Jesus is visited by kings and poor shepherds, being himself both King and Good Shepherd as the evangelists conceived him.

Prophecy Historicized[5]

Matthew's infancy account is a collage of six biblical prophecies. The coming of the stargazing astrologers from the East is foreshad-owed in Balaam's Oracle where he foretells that "a star shall come out of Jacob, and a scepter shall rise out of Israel" (Num 24:17). The prophecy in Micah 5:2 prescribes where the Messiah is to be born:

"For from you [Bethlehem] shall come forth for me the one who is to rule in Israel." A third text focuses on the Septuagint Greek passage according to which it is said that a virgin (*parthenos*) will conceive and bear a son (Isa 7:14). A fourth passage is seen as foretelling that after the sojourn of the Holy Family in Egypt, God will call them back to Palestine, for he has declared, "Out of Egypt have I called my Son" (Hos 11:1). The slaughter of the innocent male infants under the age of two is anticipated by the image of Rachel weeping for her children, "because they are no more" (Jer 31:15). Finally, by taking the Hebrew equivalent of the consonants NZR (which could refer to a "branch" or the "Nazirite vow"), Matthew implies that texts (unnamed) from the Hebrew scriptures indicate that Jesus would be known as a NaZoR-ean (Mt 2:23).

We have here a stellar example of Hebrew midrash. The evangelist creates a story out of six texts. Moreover, there is an obvious parallel between the story of the infant Moses being spared, in spite of Pharaoh's order that all of the male Hebrew children be killed, and Jesus being spared in spite of Herod's attempt to kill Jesus along with the other male Jewish infants in Bethlehem (Ex 1:16 ff.; Mt 2:16).

Neither Mark's Gospel, nor John's Gospel, nor the Letters of Paul indicate when or where Jesus was born. In fact, in John's Gospel, the people argue that Jesus cannot be the Messiah because he is from Galilee and not Bethlehem in Judea: "Surely the Messiah does not come from Galilee, does he?" (Jn 7:41). John does not try to contradict the belief that Jesus was born and bred in Galilee, and Mark and Paul (Acts 22:8) leave the impression that Jesus was born and brought up in Nazareth. Matthew and Luke, however, guided by the scriptures, think that Jesus, if he is truly the Son of David and heir to David's throne, should have been born in Bethlehem as the scripture foretold. But why? There must have been thousands of descendents of King David in Palestine at the time when Jesus lived. Were they all, including Jews of the Diaspora, supposed to descend on the tiny village of Bethlehem to register for the census?

It was the prophecy of Micah that seems to have been the determining factor in persuading Matthew and Luke that Jesus must have been born in Bethlehem. Prophecy determines history. Luke invokes the census under Quirinius as a way of getting Joseph and Mary to Bethlehem so that Jesus could be born there in fulfillment of the prophecy. And Matthew's dating is of a piece with the story about the massacre of the infants in Bethlehem. Since he dates the birth of Jesus

before the death of Herod in 4 BCE, Jesus would have been at least thir-
ty-four years of age when he began preaching in the year 30, and possibly thirty-seven years of age when he died, if Jesus' ministry lasted
three years as the Fourth Gospel seems to require.[6]

Luke holds that shortly after the birth of Jesus the family returned
to the town of Nazareth. Matthew, on the contrary, says that they all
fled to Egypt where they stayed for an undisclosed period of time.
What persuaded Joseph to settle with his wife and child in Nazareth
after returning from Egypt? It was because Archelaus, the cruel son of
Herod, was ethnarch in Judea. So Joseph did not return to his home in
Bethlehem but choose to settle in Nazareth in order to fulfill the
prophecy mentioned earlier by Matthew.

There is no easy way to reconcile the infancy accounts of Matthew
and Luke. They are using different sources with different time frames
and travel plans. That is less important than the lessons they seek to
communicate. Matthew's account is like the grand overture to a sym-
phony. In it are themes that will later play a role during the ministry of
Jesus. The gifts of the Magi symbolize who Jesus is: gold for kingship,
frankincense for divinity, and myrrh for burial and immortality. The
Magi foreshadow the coming of the Gentiles, and Herod's attempt to
kill Jesus anticipates later attempts on his life. In returning from
Egypt, the infant Jesus, guided by the dreams of Joseph, recapitulates
the history of God's chosen people reentering the Holy Land that the
biblical Joseph, also a dreamer, had left when his own brothers tried
to kill him (Ex 37:20).

Putting the best face possible on Matthew's story about the massacre of the infants and the visit of the Magi, is there not a way to
explain such a series of events as historically plausible without at the
same time invoking supernatural intervention? We might start with the
fact that Herod did not hesitate to murder anyone suspected of being
a threat to his absolute rule. A person who thinks that others are out to
kill him may not be paranoid; he may have good reason to think so.
Herod's life and throne were always in danger because of plots on the
part of his relatives and courtiers. Sometimes his fears were mere
superstitions; at other times, he had evidence that those around him
were plotting his overthrow. So Herod took the initiative and had no
qualms about eliminating his relatives or anyone else he suspected. In
view of the fact that, according to Josephus, Herod did not seem to be
in his right mind during the last days of his life when he kept murder-
ing his relatives and changing his wills,[7] had Joseph learned of

Herod's condition, he might have decided to leave the country and take employment in Egypt where carpenters were always in demand.

Also, it is not unbelievable that a few Chaldean astrologers might have been acquainted with the Hebrew Scriptures and the expectations of the Jews concerning the advent of a Messiah–King. And who would be most likely to know about the birth of a much-heralded heir to Herod's throne? It would be the child's presumed father or grandfather, that is, Herod himself. This fact may explain why the Magi went directly to Herod and asked him about his new heir with results they had not foreseen.

In spite of our best attempts to make Matthew's account historically plausible, the fact remains that his infancy story is a tissue of texts taken from the scriptures, a stellar example of prophecy historicized. Beyond that, it cannot be harmonized with Luke's infancy text describing how the Holy Family wound up in Bethlehem, with Jesus being born in a stable and laid in a manger. Luke is intent on showing how poor and forlorn Jesus was in his birth. He was born in a stable "because there was no room at the inn" (Lk 2:7). The suggestion that Jesus was rejected by his own people corresponds to the statement in the Prologue to the Fourth Gospel where the evangelist declares, "He came to his own people and they did not accept him" (Jn 1:11). For Luke, Jesus comes into the world unrecognized except by poor shepherds and angels. In Matthew's Gospel, he is recognized by the great men of the world, by the King of the Jews, and by the noble wise men.

Regarding the Day on Which Jesus Was Born

Few people question that Jesus was born in the dead of winter in Bethlehem on December the twenty-fifth, unaware that the December date was not determined until the middle of the fourth century. It was selected at that time to replace the pagan festival celebrating the birth of Mithras, the god of light and truth. Late December was also the period of the year when the days began to grow longer, following the winter solstice and the revelry that accompanied the orgiastic days of the Saturnalia. Even if Jesus had been born in Bethlehem, there was little reason for Joseph to travel there in late December. We do learn, however, that Jesus' parents went to Jerusalem every year to celebrate Passover (Lk 2:41). Since Jerusalem was always packed with tens of thousands of pilgrims at Passover, Joseph may have customarily made his way to Bethlehem, only a few miles away, where he had relatives.

This could substantiate Luke's account, according to which Jesus was born in Bethlehem on the occasion of one of his parents' visits to that area.

In other words, Jesus' birth in Bethlehem should not be absolutely ruled out, though there is no scriptural evidence for it having taken place in December. That Matthew and Luke may have honestly come by rumors of Jesus' birth in Bethlehem is quite possible. The prophecy of Micah was well known. So, basing their accounts on the scribal tradition, Matthew and Luke then tried to provide a rationale to explain how Jesus, though widely known as a Galilean from Nazareth, happened to be born in Bethlehem. Did the scripture create the historical fact or did a historical fact find support in the scripture?

If one were pressed to choose between Luke's account and Matthew's, which of the two—assuming the two cannot be reconciled—makes contact with known historical facts? Here Matthew has the edge. Herod the Great is a well-known historical figure. A wry joke going around Rome had it that it was safer to be Herod's pig—Jews do not eat pork or slaughter pigs—than to be Herod's wife or son. Herod was among the most murder-prone monarchs at a time in the Roman world when one became head of state by assassinating the incumbent. Fleeing to another country in order to escape persecution would have been an indicated avenue of escape, had Joseph learned about some kind of threat to himself or his family. Credible, too, is Joseph's unwillingness, upon returning from Egypt, to settle in Judea in view of the documented history of the unpredictable behavior of Archelaus, Herod's son, who was ruling there.

Finally, there would have to be some reason to explain why Joseph decided to settle in Galilee and choose the town of Nazareth. That would have been because Herod Antipas was engaged in the massive project of rebuilding Sepphoris. There would thus have been plenty of work for carpenters and craftsmen like Joseph. Of course all of this speculation still does not account for the care of the other children of Joseph while he, Mary, and the infant Jesus were living in Egypt.

These are but a few of the perplexing circumstances that have to be taken into account. All things considered, scripture scholars lean to the view that Jesus was probably born in Nazareth and that his parents had always lived there.[8] To this extent, they would agree with Luke insofar as he holds that the parents of Jesus lived in Nazareth before his birth and immediately thereafter. Luke says that after Mary's purification, a rite that took place forty days after the birth of a male child (eighty days after the birth of a female), Joseph and Mary "returned to *Galilee*, to their own town of Nazareth" (Lk 2:40). This, of course, would allow no time for the flight into Egypt.

What are we to do about our mid-winter Christmas pageantry and holiday sales, if it turns out that Jesus was born neither in winter nor in Bethlehem of "Judea"? Bruce Chilton, basing his research on two sources and Joshua 19:15, speculates that Jesus may have been born in Bethlehem of Galilee, just a few miles from Nazareth. It is mentioned by Joshua and appears on Map 3 in the New Oxford Annotated Bible. Whether Jesus was born in one Bethlehem or the other is of less importance for Christians than the very fact of his birth. They have the right to celebrate it on any or every day of the year in any part of the world.

Notes

[1] See note 7 below on Herod's character and madness.

[2] Most of the history about Herod that follows is condensed from Howard W. Hoehner, "Herodian Dynasty," in *The Oxford Commentary to the Bible*, edited by Bruce M. Metzger & Michael D. Coogan (New York: Oxford University Press, 1993). The article brings together the material found scattered in Josephus.

[3] Richard A. Horsley and Neil Asher Silberman, *The Message and the Kingdom: How Jesus and Paul Ignited a Revolution that Transformed the Ancient World* (New York: Grosset/Putnam, 1997), 23.

[4] Scholars regularly accept Matthew's dating of the birth of Jesus. The evangelist holds that it took place before the death of Herod the Great. The worth of this dating depends on the historical validity of Matthew's story about the massacre of the Bethlehem infants and the flight of the Holy Family to Egypt.

[5] John Dominic Crossan's most extended treatment of his belief that the gospel accounts are largely prophecy historicized rather than history remembered will be found in the Prologue, "History and Prophecy," in *Who Killed Jesus?*: Exposing the Roots of Anti-Semitism in the Gospel Story of the Death of Jesus (San Francisco: HarperSanFrancisco, 1995), 1–38.

[6] Luke says that Jesus was about thirty years of age when he began his ministry (Lk 3:23). If he was born in 6 CE, he would have been thirty-six at that time. Luke was simply wrong about Jesus being born during the census. But was Matthew right about the approximate date of Jesus' birth sometime before 4 BCE?

[7] Before he dies, "Herod's distemper greatly increased." It brings him "to do all things like a madman." He orders the nation's principal men to assemble in the hippodrome. Meeting them, "the king was in a wild rage against them all." He orders them all to be killed so that there would be mourning at his own funeral. Josephus, *The Antiquities of the Jews* 17,6,5 in *The Works of Josephus, Complete and Unabridged*. Translated by William Whiston (Peabody, MA: Hendrickson Publishers, 1995), 462b.

[8] Aside from the more radical contemporary scholars, even traditional authors, such as John P. Meier, C.H. Dodd, and Marcus Borg vacillate on the historicity of Jesus' birth in Bethlehem. Michael Grant doubts that he was born there; see *Jesus: An Historian's Review of the Gospels* (New York: Scribner, 1977), 72.

Chapter Four

JOHN THE BAPTIST

Humble, Harsh, Hurried

According to Luke's Gospel, Jesus and John the Baptist meet before either of them is born. Mary, the mother of Jesus, having learned that she will soon become pregnant plans to visit her elderly relative Elizabeth who was in the sixth month of her pregnancy.[1] By the time Mary reaches the home of Elizabeth and her husband Zechariah she too is carrying an unborn child in her womb. No sooner has she entered the home of Elizabeth than the older woman feels the child in her womb leap for joy, and she exclaims in wonder, "And why has this happened to me that the mother of my Lord comes to me?" (Lk 1:43).

The unborn John here recognizes Jesus and through the mouth of his mother calls him "Lord." Thus begins the saga of the relationship between John and Jesus. Did the two of them ever meet again before the time of Jesus' baptism by John in the River Jordan?[2] The Gospels offer no light on this subject, but because Mary and Elizabeth were not only relatives but close friends, it is reasonable to suppose that Jesus and John met again during their childhood and adolescent years. As they grew to maturity, they must have discussed with one another the future of the Jewish nation.[3] On the other hand, when John and Jesus did meet again by the River Jordan, John, in the Fourth Gospel, declares twice, "I myself did not know him" (Jn 1:33). What the evangelist may mean in attributing these words to the Baptizer is that until John saw the Holy Spirit "descending from heaven like a dove" and settling over the head of Jesus, he did not realize that Jesus was the expected Messiah, or "The One Who Was to Come" (*Ho Erchomenos*).

In Matthew's Gospel, John recognizes Jesus' superior status even before he baptizes him and beholds the theophany of the descending dove. For when Jesus enters the water to be baptized by John, "John would have prevented him, saying, 'I need to be baptized by you, and

35

do you come to me?'" (Mt 3:14). This statement can only mean that John already knows Jesus and holds him in high esteem.

Jesus' encounter with John even before they are born may be a midrash introduced by Luke to stress the superiority of Jesus over John. When the Gospels were written during the last third of the first century, the disciples of John were still numerous and widespread. Thus, we read in the Acts of the Apostles that Apollos, a native of Alexandria, "knew only the baptism of John" (Acts 18:25), and when Paul comes to Ephesus, a long way from Palestine, he finds a number of people who knew something about Jesus but had been baptized only "into John's baptism of repentance" (Acts 19:3).

Whose Baptism?

Reading between the lines, one can sense a certain amount of tension between the followers of Jesus and the disciples of John. Eventually, Jesus learns that some Pharisees have heard the rumor that "Jesus is making and baptizing more disciples than John" (Jn 4:1). This prompts Jesus to leave the area where John is baptizing and repair to Galilee, passing through Samaria on the way. The fact that Jesus leaves the area where John is baptizing indicates that he does not want to appear as John's rival.

We have very little contemporary information about the activities of Jesus and John beyond what we learn from the New Testament. But the Jewish historian Josephus does mention both John and Jesus. John receives extended treatment in the historian's *The Antiquities of the Jews*, but Jesus is mentioned only in passing in the single unquestionably authentic passage, that is, in 20,9,1.[4] There he is identified as the brother of James, the first Bishop of Jerusalem, who was stoned to death with some others at the instigation of the high priest Ananus during the interregnum between the death of the Roman governor Festus and the arrival of his successor Albinus. Another passage calls Jesus a wonderworker and "the Christ." It also refers to the postresurrection appearances (*The Antiquities* 18,3,3). These three affirmations are generally thought to be the work of a Christian hand, phrases inserted into the text at a later date.[5]

The Parting of the Ways

The Baptist was an old-style Hebrew prophet wearing rough clothing and surviving on desert food. He called for a movement of national repentance that would usher in the Messianic Age. Like the Dead Sea Scrolls Community, he situated himself far from the Temple in Jerusalem and its corrupt Sadducean high priests.[6] When he sees the Jerusalem Sadducees and Pharisees coming to hear him, he lashes out at them:

> You brood of vipers! Who warned you to flee from the wrath to come? Bear fruit worthy of repentance. Do not presume to say to yourselves, "We have Abraham for our ancestor"; for I tell you, God is able from these stones to raise up children to Abraham. Even now the ax is at the root of the tree; every tree that does not bear good fruit is cut down and thrown into the fire (Mt 3:7–10).

John and his disciples fasted and led austere, ascetical lives. Jesus, on the other hand, while he believed the Messianic Age was stirring in the wings—something called "the kingdom of God"—did not fast and did not remain in one place. Jesus traveled and projected the image of a far more humane, even urbane, messenger than did John.

Upon hearing about the activities of Jesus, John is disturbed. Rumors come to him that Jesus and his disciples do not fast, that Jesus is a glutton and wine drinker, and that he feasts and consorts with the hated tax collectors and sinners (Mt 11:19).

So John sends a delegation of his own disciples to check on Jesus and try to find out what truly is the case. Their first question, when they found Jesus, is, "Are you the one who is to come, or are we to wait for another?" (Lk 7:19). In other words, "Are you the expected Messiah?" What kind of Messiah begins his public ministry by providing six large vats of wine at a wedding feast when the celebration is almost over? What kind of Messiah eats and drinks with known public sinners? As far as his personal conduct is concerned, Jesus gives his standard answer: "Those who are well have no need of a physician, but those who are sick. I have come to call not the righteous but sinners to repentance" (Lk 5:31). You cannot convert sinners by standing at a distance and simply barking at them. One must get in amongst them, win their confidence, and then hope to turn them around. We now see why Jesus was interested in meeting with, eating with, talking with, and eventually converting the tax collectors. Agents in the employ of Rome and Herod Antipas, they served as middlemen in oppressing peasant farmers and by indirectly helping in the confiscation of their farms when they were unable to bear the burden of taxes laid on them.

Where sinners were concerned, Jesus and John used diametrically opposed methods. Remaining in one well-known place, John launched out and attacked the sinners who came to him. Jesus went out after them and often dined with them. He won over the arch-tax collector Zacchaeus not by berating him, but by inviting himself to stay at his house. He needed to "have a talk" with him. The result was that Zacchaeus agreed to give half his possessions to the poor, and "if I have defrauded anyone of anything, I will pay back four times as much" (Lk 19:8). Jesus not only banqueted with Levi, another tax collector, also known as Matthew, but finally also accepted him as one of his twelve apostles (Lk 5:27–29).[7] It is hard to imagine John the Baptist sitting down to eat with known sinners, allowing a sinful woman to touch him (Lk 7:38), and in violation of the purity laws touching a leper (Mk 1:40). Jesus, on the other hand, was interested in the sheep that have gone astray or who were despised by others. They were the ones that needed help. Those already in the sheepfold could take care of themselves.

On a less personal, pastoral level, Jesus' reply to John the Baptist concerning the type of life he was leading is indirect. He does not answer the question implied in John's inquiry, "Are you the Messiah?" Instead he calls attention to the fact that since he started his ministry, "the blind receive their sight, the lame walk, the lepers are cleansed, the deaf hear, the dead are raised, the poor have the good news brought to them. And blessed is anyone who takes no offense at me" (Lk 7:22–23).

This last remark is important. Jesus is asking John, via his emissaries, not to be put off or scandalized because he waives some of the purity rules and eats with sinners,[8] which has to be judged in the context of the cures that are taking place. We have no evidence that John the Baptist was a healer of physical ills. Jesus was. As he says when he is accused of casting out demons through the agency of Beelzebul, the ruler of demons, "But if it is by the finger of God that I cast our demons, then the kingdom of God has come to you" (Lk 11:20). If Jesus' physical cures prove that he has God's approval, then his friendship with sinners cannot merit God's disapproval. The healings and his work among sinners rise or fall together.

Jesus surely felt that John had a right to an explanation of his own conduct. After all, John was an authentic prophet, and even more than a prophet, since he had been appointed by God to announce the advent of the kingdom, a blessing which the Jerusalem scribes and Pharisees turned their backs on "by refusing to be baptized by [John]" (Lk 7:30). Indeed, among the children born of woman none is greater than John, at least on the strictly human plane. But, then, the least member of the kingdom is greater than John (Mt 11:11; Lk 7:28). One would expect that John would automatically be a member of the kingdom by reason of his role as precursor, and it is unlikely that Jesus would want to exclude him. What is "greater than John" as a mere precursor would be his incorporation into the kingdom.

However, if the evangelist means that the least member of the community of those who believe in Jesus is greater than John, this could mean that in the estimation of Matthew and Luke—the put down is missing in Mark—the teaching of Jesus is superior to John's and the New Covenant inaugurated by Jesus "supersedes" the old one promulgated by Moses. What is likely is that the words put in the mouth of Jesus reflect the later rivalry between the disciples of John and the followers of Jesus. If the text is taken to mean that the least member of the community of those who believe in Jesus is greater than John, it would be at variance with what one expects the attitude of Jesus toward John would be. We must keep in mind that the evangelists have their individual agendas and polemical axes to grind.[9] Even though Jesus' approach to the coming new age was quite different from John's, it is hard to believe that he ever thought of John as inferior or as a rival.

The Execution of John

Herod Antipas, in whose territory John the Baptist carried out his baptizing ministry, had John beheaded rather than stoned to death or crucified. We have no indication that Antipas ever crucified anyone, possibly because his Roman overlords reserved that right to themselves. Stoning, a peculiarly Jewish form of execution, would have been inappropriate in John's case, for he was neither a blasphemer nor a heretic in the eyes of the common people. On the contrary, he was regarded as a great prophet in the line of Elijah and Jeremiah. So, wishing to do away with him, Antipas cut off his head.

Matthew, following Mark, dramatizes the antecedents to John's death. John has publicly upbraided Herod for marrying his stepbrother Philip's wife, Herodias, while Philip is still alive. Therefore, there is no question of a levirate marriage (Deut 25:5). The story about Salome, the daughter of Herodias, is well known. She performed an artistic dance that so pleased Herod Antipas that he offered to grant her anything she desired. So she asked for the head of John the Baptist. The story will be treated in some detail in chapter twenty-one. We know the girl's name, courtesy of Josephus [*The Antiquities* 18,5,4]. "Salome" has become the title of an opera by Richard Strauss and, a play by Oscar Wilde, and Gustave Flaubert's story, *Herodias*, exploits the same theme.

Probably the vindictiveness of Herodias had something to do with the execution of John the Baptist, but when Josephus gives an account of the reasons for John's death, he does not mention Herodias. He says that Herod had the Baptist slain because he "feared lest the great influence John had over the people might put it into his power and inclination to raise a rebellion; for they seemed ready to do anything he should advise" (*The Antiquities* 18,5,1).

How did the execution of John play out in Jesus' plans? Because he, too, was followed by great crowds, and because his ministry was carried on for the most part in Galilee, part of Herod's territory, he had every reason to fear him. In fact, some friendly Pharisees had warned Jesus to flee from Herod's domain. "Get away from here," they urged, "for Herod wants to kill you" (Lk 13:31). Jesus apparently does just that. Mark says, "From there he set out and went away to the region of Tyre. He entered a house and did not want anyone to know he was there" (Mk 7:24). Jesus was constantly aware that his life was in danger. So it should not be surprising that he foresaw that he might be killed. At first, he thought that those who would destroy him would be the Temple authorities, "the elders, the chief priests, and the scribes" (Mk 8:31), not the Pharisees.

Somewhat later, he learns of a plot to betray him (Mk 9:31). Finally, no doubt on information he had received from friends close to the high priests in Jerusalem, he learns that, after he had been betrayed and captured, the chief priests intend to hand him over to the Roman authorities with a charge equivalent to planning an insurrection (Mk 10:33). Luke says that the chief priests accused Jesus of claiming to be "a king" and that "He stirs up the people by teaching throughout all Judea, from Galilee where he began even to this place" (Lk 23:2; 23:5). Part of the charge, taken in the proper sense, would not have been untrue. Jesus did "stir up the people," but not with a view to insurrection. He wanted the rich to share with the poor in a kingdom of justice and mercy, "under God as King."[10]

Some scholars have questioned the claim of the evangelists that Jesus knew in advance that he would be killed and even said what kind of death he would undergo. It is called prophesying *ex eventu*, foretelling the past after it has happened. Still, if Jesus did not suspect that he might be killed, especially after the execution of John the Baptist, he would have been utterly naive. He may not have foretold that he would rise from the dead on the third day, but on the basis of information passed on to him by many friendly sources, he could eventually have even guessed what kind of death he would suffer. Once it looked as though he would be turned over to the Romans, he could expect to be scourged and crucified, since flogging was a routine form of torture before hanging a man on a wooden beam. Had Herod arrested him, he could expect to be beheaded, which was easier than stoning or crucifixion. Had unfriendly Jews used violence against him, his death would probably have taken the form of stoning. They once tried to stone him by attempting to hurl him off a cliff so that he would be killed by falling on the rocks below. Precipitating a man headlong over a cliff or from a tower was a form of stoning (Lk 4:29; Acts 1:18).The fourth century Christian historian Eusebius writes that James, the brother of Jesus, was killed in this way when "he was thrown from the parapet and clubbed to death."[11]

It would not have been easy for Jesus to get the death of John the Baptist out of his mind. Among the authentic sayings of Jesus, I would include the verse in which he declares, "I have a baptism with which to be baptized, and what stress I am under until it be accomplished!" (Lk 12:50). It was not to be a baptism with water but a baptism in his blood. When James and John ask to share in Jesus' glory, he warns them, "Are you able to drink the cup that I drink, or be baptized with the baptism that I am baptized with?" (Mk 10:38). The "cup" here, like the cup that held the hemlock that Socrates had to drink, stood for suffering and death.[11] The menace of death, like the sword of Damocles, hovered perilously over Jesus' head. As he waited, imprisoned in the palace of Caiaphas, expecting to be turned over to Pilate for execution, did his mind go back to John the Baptist whose death, however gruesome, was quick and easy? The anticipation of his own end was sufficient to induce terror. Did all the excess of pain have some deeper meaning? Would he be given a decent burial as John was? Herod allowed John's disciples to pick up the body and bury it honorably (Mk 6:29). Or would Jesus' body be thrown into a shallow pit and covered over with a thin layer of dirt by a pair of brutal Roman soldiers?

These thoughts were sobering. At the end, Jesus and John might have looked on their lives and ministries as failures. They were both put to death. The people regarded John as too austere and Jesus as too permissive. No matter what they did or how they behaved some found fault: "We played the flute for you, and you did not dance; we wailed, and you did not weep" (Lk 7:32). John came eating no bread and drinking no wine, and they thought him a mad man, and said, "He has a demon." Jesus came eating and drinking, and they said, "Look! A glutton and a drunkard" (Lk 7:32–34).

Let wisdom be the judge. She knows who her children are, who belong to the kingdom, and who not. One prophet uses vinegar, another honey. At the midpoint of his career, Jesus felt that he and John complemented one another. He could not conceive them as rivals, but only as agents of the one divine Spirit.

Notes

[1] Elizabeth and her husband Zechariah are traditionally thought to have lived in the village of Ain Karin, about five miles west of Jerusalem, near Emmaus. If so, Mary traveled a long way from Nazareth to visit Elizabeth in time for the birth of John the Baptist. Luke does not tell us how Mary got there. The impression given is that Mary traveled alone and in haste. It is highly improbable that a young girl would risk such a long and dangerous journey alone and return by herself. If the story is authentic, she must have been in the company of others until the time she actually entered the home of Zechariah and Elizabeth.

[2] Artists, basing their inspiration on Luke's Gospel, represent Jesus and the future John the Baptist playing together as children. In this case, the artist goes beyond the literal sense of the text and develops a likely scene on the basis of the information he has.

[3] If, as young men, Jesus and John the Baptist communicated with one another, they could not have avoided talking about religion and politics. The two themes were inseparable in the minds of men in those days.

[4] Josephus, before describing the execution of John the Baptist, has many laudatory things to say about him, including the interesting note that he expected of those to be baptized that "the soul be thoroughly purified beforehand by righteousness (*The Antiquities of the Jews* 18,5,2). Baptism did not "take away" sin. It was, rather, a sign expressive of the fact that the person to be baptized had already had a change of heart, or metanoia. Contemporary Baptists have a similar view.

[5] Shlomo Pines has uncovered what looks like an authentic, unaltered version of Josephus' passage on Jesus. It was found in the writings of a tenth-century author named Agapius. See *An Arabic Version of the Testimonium Flavianum and Its*

Implications (Jerusalem: The Israel Academy of Science and Humanities, 1971). The Agapius version omits words and phrases expressing excessive praise of Jesus and doctrinal assumptions, such as, that he was the Christ, rose from the dead, and did ten thousand marvelous things, as the prophets had foretold.

6 Hershel Shanks calls attention to the fact that, "The waters of the Jordan, where John performed his baptisms, are only a stone's throw from where the [Dead Sea] Scrolls were found." But he warns that physical proximity to the habitat of the Qumran community and the use of similar biblical texts as warranty for the legitimacy of their respective missions are not sufficient evidence that John the Baptist, in spite of his scorn for the Temple hierarchy, was ever a member of the Qumran sect. *The Mystery and the Meaning of the Dead Sea Scrolls* (New York: Random House, 1998), 78–79.

7 The tax collectors mentioned in the gospels were mostly operating in Galilee. They would have been in the employ of Herod Antipas rather than working as immediate agents of Rome. Rome, of course, got its share of the money and produce harvested by Herod's publicans. Tax collectors should be distinguished from toll collectors.

8 To what extent did Jesus skirt a literal observance of the purity laws? Even though there is no indication in the gospels that he even entered a *mikveh*, that is, took a ritual bath after touching a leper or being touched by a woman with a flow of blood, this does not mean that he failed to do so. True, he seems to have been fairly permissive regarding the food he ate (Mt 15:11), and he not only healed on the Sabbath, but stoutly defended his disciples when they harvested grain on the Sabbath (Mt 12:1–5). Luke says that a Pharisee who asked Jesus to dine with him "was astonished to see that he did not first wash before dinner" (Lk 11:38). Again, regarding circumcision, he mentions it once in John's Gospel and not at all in the Synoptics. In John's account, he refers to it as part of "your law," and says that "Moses gave you circumcision," as though he were distancing himself from the practice (Jn 7:22–23). But this distancing almost certainly reflects the view of the evangelist, not that of Jesus.

9 Whatever Jesus may have thought about the relationship of John the Baptist to the New Covenant, Matthew's text clearly implies supersessionism, the belief that the older Covenant between God and God's people had been superseded by the new. Therefore, the Old Covenant was no longer valid and pleasing to God. The idea is extremely offensive to Jews. "The Declaration on Non-Christian Religions" in the Second Vatican Council (1962–1965) roundly rejected the idea that Jewish religious practice is no longer pleasing to God, and Pope John Paul II has emphatically done the same.

10 Jesus' idea of the kingdom of heaven was that it was to be ruled by God alone with no earthly king to dominate others. It was a return to the way Israel was governed before there were kings and despots. The prophet Samuel had warned about the dangers of kingship. Set up a king to reign over you, and he will take the best of your fields, your grain, your cattle, yours sons, "and you shall be his slaves" (1 Sam 8:17). With such an attitude toward kingship, the idea that Jesus would have aspired to be Messiah–King becomes unthinkable.

11 "The cup," both for Socrates and for Jesus spells suffering and death. See Phaedo 116c, and the Synoptic Gospels: "Abba, Father, for you all things are possible; remove this cup from me; yet, not what I want but what you want" (Mk 14:36).

PART TWO:

Jesus of Nazareth

Chapter Five

JESUS: A MAN FOR OTHERS

Mission to the Disinherited

Many are not fully aware of how politically subversive the teaching and program of Jesus were. In the Middle East of his day, as in our own day, everything was political. This is a side of his activity that has been overlooked until quite recently. Jesus may have been a mystic, but the kingdom he preached was not primarily one that the virtuous would enter after death. He prayed and taught others to pray that God's kingdom would come on earth, as it exists ideally in the mind of God. In the pages that follow I will concentrate on a few salient features of his ministry that contributed to his arrest and execution as a threat to the existing *political* order. He strived to keep a low profile, which became impossible when, as a prophet, he challenged the complacency and insensitivity of the rich and spoke of the coming of a kingdom that to Roman ears sounded like the coming of a new order to supplant Roman rule. Then, he offended the ultra-conservative religious factions by consorting with sinners and the *'am ha-'aretz*, the religiously uneducated peasants, who "know not the law" (Jn 7:49).

1. Who Did Jesus Think He Was?

a. The Name

Palestinian Jews of Jesus' day would not know to whom you were referring, if you spoke of Jesus and pronounced his name as Gee-zus. His Hebrew name was Yehoshua shortened in Aramaic to Yeshua or even Yeshu. Since there is no "sh" sound in Greek, Yeshu became Yesu, Latinized to Iesus or Anglicized as Jesus. *Yehoshua* in Hebrew means God saves or God will save, an appropriate name for one who would be known as Savior. What's in a name? There was power in the name of Jesus. His disciples casted out devils in his name, and there were exorcists who were not even members of the apostolic band who used the name of Jesus successfully to rout the demons (Lk 8:49). For

47

the saints the name of Jesus was sweet as honey and like oil poured out, silent, smooth, and holy.

The Jews, who would not pronounce the sacred name of God, the tetragrammaton, YHWH, had many substitutes, chief among them were "Adonai," My Lord, "El Shaddai," The Almighty, or "Elohim," the plural of majesty, or God and the whole heavenly court. Jesus, basing his special name for God on his own experience, called God "Father," and he urged others also to think of God as a loving parent. The paradigm prayer begins with the words, "Our Father," where the "Our" is as important as the "Father," since it stresses the community aspect of the brotherhood of men and women, with Jesus as their brother, under God as Father.

Of no small importance is the way Jesus did not address God. He did not speak of God as the impersonal Ground of Being, nor as the remote and incomprehensible Almighty Other, nor as the God of Wrath.[1] He called God *Abba* which is not only a child's way of speaking to its father, but also the manner in which a grown man might address a much loved parent. *Amma* would be the way Jesus addressed his mother in the privacy of their home, and she probably called him *Yesha*. During his public ministry he was called many things—not all of them complimentary. The more common forms of address were "Master," "Teacher," and "Rabbouni." The latter expressed deep affection and was used spontaneously by Mary Magdalene when she encountered the risen Jesus just outside his tomb.

b. What Did Jesus Call Himself?

In the Synoptic Gospels Jesus twice referrs to himself as a prophet: "Prophets are not without honor except in their own country" (Mt 13:57); and "it is impossible for a prophet to be killed outside Jerusalem" (Lk 13:33). But most often he spoke of himself as "Son of Man." The evangelists endowed the words with messianic overtones, leaning heavily on the Book of Daniel[2] and terminology found in the First Book of Enoch.[3] But in Ezekiel God addressed the prophet as "son of man" (lower case) nearly a hundred times, and the book always stresses the prophet's mortality and finitude as a mere human being. Very often Jesus used the words as a substitute for "I," or the first person singular of the personal pronoun. At other times "Son of Man" referred to humanity in general; or Jesus would use it to describe himself as just an ordinary human being, born of woman. This was his way of identifying with all that is human. He drew back from such titles as "Messiah," "King," or "Lord." They were loaded with conceptual baggage that suggested domination. He did not want to be placed on a pedestal and have incense offered to him, separated from the people in isolated grandeur.

c. Keeping a Low Profile

When Jesus asks his apostles, "Who do men say that the Son of Man is?" the answer he receives is that some thought he was John the Baptist redivivus, or Elijah, or Jeremiah, or one of the prophets (Mt 16:14). It was not that Jesus was John the Baptist who had been killed by Herod Antipas, but people thought that the spirit of John or one of the prophets was acting in him. His enemies said that the spirit that moved him was that of the demon Beelzebul (Mt 12:24). In either case, we have a form of spirit induction, which is a lesser form of spirit possession.[4]

Without affirming or denying that some form of spirit was acting in him, Jesus then asks a second question, this one directed to the apostles themselves: "But who do *you* say that *I* am?" The first thing to note here is that Jesus replaces the "Son of Man" with the personal pronoun. What the evangelist is leading up to is his conviction, put into the mouth of Peter, that Jesus is not just a man moved by the spirit of somebody else, but a spirit in his own right, namely, the Messiah in person, the Expected One (Mk 8:29; Lk 9:20).[5] Matthew's Peter declares that Jesus is not only the Messiah but the "Son of the Living God" (Mt 16:16). Because Peter was so perceptive, Jesus, in Matthew's Gospel, praises him and confers on him the "Power of the Keys to the Kingdom of Heaven."[6]

This accolade is missing in Mark and Luke. Even Matthew allows that Jesus "sternly ordered them" not to proclaim him Messiah. He wanted above all to keep a low profile in this matter. To call him "Messiah" was too dangerous. The title meant "king" in the eyes of scribes as well as the common people, and the surest way to end a promising career was to give Herod Antipas or Pilate the impression that Jesus of Nazareth was claiming the title which Rome alone had the authority to confer on its carefully selected client kings.

In John's Gospel Jesus, God's Logos, is the personification and embodiment of Divine Wisdom. He does not hesitate to call attention to his "works," and he declares unabashedly that he is the Way, the Truth, and the Life. But in the Synoptic Gospels, especially in the Gospel according to Mark, Jesus is reluctant to make any high-sound-ing claims for himself. After curing the lame, the blind, or the diseased, he usually forbids those he has healed to publicize their good fortune. They might be told to report to a priest but then they are to go home and tell no one else (Mt 8:4; Mk 1:43). When a demon identifies Jesus as "the Holy One of God," he rebukes him, ordering him to be silent and leave the man (Mk 1:25). When he stands before Caiaphas and the High Priest asks if he is the Messiah, in Luke's Gospel Jesus simply refused to answer, and in Matthew's his reply is ambiguous.[7] There can be little doubt that the evangelists believed that Jesus was the promised Messiah–King. Mark even has him admit it (Mk 14:62). What is less certain is that Jesus would have agreed with him.

2. Jesus as Prophet and Teacher

Quite independent of who Jesus thought he was, or who the evangelists thought he was, scholars believe that we have a fairly reliable account of his early teaching in the Q Gospel, said to be an early common source (*Quelle*) for some parallel passages in Matthew and Luke. As a Sayings Gospel, Q or more properly Q[1], presents Jesus as a wisdom teacher. It contains no account of his passion, death, and resurrection. This leads one to suppose that the sayings of Jesus gathered in this source were collected before his death and therefore represent his teaching before it was reworked by the evangelists in the decades after his resurrection.

a. Love of Friends and Enemies

Much of the material that Matthew includes in his Sermon on the Mount appears in Q[1]. It represents part of the earliest undistorted layer discerned by John S. Kloppenborg and Burton L. Mack.[8] The Jesus we meet there challenges us as he certainly challenged his contemporaries with a disturbingly radical doctrine. What he is preaching is a complete reversal of what is typical and, for the most part acceptable, human behavior. The recurring phrase, "You have heard it said, but I say to you," presents us with a program that is *super*-natural in the sense that Jesus is asking his followers and hearers to conduct their lives in a way that challenges the old axiom, "You can't change human nature." What does the accepted adage say? "'You shall love your neighbor and hate your enemy.' But I say to you, Love your enemies and pray for those who persecute you" (Mt 5:44). What do most people do when they are cursed and persecuted? They immediately seek

to retaliate or find some way of getting "even." Jesus wants his followers to do the exact opposite, to return love for hatred. Even offer the
left cheek of friendship to one who in anger or contempt strikes you
on the right cheek (Mt 5:39).

Jesus does not seem to be asking his disciples to be cowering or
chicken-hearted in the face of injustice or outrage. What he wants is a
habitual attitude of benevolence. To return insult for insult serves only
to perpetuate and escalate the cycle of violence in word and deed. It
would be a far better world if people managed to put into practice even
half of what Jesus recommends.

b. Sharing

Another startling counter-cultural attitude is Jesus' view concerning the folly of depending on wealth and material possessions, a theme
to be developed at considerable length later in this book. In the Parable
of the Rich Fool, Jesus tells the story about a wealthy man who has
nothing better to do with his wealth than to pull down his barns and
build new ones to warehouse his grain and cattle, saying to himself,
"'Soul, you have ample goods laid up for many years; relax, eat, drink,
and be merry.' But God said to him, 'You fool! This very night your
life is being demanded of you. And the things you have prepared,
whose will they be?'" (Lk 12:19–21).

Tie this story to Jesus' advice to the rich young man. He says that
if the young man wants to be perfect and follow him he should sell
everything he owns, "and distribute the money to the poor" (Lk 18:
22). There were many poor people in Galilee in Jesus' day, but Jesus
was not urging the man simply to distribute his wealth indiscriminate-
ly. He was telling him that, if he joined his movement, he was to share
his wealth with the poor communities Jesus initiated. This, in fact, was
exactly what was done in the early Jerusalem Church when those with
money and property sold what they had and laid the proceeds at the
feet of the apostles (Acts 5:2). The money would then be shared with
the poor of the community, on whose behalf Paul collected money
during his missionary journeys (1 Cor 16:1–4).

This idea of sharing may explain the two miracles of the multiplication of the loaves and fishes in the first two Gospels. By offering the
example of sharing with the multitude the loaves and fishes that his
disciples bought from a young fish monger, Jesus encourages others to
share the food they have brought into the wilderness with those who
have brought none. In the end several baskets of remnants are left over

after all have eaten (Mk 6:35–44, 8:1–10). When poor people share their meager resources, it usually turns out that there is enough for everyone.

Jesus was convinced that leading an insurrection would never succeed in ousting the Romans from the land God had given his Chosen People, nor would driving them out necessarily better their lot. What he proposed instead was to teach them to make do with whatever resources the impoverished people of the land could muster. The solution to their grueling poverty was to pool their goods in a kind of cooperative, so that the more fortunate would share what they had with those who had even less. This was the test Jesus set before his disciples.

c. The Social Significance of the Parables

Those who read the parables of Jesus from a strictly spiritual and theological point of view often fail to notice the underlying social and economic conditions that were presupposed or taken for granted in the stories. Most Christians are familiar with the Parable of the Tenant Farmers. When the absentee owner of the vineyard in which the tenants labored sends his servants and, eventually, his own son to collect his share of the produce, the tenants mistreat the servants and kill the son, thinking that in this way they could inherit or recover the land they have been working. They are greatly mistaken. For they succeed only in having the owner "put those wretches to a miserable death and lease the vineyard to other tenants who will give him the produce at harvest time" (Mt 21:41). Matthew has turned this story about the futility of violence as a way to recover the land into a thinly disguised allegory about the rejection of Jesus by those Jews who in the past killed God's prophets and, more recently, God's only Son. God has handed the vineyard over to new tenants, namely, to the members of the new Israel, the Christian Church.

This is one of the many examples of "supersessionism," according to which the Christian Church has inherited the promises made to Abraham and dispossessed the Jews. "For many will come from east and west and will eat with Abraham, and Isaac, and Jacob in the kingdom of heaven, while the heirs of the kingdom will be thrown into exterior darkness, where there will be weeping and gnashing of teeth" (Mt 8:11–12). Matthew's working of The Parable of the Tenant Farmers reflects also the economic situation of the poor Jews in first-century Palestine. They had lost their land and were now reduced to

being day laborers on what had once been their own farms and vine-
yards. If the only heir to the property died, there was a good chance
that they might be able to get their property back. But, Jesus warned,
if they used violence and murder, they must be ready to suffer the consequences.

The same lesson is outlined in the Parable about the king who
invites some guests to share in the wedding banquet of his son. What
does the king do when those who are invited beat and kill his messen-
gers? Enraged, he "sent his troops, destroyed those murderers, and
burned their city" (Mt 22:7). Violence is not the answer to the plight
of the poor and oppressed Galilean peasants.

Even the Parable of the Laborers in the Vineyard has an economic underpinning. The landowner pays those who worked for only an
hour the same wage he had paid the ones who had worked all day. The
latter complain. The owner, however, puts them in their place: "Am I
not allowed to do what I choose with what belongs to me?" (Mt
20:15). From one point of view the owner is being exceedingly generous to the ones who came late. But his action can also be seen as arbi-
trary and calculated to be an affront to those who have worked all day.
The powerful and the rich are not bound by the ordinary laws of rec-
ompense. They can do what they want with their money and with
"what belongs" to them.

The story, incidentally, reveals the desperate condition of the
peasants in a marginalized, agrarian economy.[9] Their mortgaged farms
had been taken over by absentee landlords in an ancient example of
agribusiness. Although this situation is rarely mentioned directly in
the gospels, it was something that Jesus could not ignore. Consoling
peasants with promises of happiness after death did nothing to better
their daily lot. Jesus had to have some kind of program that would
result in changing the system. Waiting for God or militant activists to
bring freedom and prosperity would not improve conditions. Jesus'
own solution was sharing. Beginning small, his program would result,
eventually, in an equitable and large scale redistribution of wealth and
the riches of the soil. It was this last threat the wealthy landowners
would not tolerate, and it contributed mightily to Jesus' downfall.

The institution of slavery was taken for granted in ancient society. The Jews held slaves but were expected to treat them fairly. Jesus
tells of a propertied man who goes away on a journey. He leaves sixteen talents to three of his slaves, one receiving ten talents, another
five, and a third one. They are to invest the money and make a hun-

dred percent profit for the owner. Upon returning, he punishes the slave who has buried his one talent and failed to double the owner's assets. When hailed before his lord, the slave pleads, "Master, I knew that you were a harsh man, reaping where you do not sow, and gathering where you did not scatter seed; so I was afraid, and went and hid your talent in the ground" (Mt 25:24–25). The response of the owner is typical. He confirms the evaluation of the slave: "You knew, did you, that I reap where I did not sow, and gather where I did not scatter? Then you ought to have invested my money with the bankers, and on my return I would have received what was my own with interest." For a Jew, taking interest was strictly forbidden. So it would seem that the owner was a renegade Jew. He was not simply "harsh," but ready and willing to increase the value of his holdings by investing at interest, something an observant Jew would not do in dealing with other Jews.

The parables of Jesus can be read in various ways.[10] Several include an anti-Jewish slant that challenges the reader to rediscover the original context in which Jesus delivered them.

d. Table Fellowship

John Dominic Crossan calls Jesus' program one of open commensality.[11] The word "commensality" does not appear in most dictionaries, at least not yet. What it refers to is the practice of people eating together at the same table (*mensa*). Jesus was fond of using this image to describe what living in an ideal society—what he called the kingdom of God—would be like. To begin with, there would be no class distinctions. Even sinners would be welcome. "Sinners" in Jesus' day were not simply those who lied, stole, or committed adultery. As a class, the designation could also include those suffering from God's disfavor as it was conceived in first-century Jewish Palestine: usurers, Gentiles, those married to Gentiles, divorced women, prostitutes, those choosing not to marry, homosexuals, lepers, the blind, the seriously disfigured, Samaritans, and those burdened with some kind of legal or ritual impurity. A woman suffering from a flow of blood was impure, and the person she touched, Jesus in one instance, was rendered impure (Mt 9:20). Jesus himself is accused of allowing his disciples to eat with unwashed hands and pluck and shuck grain on the Sabbath (Mt 12:1; Mk 7:2–6). He defends them, saying, "[Evil intentions] are what defile a man, but to eat with unwashed hands does not defile" (Mt 15:20). Luke includes an occasion when Jesus himself failed to wash before eating (Lk 11:38).

The above are instances of ritual impurity. What distressed the more rigorously righteous among Jesus' adversaries and, perhaps, some of his friends, was his willingness to eat with tax collectors (*telōnai*). But as Richard A. Horsley has warned (*Jesus and The Spiral of Violence,* p. 81), a toll collector like Matthew who sat in a booth, *telonion* (Mt 9:9), is not to be confused with an arch-publican, like Zacchaeus, an *architelonēs* (Lk 19:2). This is not to say that there may not have been some true publicans at the banquet Matthew (Levi) prepared for Jesus, when the guests were tax men (Lk 5:29). Why, then, did Jesus keep company and practice table fellowship with toll collectors? Aside from the fact that by meeting with them he could hope to induce them to be more honest in their dealings with others, he was also modeling what he understood by open table fellowship. He would exclude no one, not even sinners, from his table. God sends his rain on the just as well as on the unjust, on the saved as well as on sinners (Mt 5:45). Thus, in one of the parables Jesus tells about a host whose invited guests failed to come to dinner. He then sends his servants out into the city to bring to the dinner "both the good and the bad" (Mt 22:10).

The real test of openness is what kind of people you are willing to eat with. The rich invite the rich to their table. This is not Jesus' idea of fellowship in the kingdom of God. If you are going to give a party, do not invite those who can return the favor, but bring in "the poor, the crippled, the lame, and the blind" (Lk 14:13). Table fellowship is the touchstone of Jesus' radical egalitarianism. We are all children of the same Father–God. So, while certain people in any society must play functional roles, when it comes to eating, all are equal. Jesus would probably have preferred a round table with no privileged places. Noticing how the guests at a wedding banquet jostled one another in order to be seated in the places of honor, he warned against such maneuvers. If there must be places of honor, the disciples of Jesus should prefer the last places at table. Then if the host comes, he may say, "Move up higher."

e. Healing Without Charge

A second plank in Jesus' program has to do with healing.[12] There were many healers in Jesus' day. Whether they were imposters or honest dealers, they took money for their services. Neither Jesus nor his disciples profited from their healing ministry. Jesus likely was able to cure certain kinds of physical, emotional, and neurological ailments. Apparently even his disciples had some success in healing. Upon returning from one of their missions, they declare, "Lord, in your name even the demons submit to us" (Lk 10:17). However, it was the society as a whole that was sick. The rich had become inordinately rich while the poor landless peasants were all but destitute. It was not wealth itself that Jesus decried but the way it was obtained along with the lack of concern on the part of the rich for those in need. The Parable of the Rich Man and Lazarus calls attention to this situation. A sick, poor man crouches each day at the gate of Dives, the rich man. He longs to satisfy his hunger with the crumbs that fall from the table of Dives. But the rich man takes no notice of Lazarus and his desperate need. He walks past him each day as though he does not exist. Both men die. The rich man who had been clad in purple and who dined sumptuously is now in Hades without a drop of water to slake his thirst. Meanwhile, the formerly ulcerous Lazarus is at peace with the angels in the bosom of Abraham (Lk 16:19–31).

Neither this tale nor the Parable of the Last Judgment in Matthew's Gospel should be taken as positing anything dogmatic or definitive about the eternity of punishment meted out to those who, due to some sin of omission, will be imprisoned forever in the eternal fire "prepared for the devil and his angels" (Mt 25:41). Matthew's Jesus uses colorful language in his typical "thought experiments," to highlight the often overlooked fact that there are times when sins of omission are seriously wrong. He is not addressing great criminals guilty of planned murder, rape, grand larceny, or genocide. He wants his followers to examine their own lives and attitudes toward the oppressed and underprivileged. We can so easily blindside ourselves to omissions that can have far-reaching consequences for others.

f. Caring for Others

St. Paul, faithfully echoing the mind of Jesus, writes, "Do nothing from selfish ambition or conceit, but in humility regard others as better than yourselves. Let each one of you look not to your own interests, but to the interests of others" (Phil 2:3–4). Prefer the welfare of others to your own self-interest. That is the heart of Jesus' message. It almost seems like going against nature, as indicated earlier. And in a way it is. In the animal world and in the world of uncaring human beings, the way to survive and prosper is to get all you can, seek the first place against all others, and make no provision for loving kindness. No wonder Nietzsche, an inspiration for the Nazis, thought that the morality of Jesus was for slaves. *Der Übermensch* is a man of steel whose higher morality scorns the ordinary categories of bourgeois good and evil. The Thousand-Year Reich lasted for less than twelve years, while Jesus' ideal of love in action still motivates millions of men and women who devote their lives to bettering the human condition with no provision for personal gain. In spite of all the shortcomings of our modern democracies, there are those who have taken Jesus' radical egalitarianism to heart. They are not deterred by the accommodations institutional Christianity has made to the spirit of the world and secularity. Even those who try to ignore the still small voice of conscience cannot completely eliminate from their minds what they have been told about the words and example of a man who lived two thousand years ago and loved both saints and sinners. Jesus truly was a man for others.

In a rigidly structured class society in which the rich and the educated thought of themselves as belonging to a different race than the poor, the illiterate, and the unwashed, Jesus sought out the least and treated them as royalty. If you want to be first, go to the end of the line and be first in love and kindness. When the kingdom comes, God may call an about face. Then the last will be first and the first will be last.

But even Jesus would correct his own example. For in the ideal commonwealth there would be no firsts or lasts. The concept of ranking was entirely alien to his mentality. In his kingdom you do not compare yourself with others nor do you even think in terms of personal privilege or worth. Returning to the Parable of the Laborers in the Vineyard, we might see it in a context different from the one proposed above. Look on it as a lesson in God's unconditional love for all creatures. Worthiness has nothing to do with God's free gifts. Should the man who has served God faithfully all his life resent the fact that the one who repents on his deathbed also inherits the kingdom? No one can really "earn" eternal life and membership in the kingdom of heaven. There might be yet another reason why Matthew included this parable (it is not found in the other gospels). He may have had in mind the complaints of certain Jewish Christians, heirs to a two thousand year tradition, who were displeased that uncircumcised Gentile converts—latecomers to the tradition—were put on a par with them and were to inherit the long-expected kingdom.

Jesus' parables are meant to be disturbing. For centuries they have elicited from scholars and non-professional Bible readers alike an endless variety of interpretations. We have offered a few of our own. The Bible is a book that challenges us to interact with it. Jesus himself was a person with whom his contemporaries and later generations were expected to interact and enter into dialogue. His stories are provocative and can be read in myriad different ways, even as Jesus himself can mean different things to different people.

3. Jesus as a Wisdom Teacher

We are not born into this world to mark time. In the spiritual life, not to advance is to fall behind and eventually to end with nothing. "For to all who have, more will be given, and they will have in abundance; but from those who have nothing, even what they have will be taken away" (Mt 25:29). If you bet on a horse and lose, you forfeit any potential gain and the original deposit itself. The accumulated earthly treasure of those who lead wasted lives seeking material gain adds up to nothing in the world to come, and they are equally without the spiritual coin of the realm. Time is precious. We have only so many hours to love and serve God and care for others. Jesus says, "I must work the works of the one who sent me while it is day; for the night is coming when no one can work" (Jn 9:4). Paul calls this "making the most of time" (Eph 5:16). As Jesus sets his face to go to Jerusalem, he knows that his days are numbered, that the time is short. "Listen," he says, "I am casting out demons and performing cures today and tomorrow, and on the third day I finish my work" (Lk 13:32). We all face that "third day" when no one can work. Greek and Roman bons vivants, if they were Epicureans of the popular variety, might cry, "*Carpe Diem*! Eat, drink, and be merry today, for tomorrow you die." They intended to squeeze all the pleasure they could out of each moment. For Jesus, however, the task was to accomplish as much good as possible for the welfare of others during the days and hours left to him.

We can so easily be deceived by the tinsel and pretense of the good life that we waste our days, fascinated with the emptiness of the human comedy. Jesus is never so serious as when he warns, "Do not store up for yourselves treasures on earth, where both moth and rust consume and where thieves break in and steal, but store up for yourselves treasures in heaven, where neither moth nor rust consumes and where thieves do not break in and steal. For where your treasure is, there your heart will be also" (Mt 6:19–20).

Along with several other sayings, this last one might seem to be otherworldly. Is Jesus not saying that going to heaven is the fruit of a virtuous life? Heaven, however, is not some place outside and beyond us. It refers to the treasure house of the spirit within, as well as to the ideal set of social conditions outside of us. If there is anything we can take with us at the moment of death it is the store of values that have been internalized and incorporated into the deep self so that they become second nature. It is not a question of striving to be virtuous in order to obtain a reward after death. If we must speak of rewards, there is a lot of truth in the saying that virtue is its own reward. Heaven can be now for those who lead unselfish lives. At the Last Supper on the eve of his passion and death, Jesus speaks to his apostles about his joy: "I have said these things to you so that my joy may be in you, and that your joy may be complete." It is a joy that no man can take from them (Jn 15:11, 16:22, 17:13). Even when faced with death, Jesus' joy does not desert him.

If these quotes seem like preaching, they are nevertheless the preaching of Jesus, and to that extent they are autobiographical. Jesus most certainly lived what he preached and preached what he lived. It greatly upset the rich and the powerful who sensed immediately that they would be at risk if his program succeeded. As I will try to show below, this fear, rather than theological considerations, was the principal factor in his arrest and execution. The fact is that, humanly speaking, Jesus died too soon. His early death was an unfortunate interruption of a teaching career that should have gone on for many more years. A longer lifespan would have given him the opportunity to guide the growth of his community and answer questions about his original intentions, such as those raised by St. Paul regarding the exemption of Gentile converts from circumcision and all the requirements of Torah.[13] As it is, we have to depend on texts written forty to sixty years after Jesus' passing that respond to conditions that arose outside of Palestine after the fall of Jerusalem and the destruction of the Temple.

4. Why Was Jesus Crucified?

Why was Jesus not he beheaded as was John the Baptist or stoned to death like the deacon Stephen? It was not because the Jews had been denied the right to inflict capital punishment on a man or a woman. Stephen had been stoned with no adverse consequences for those who executed him. A woman taken in adultery could be stoned according to the Law of Moses, and Herod Antipas, a Jew, beheaded John the Baptist. What the Jews under Roman rule could not do was crucify a man. Why, then, was Jesus crucified?

a. The Charge of Subversion

The reason for the type of death Jesus suffered was indicated by the wording of the advisory, or *titulus*, placed at the head of his cross. It read, "Jesus of Nazareth, King of the Jews." This meant that his crime was subversion. He was put to death on the charge of having claimed to be "King" in a Roman province under the lordship of the Emperor. But, had he ever made such a claim? If he had, he would by that very fact have claimed to be king and the rightful heir of King David and his throne. His "claim" was a crime punishable by death according to Roman law.

In determining whether Jesus ever claimed for himself the role of Messiah, we should not be confused by what the evangelists thought and wrote about him. The point at issue is whether Jesus claimed to be, or thought he was, the Messiah. Academic, as contrasted to Church-related, commentators lean heavily toward the opinion that Jesus did not make any such claim. This opinion did not prevent gospel writers, such as the author of Mark's Gospel, from opening his account with the declaration, "The beginning of the good news of Jesus Christ," that is, Jesus the Messiah, Jesus the King.

So, when Pilate asks Jesus, "Are you the King of the Jews?" (Mk 15:2), the Roman governor must have been concerned. Anyone claiming to be king without appointment by the Emperor was by that very fact in rebellion and subject to the death penalty by crucifixion.

Standing before Pilate, the high priests accuse Jesus: "We found this man perverting the nation, forbidding us to pay taxes to the emperor, and saying that he himself is the Messiah, a king" (Lk 23:2). The accusation would have been enough for Pilate to act and send Jesus to the cross; however he already previously conspired with the Temple hierarchy to arrest Jesus and execute him. (See chapters twenty-two and twenty-four of this book).

b. What Kind of Kingdom?

Jesus made no attempt to conceal the fact that what he preached was the coming of a kingdom, traces of which were already in evidence. Twenty centuries of preaching "the kingdom" have obscured the fact that the kingdom Jesus was talking about was not primarily or exclusively a heavenly one to be enjoyed by the faithful after death. Jesus might assure Pilate that "My kingdom is not *of* this world," but it was to be very much *in* the world.

What was the nature of this kingdom? In the new age that was dawning the rich and the powerful would find no place in it, as long as they clung to their wealth and had no concern for the less fortunate members of their society and were unwilling to share their abundance with them. The poor and the meek, meanwhile, would be included and would "inherit the land" (Mt 5:5). "The land" here, *hē gē*, almost certainly refers to the land of Israel, the original territory ruled by King David and his son Solomon, and secondarily to the peasant farms that had been appropriated by the rich absentee Jewish and Gentile landowners. Those who were first in rank and wealth would be last, and those who were now oppressed and sorrowing would be comforted and could rejoice, which is the message of the Eight Beatitudes (Mt 5:3–11). Luke's shorter version is even more threatening to the privileged members of the nation: "But woe to you rich for you have received your consolation. Woe to you who are now full, for you will be hungry. Woe to you who are laughing now, for you will mourn and weep" (Lk 6:24–25).

What Jesus is preaching is a complete reversal of fortunes. One can imagine how rumors of such a turn around would be received and interpreted by the rich and powerful. What Jesus was fostering was nothing short of revolution. Look at the kind of people who were going to constitute the main body of the population when the kingdom would come: the unlettered, sinners, the sick, the destitute, society's outcasts. Jesus' program certainly gave the privileged classes something to think about, and to stop.

c. Religious Opposition

If the well-to-do found Jesus' vision of the kingdom a threat to themselves and their possessions, ultraconservative religious figures were equally shocked and alarmed by his words and deeds. They could accept John the Baptist as an austere prophet in the traditional mold. He drank no wine, ate no bread, and subsisted on locusts and wild honey. But this Jesus had the reputation of being a party person, a wine-bibber and glutton. He ate and drank with sinners, not just the ritually unclean but with extortionists like the publicans, the hated tax collectors. On one occasion he even allowed a woman who was a public sinner, who had let her hair down, to touch him, wash, and even kiss his feet. Women traveled in his company of disciples, supported him out of their means, talked Torah with him on an equal footing with men. He was even said to have defended a woman taken in adultery.

However innocent these actions were, they could easily be made to sound outrageously unbecoming in a Hebrew teacher. Thus, even Jesus' good deeds were seen as tainted in the eyes of the sanctimonious. Why did he deliberately cure people on the Sabbath when there were six other days on which to perform cures? As indicated above, he seems at times to have disregarded the custom of hand washing before eating and defended his disciples when they ate with unwashed hands (Mt 15:20). So, whatever his coming kingdom was to be like, it would surely be one in which an ultra-observant Jew would not feel at home, especially because Jesus had announced that publicans and sinners were already entering it while the righteous scribes and Pharisees were staying away. As for observing the food laws, had they heard right when it was rumored that Jesus had said something to the effect that what people ate did not matter as long as those people were just, compassionate, and pure of heart? (Mk 7:20–21).

d. The Last Straw: Challenging the High Priests and Rome

If the words and actions of Jesus succeeded in marshaling against him the wealthy and the righteous, he had yet to attack and act against the Temple hierarchy and Rome's political interests. It was only during the closing days of his final stay in Jerusalem that he is reputed to have done two things to seal his fate. First, according to the Synoptic Gospels, he carefully planned to enter Jerusalem in ceremonial fashion riding on a borrowed donkey. In this way, he would intentionally implement the prophetic model described by Zechariah: "Look, your king is coming to you humble and riding on a donkey, and on a colt the foal of a donkey" (Mt 21:5; Zech 9:9). He would surely have known that his followers would recognize the gesture and hail him as King and royal Son of David. Secondly, he is reported to have knotted a whip and single-handedly driven the money-changers and the animals out of the Temple yard. In the process, he upset the counting tables and sent the coins stacked on them flying off in all directions.

Why did Jesus engage in such an obviously provocative action, one that directly attacked the Temple high priests and the monetary exchange operation they sanctioned and by which they probably profited? Was he trying to do something that was guaranteed to result in his arrest and execution? Did he think that such a symbolic action would provoke divine intervention, or perhaps encourage others to join him and create a mass protest against the Temple hierarchy?

I refuse to believe that Jesus was that naive. Did he really attack the Temple physically? The Gospels tell us that he was overheard saying that the Temple would be destroyed with not a stone still standing upon another (Mk 13:2; Mt 24:2; Lk 21:6). This information may be interpreted as "attacking" the Temple, not physically but verbally, by predicting its destruction. It is of the utmost importance to note that when Jesus was interrogated before the Sanhedrin, he was not charged with having overthrown the tables of the money-changers, but of having said that the Temple would be destroyed, or that he could or would destroy it. The witnesses could not agree on just what he had said. But *there is not a word in any of the gospels indicating that the disturbance Jesus is supposed to have caused in the Temple area was introduced as a reason for his arrest and condemnation.* That is strange. It throws into question the historicity of the money-changer incident. Jesus did not likely go on a one-man rampage, violently overthowing the tables of the money-changers, driving out all of the animals, and then quietly walking away unscathed under the very noses of the watchful Temple police!

On the other hand, if Jesus had predicted, or merely speculated about the destruction of the Second Temple, his words may have been interpreted as an oncoming attack on the Temple. To prophesy against the House of God, God's dwelling place, was equivalent to blasphemy, and this may have been the basis for the charge of blasphemy that was introduced into the trial of Jesus. Even if Jesus had claimed to be the Messiah, he could not be accused of blasphemy on that charge alone. But prophesying against the Temple and foretelling its destruction was something else.

Turning now to Jesus' triumphal entry into Jerusalem astride a donkey, I must begin by stating that several considerations militate against his having planned such an obvious affront to Roman authority. Matthew and Luke, following Mark, say that Jesus had arranged with some acquaintance to provide him with a donkey when he would have need of it. So he sent two of his disciples to a nearby village to bring him the donkey to ride on in a triumphal entry into Jerusalem (Mk 11:1–7; Mt 21:1–3; Lk 19:29–35). What Jesus could not have failed to foresee was that news of this escapade would within minutes come to the attention of the military commander of the cohort quartered in the Antonia Tower where the ever-vigilant Roman garrison was stationed. Pilate, who was staying in Jerusalem at the time, would then be informed in short order about what had happened, namely, that the Galilean prophet was entering the city in triumph and was being hailed as King of the Jews and heir to David's throne.

The Fourth Gospel records this event with no indication that Jesus had planned in advance a regal entry into the city. During the week or ten days before his arrest, Jesus would travel each day from the village of Bethania to Jerusalem in order to preach and teach in the Temple area. On one of these trips, he is met by an enthusiastic crowd. The people hear that he is on his way to the city again. Thus, John writes: "The next day the great crowd that had come to the festival heard that Jesus was coming to Jerusalem. So they took branches of palm trees and went out to meet him, shouting, 'Hosanna! Blessed is the one who comes in the name of the Lord—the king of Israel!'" (Jn 12:13). Probably to avoid being crushed by the press of the crowd, "Jesus *found* a donkey and sat on it." There is nothing planned in this account. The donkey was found half way through the procession. Probably his enthusiastic followers in the crowd hailed Jesus as "King of Israel." The accolade, however, would have been more of an embarrassment to Jesus than a blessing, because he could foresee where it would lead.

e. An Ounce of Prevention

Jesus did not have to perform two highly provocative actions, such as those outlined above (and rejected as not literally historical) to run afoul of the Temple authorities and Rome, the sole superpower in the Mediterranean basin. His entire program was seen as subversive by those who thought they had the most to lose. If Jesus had his way, privilege would have ended and roles would have changed, eventually ensuring that the rich shared their wealth with the poor. In the bargain, the underclass would emerge and set the agenda in the new-age kingdom under God. There would be no kings or procurators, and no large landowners and absentee landlords, because the earth's riches would be shared equally by all. Among those who were at risk when that day came were those very landowners, whether Greeks or Romans or Jews. Among the latter were the wealthy Sadducean High Priests who wanted Jesus stopped. Was Jesus' execution a mistake? Not in the eyes of Caiaphas and Pilate. They regarded the existence and activity of Jesus as a threat to public order, the status quo, and the sovereignty of the Emperor.

From all of the above, it seems clear that Jesus did not preach a strictly otherworldly kingdom, and that the *religious* charges against him were not the main reason for his condemnation by the high priests—at least they were not sufficient to warrant his being stoned to death. If that kind of execution were carried out on religious grounds, the common people would blame the highly unpopular Temple authorities. It was far better to have the Romans, whose military strength could not be challenged, eliminate the troublesome Galilean on political charges. Behind issues of both religious and political grievances lay the economic one and the fears of those who did not trust the masses and the influence that a charismatic populist leader could have on them.

5. Was Jesus an Apocalypticist?

Mitchell D. Reddish distinguishes between prophetic eschatology and apocalyptic eschatology.[13] The former concerns events that are to take place in the ordinary course of human affairs under the guidance of the God of history. The latter entails supernatural interventions, other-world journeys, and revelations given to privileged individuals concerning the future. I do not believe that Jesus was an eschatologist in the second sense. This is an important distinction in determining whether, in his so-called Eschatological Discourse, Jesus maintained that after a great war, he would come in power to judge the nations. The angels would gather the elect from the four corners of the earth, and heaven and earth as we know them would pass away (Mk 13:27, 31). Jesus seems to have had in mind a crisis in Jewish affairs. But it would not include an accompanying cosmic catastrophe, followed by his return to earth, the General Resurrection, the General Judgment, and the end of time.

Always aware of the restlessness of those impatient patriots who were itching for an opportunity to challenge Rome militarily, Jesus could foresee nothing but disaster. He knew that war is accompanied by untold hardships, even for non-combatants, who suffer famine, disease, the loss of their homes, and the death of loved ones. The high priests' council had warned Caiaphas that if there were to be an insurrection, both the nation and the Temple would be at risk (Jn 11:48). As women and children flee the war zone, hardships multiply, especially in winter during the rainy season. "Then those in Judea must flee to the mountains, the one on the housetop must not go down or enter the house to take anything away; the one in the field must not turn back to get a coat. Woe to those who are pregnant and to those who are nursing infants in those days! Pray that it may not be in winter. . . . And if anyone says to you, 'Look! Here is the Messiah!' Or 'Look! There he is!'—do not believe it." Jesus, or the evangelists speaking for him, declares that in those days, "The sun will be darkened, and the moon will not give its light, and the stars will be falling from the heavens, and the powers of the heavens will be shaken. Then they will see the Son of Man coming in the clouds with great power and glory" (Mk 13:24–25).

Is Jesus talking here about two events, about a war and then about the celestial phenomena that are to precede his own second coming? The Synoptic Evangelists introduced the idea of two events: a war and a final catastrophe when Jesus would return again in the clouds as the victorious Son of Man. A good case can be made to show that Jesus was referring to a single event accompanied by *symbolic* astronomical effects? To begin with, the celestial phenomena are not to be taken literally. To stress the enormity of the disaster that could affect Jerusalem during an all-out war with Rome, Jesus uses conventional language of the kind common in the writings of the Hebrew prophets and in the more recent eschatological tracts.

Thus, referring to the destruction of Babylon, Isaiah says that when "the Lord *comes*," the sun will be darkened and the moon will not give its light" (Isa 13:10). To be noted is that the destruction of Babylon is spoken of as "the Day of the Lord," or "the *Coming* of the Lord." Joel, speaking for God, says, "I will show portents in the heavens and on the earth blood and fire and columns of smoke. The sun shall be turned to darkness, and the moon to blood, before the great and terrible day of the Lord *comes*" (Job 2:30–31). Ezekiel, too, introduces heavenly signs and portents in the sky to symbolize a time of great crisis. Such emotive, figurative language expresses what the prophet feels in the face of disaster. In none of the above instances does God "come," neither does the sun fail nor the moon turn to blood.

But like the disasters that overtook Babylon and Egypt, the fall of Jerusalem was a tragedy of such proportions that the evangelists, probably echoing Jesus, felt justified in linking it with celestial portents. Nature itself is poetically portrayed as weeping in sympathy with the misfortunes of the nation: The sky is falling! The end is near! The Son of Man will soon appear! The sorrows and sufferings brought on by the war with Rome, including the destruction of the Temple, were seen as eliciting a sympathetic response in the heavens, as the sun is darkened and the moon fails to give her light. The words used by the evangelists are almost identically the ones found in Isaiah, Joel, and Ezekiel. For their part, the New Testament authors could view the destruction of the Temple as an example of "the Lord *coming* in power." It was seen as a belated vindication of Jesus who had been rejected by the Jews.

I conclude, then, that Jesus believed that one phase of Jewish history would soon come to an end in pain and suffering. But he did not intend the colorful language about heavenly portents to refer to a cosmic catastrophe ushering in the Last Judgment, or to his own Second Coming, though the evangelists interpreted him to mean exactly that. On the contrary, he was speaking from the point of view of a prophetic eschatologist, not as a radical apocalypticist. John the Baptist not only believed that the present age was coming to an end, but spoke, as well, of an apocalyptic "wrath to come" when God, as final Judge, would cut down those individuals who bore no fruit and cast them into the fire (Mt 3:7–10). This statement implies an extraordinary divine intervention at the end of time. It is imperative, then, that everyone shape up against that dreadful Judgment Day. To prepare for it, they must refrain from dishonesty, extortion, and all the other kinds of moral disorders, in favor of good works and acts of charity. Paul shared this apocalyptic view in his early writings. But it could not have been Jesus' vision of the distant future, for in his preaching he was laying the ground for an earthly kingdom that would survive every possible human disaster, rather than for a short-term commonwealth whose members would soon be raptured into heaven.

6. Death and Defeat

The death of a young and beloved public figure—one thinks of the assassination of John F. Kennedy—focuses all eyes on the tragic event. All too often the attention given to the hero's last moments leaves in the shade the substance of his or her life. The Christian tradition has freighted the death of the young Jesus with a redemptive meaning that can easily blur the importance of his life and teaching up to that final hour. His death was one piece of his life, with all that had gone before. It was like the point that terminates a line and is not distinct from it, being but the cut off point of a career dedicated to God and the service of others. If Jesus had died accidentally, without prolonged pain or suffering, it would not diminish the salvific worth of his dedicated life.[14]

There is nothing magic about the death of Jesus. It changes nothing in the life of any one of us, unless his teaching and example affect our own way of thinking and acting. His death did not temper the wrath of God, a wrath that never existed save in the minds of those whose idea of God was based on their image of an oriental despot. He was not sent to die on the cross by a Father who required that his Son die the most shameful and agonizing death man has devised to placate himself.

St. Augustine felt that the vast majority of human beings (the *massa damnata*,) were on their way to perdition.[15] Those who are spared from eternal damnation owe their salvation to the saving death of Christ who took upon himself the punishment that we all justly merited as children of Adam. St. Paul, who had a flare for vivid, rhetorical imagery, says that Jesus became sin and a curse for our salvation (2 Cor 5:21; Gal 3:13). He became a kind of lightning rod by taking in his body the full force of God's anger, thus shielding us from the avenging "wrath." Writing almost a century ago, Annie Besant made a collection of the reasons offered by nineteenth-century divines to account for the cruel death of Jesus.

> Stroud makes Christ drink "the cup of the wrath of God."
> Jenkyn says, "He suffered as one disowned and reprobated
> and forsaken by God." Dwight considers that he endured
> God's "hatred and contempt." Bishop Jeune tells us that
> "after man had done his worst, worse remained for Christ
> to bear. He had fallen into his Father's hands." Archbishop
> Thompson preaches that "the clouds of God's wrath gath-
> ered thick over the human race: they discharged them-
> selves on Jesus only." He "became a curse for us and a ves-
> sel of wrath."[16]

What we have here is a classical instance of rhetorical overkill. Some people are fascinated with the grotesque. The sufferings of the damned in hell are described so vividly by revivalist preachers that you would think they had been there. People like to be frightened. That is why they go to horror movies and auto races with smash-ups at a hundred miles an hour. At least the excitement relieves the boredom of everyday living. The suffering of Jesus crucified are so real for anyone who can endure meditating on the horror of it that there is little need to multiply terrifying images to describe what it was like. Looking at the crucified Jesus, or any other victim of violence and calculated cruelty, we ought to weep for man's inhumanity to man. The cross is not something out of the past. Paul carried it in his heart wherever he went. The cross is an ever-present reality wherever there is rank injustice, torture, hate crimes, racial injustice, and rule by brutality and terror.

What the cross did, and still does, is showcase Jesus' fidelity to his mission of service and justice for all. It entailed an all-out effort to better the human condition and improve the material and spiritual quality of life against all but insuperable odds. Eventually he came to understand what the risks were and what they could lead to, "even to death on a cross" (Phil 2:8). Shocking as it may seem to pious ears, I would be greatly surprised if Jesus, hanging on the cross, knew beyond all shadow of doubt that his death was the condition sine qua non for the salvation of the entire human race. Even if it was just that, part of his suffering was not to know whether it had any larger redemptive meaning. That interpretation was placed on it and on his death by others who drew heavily on the fifty-third chapter of Isaiah: "But he was wounded for our transgressions, crushed for our iniquities; upon him was the punishment that made us whole, and by his bruises we are healed" (Isa 53:5). If Jesus was to plumb the depths of human dereliction, the experience of "feeling" abandoned by God was part of his self-emptying. The feeling did not make it so. The resurrection, as later writers would declare, was the refutation of abandonment, while the worldwide dissemination of Jesus' teaching was and is a vindication whose success stands in inverse proportion to the apparent depth of his defeat.

In spite of the bizarre beliefs that have been held and the dreadful deeds that have been carried out in the name of Jesus, his spirit is still very much alive in many of our institutions. Democracy, based on the assumed equality before God of all citizens, while honored in the breach, is a legacy of Jesus' abolition of the distinction between masters and slaves (Jn 13:14). The corporal and spiritual works of mercy have been institutionalized in many of our medical and psychiatric services, albeit with the unhealthy innovation of healthcare-for-profit. Alongside the abuses, the Western democracies have a general consensus, frequently backed by laws, concerning the importance of fairness, tax relief for the poor, welfare for the indigent and disabled, and retirement benefits for the aged. These are mostly novelties in the history of the human race, and they owe their inspiration and existence largely to the life and teaching of Jesus of Nazareth and his Jewish roots.

7. Paul's Post-Ascension Jesus

a. His Continued Existence as the Transcendent Nonethnic Christ

St. Paul, speaking of the vision he had at the time of his conversion, was convinced that Jesus, as the Christ, was still alive and active in the world. He had not gone off into the Absolute Elsewhere. In the Hebrew tradition, "Christ" was the title given to a man who was to have a special role to play in the redemption of Israel, specifically in freeing it from foreign domination. But whether he was a king or a priest or a conqueror, or all three put together, he was only a human being with a service to perform. The Christ in whom Paul lived and moved and had his spiritual being was much more than an ethnic hero who, among other actions, was to free Israel from Roman and all foreign domination. That particular role did not command the interest of Paul, a Jew of the Diaspora, and it was much too limited a concept for Jesus, which is one of the reasons why he hesitated to embrace the role of Christ, or Messiah.

The Living Christ whom Paul encountered was a universal spirit, more like the indwelling Holy Spirit than a man with a divinely assigned political role to play. The latter type of Messiah might live in the memory of those who honored him, but the Life that was in Jesus literally indwells those who believe in him now. So Paul will say in one way or another, "It is no longer I who live, but Christ who lives in me" (Gal 2:20). He is talking here about a metaphysical transformation, affecting his status in being, something the mere memory of an historical figure cannot bring about.

Paul most often writes of Jesus Christ, rather than of Jesus alone. To speak merely of Jesus would be to relate to him in a human way. That, says Paul, is what he does not do. For, "even though we once knew Christ from a human point of view [according to the flesh, *kata sarka*], we know him no longer that way" (2 Cor 5:16). What, then, was the Life that elevated Jesus above ordinary humanity? It harks back to the Wisdom literature of the Hebrew Scriptures where *Sophia* is presented as a kind of primordial divine emanation, "set up, at first, before the beginning of the earth" (Prov 8:23). In the Wisdom of Solomon, Wisdom is said to be, "the breath of the power of God, and a pure emanation of the glory of the Almighty" (Wis 7:25). It may not be God strictly speaking, but it is in some sense "divine,"[17] somewhat like the ten *Sefirot* in relation to *Ayn Sof* in the Jewish mystical tradition, or the Divine Energies in the Greek and Russian Orthodox tradition.

Does Paul subscribe to the full divinity of the man Jesus? Was Jesus God? In this connection it is important to keep in mind that Paul wrote nearly three centuries before there was any kind of consensus regarding terminology. The idea of a divine person, (*hypostasis*,) subsisting in two distinct natures had not yet been worked out. Paul was writing in a Jewish context with Greek philosophical overtones. In his Letter to the Philippians, he seems to affirm the preexistence and divinity of one aspect of the of the compound name "Jesus/Christ." But it does not seem likely that he would have applied the divinity univocally to God who was "in Christ reconciling the world to himself" (2 Cor 5:19) and the humanity of the historical Jesus. What had been "in the form of God" and lowered itself was not the preexisting humanity of Jesus. As a human being with a beginning in time, Jesus had to have a limited human form and personality with special characteristics recognizable by his friends. That personality, as distinct from the person, was time-bound, contingent, and mortal of its very nature. What rose from the dead was a transfigured and glorified humanity, one that had been assumed by the divine principle and was now revealed in all its glory. It was a glory first intimated in the Transfiguration of Jesus on Mt. Tabor, and one that would be revealed after death to and in all loyal disciples. Thus, Paul wrote in Romans (8:18): "I consider that the sufferings of this present time are not worth comparing with the glory about to be revealed to us."

b. The Specter of Subordinationism

Paul, relying principally on what he could learn from the Wisdom literature of the Hebrew Bible, is groping for a way to express the relationship between the human and the divine as they coexist in the man Jesus. Did he embrace, consciously or unconsciously, some form of subordinationism? Although the Gnostics and the Middle Platonists of Paul's day were emanationists, where the various emanations were inferior to the Source, they may still be called "divine." The debate about subordinationism would not become a live theological issue until the time of Arius, who denied that the Son was consubstantial with and equal to the Father. The humanity of Paul's Jesus may not have preexisted his conception and birth into the world, but the life that was in him did. That life, God's life, "was in Christ." It was immanent in Jesus during his lifetime and united with him in his risen life. In the Letter to the Colossians, a work of Pauline inspiration, Christ, as God's Son, is said to be "The image of the invisible God, the first-born of creation. For in him all the fullness of God was pleased to dwell" (Col 1:15, 19). God indwells Christ as in a tabernacle or temple, but that does not make the container the contained, nor is being an image substantially identical with its actual counterpart. Man, created in the image of God, is not thereby God. There is a tinge of subordinationism when Colossians describes Christ as "the firstborn of all creation" (*protoīokos pāses ktiseos*), which seems to imply that Christ is first among creatures, and not "very God."

Paul's Christ differs from John's Logos; for the latter not only dwells "with God" but "is God" (Jn 1:1). Paul's Christ is more like the Sophia (*hokmah*) of Proverbs which, though it acts as a master worker beside God (Prov 8:30), nevertheless confesses, "The Lord created me at the beginning of his work" (Prov 8:22).

Later dogmatic declarations would to a degree help clarify some of the ambiguities inseparable from Paul's early speculations without eliminating the mystery of what is called the Hypostatic Union. Peter in his Pentecost speech in Acts says twice of Jesus that "God raised him up" (Acts 1:24, 32) and that he now "sits" at the right hand of God (1:34). Sitting at the right hand of God does not, *eo ipso*, mean that Jesus, as the Christ, is identically God. The method employed in this study does not allow us to pursue the preceding type of theological speculation any further. Our concern is with the humanity of Jesus, a "Jesus before theology," somewhat analogous to the program of

Albert Nolan in his ground-breaking book, *Jesus Before Christianity*, which his publisher introduced as a "portrait of Jesus . . . as he was before he became enshrined in dogma and ritual."[18]

Notes

[1] Paul Tillich's "Ground of Being" is impersonal in the sense that God is not an entity or object. The absolutely ultimate reality transcends the subject–object dichotomy. God cannot be "a being among others." See *Systematic Theology* II, 15 (University of Chicago Press, 1957). Rudolf Otto's "Wholly Other," as described in *The Idea of the Holy* (New York: Oxford University Press, 1958) is similar to Tillich's "Ground" in that the *Mysterium tremendum et fascinans* is beyond description, not unlike the Jewish notion of the ineffable numinous character of YHWH.

[2] Daniel 7:13 reads; "As I watched in the night vision, I saw one like a human being coming with the clouds of heaven and he came to the Ancient One and was presented before him. To him was given dominion and glory and kingship, that all peoples, nations, and languages should serve him. His dominion is an everlasting dominion that shall not pass away, and his kingdom is one that shall never be destroyed."

In the phrase *hos huios anthropou*, like a Son of Man, the keyword is "like," What looked like a Son of Man was not a human being. Alan E. Segal thinks that the figure is "one of the principle angels in whose form God deigns to appear." *Paul the Convert: The Apostolate and the Apostasy of Saul the Pharisee* (New Haven: Yale University Press, 1990), 53.

There is also a secondary meaning suggested: The vision of the Son of Man coming in the clouds is the fifth after four previous visions of four beasts: a winged lion, a bear, a four-headed leopard, and a dragon. They correspond to four previous kingdoms, those of the Babylonians, Medes, Persians, and Greeks. The fifth, the Son of Man kingdom, stands for an empire with a human face, a humane kingdom of righteousness. Eventually, the "holy ones" will come into possession of it and they will be able to dwell in it forever and ever (Dan 7:18).

[3] The last judgment parable in Matthew's Gospel (Mt 25:31–6) borrows from the "Similitudes" in 1 Enoch. The Son of Man, God's Chosen One, will sit on his throne of glory to judge the wicked and disobedient angels. The faithful angels "will take hold of them on the great day and throw them into the furnace of living fire" (54). The Son of Man in Enoch is an individual who will serve as universal redeemer and judge of the nations. Cf. Mitchell C. Reddish, ed., *Apocalyptic Literature: A Reader* (Nashville: Abingdon Press, 1990), 163–187.

[4] Stevan Davies in *Jesus the Healer* (New York: Continuum, 1995), presses his case for seeing Jesus as a man periodically moved by the Spirit so that he was, as it were, beside himself and spoke almost as a medium between his spirit control and his hearers. He has in mind Mark 3:21.

[5] The Dead Sea Scrolls community foresaw the advent of two Messiahs, one a priest of Aaronic lineage, the other as a king of Davidic descent. The royal Messiah would defer to the priestly one. See Geza Vermes, *The Complete Dead Sea Scrolls in English* (New York: Alan Lane, The Penguin Press, 1997), 86. The evangelists combined the two Messiahs into one. A king, because of his Davidic descent, Jesus was also, by reason of his sacrificial death, a priest according to the order of Melchizedek (Heb 5:5).

[6] Matthew's is an ecclesial gospel. It reflects a level of institutional organization that is lacking in the other gospels. Mathew alone speaks of "the Church" as a governing body (Mt 16:18, 18:17, 21).

[7] While Jesus answers "I Am" to the question Caiaphas puts to him, "Are you the Messiah?" in Mark's Gospel, his reply in Luke's is a nonanswer. "If I tell you, you will not believe, and if I question you, you will not answer" (Lk 22:67–68). In Matthew, his answer, *su eipas* (you say), is almost equivalent to a question, "Is that what you say," or "Is that so?" Jesus uses a similar tactic in John's Gospel. Pilate asks him, "Are you the King of the Jews?" Then Jesus asks him, "Do you ask this on your own, or did others tell you about me?" (Jn 18:34).

[8] For the text of Q, see Burton L. Mack, *The Lost Gospel: The Book of Q and Christian Origins* (San Francisco: HarperSanFrancisco, 1993), and an earlier work by John S. Kloppenborg, *The Formation of Q* (Harrisburg: Trinity Press International, 1999: original 1987). Q contains none of the elaboration found in the narrative gospels that deal with the passion, death, and resurrection of Jesus.

[9] William Barclay, *The Gospel of Matthew* (Philadelphia: Westminster Press, 1958), II, 245–246, holds that day-laborers would arrive at a hiring hall at daybreak waiting for someone to offer them work. Some might by lucky and be hired immediately. Others might be called to work only an hour before quitting time. But they both had families to feed, and if they received only a pittance for an hour of work after waiting all day, their children would go hungry. Hence became the custom of paying all needy workers "a day's wage," whether they worked for long hours or not.

[10] Richard O. Ford, *The Parables of Jesus: Recovering the Art of Listening* (Minneapolis: Fortress Press, 1997) gives examples from a psychologist's point of view regarding the paradoxical and disturbing nature of many of Jesus' parables.

[11] On "Commensality," See John Dominic Crossan. *Jesus: A Revolutionary Biography* (San Francisco: HarperSanFrancisco, 1994), 66–70.

[12] On "Healing and Eating Together," See Crossan, *Jesus: A Revolutionary Biography* (San Francisco: HarperSanFrancisco, 1994), 106–108.

[13] On the distinction between "Prophetic and Apocalyptic Eschatology,"see Mitchell G. Reddish, ed., *Apocalyptic Literature: A Reader* (Nashville: Abingdon Press, 1990), 19–20.

[14] Jesus could have lived longer had he stayed away from Jerusalem or gone to preach among the Jews of the Diaspora. In John 7:35, this latter idea, that he might leave and go elsewhere, was even suspected by some. But, like Socrates, who refused to leave Athens even in the face of death, Jesus had no intention of abandoning his mission to his fellow Jews.

[15] The collection of St. Augustine's writings contains sixteen volumes of his work, roughly 1,200 pages each. So it may be unfair to single out one passage dealing with the *massa damnata*. But it is true that Augustine was haunted by the specter of sin, especially sins of the flesh. In any case, the passage referred to will be found in *The City of God* XXI, 12: "Because of Adam's sin the whole mass of the human race is condemned; for he who first gave entrance to sin has been punished with all his posterity who were in him as in a root, so that no one is exempt from this just and due punishment, unless delivered by mercy and undeserving grace." The Marcus Dods translation, with an introduction by Thomas Merton (New York: The Modern Library, 1950), 783.

[16] Annie Besant, *Esoteric Christianity*, (Wheaton, Il: The Theosophical Publishing House, 1953), 135.

[17] J.–M. Hervé, *Manuale Theologicae Dogmaticae*, writes, regarding the communication of properties, *communicatio idiomatum* that it is permissible to say that the divine nature became incarnate, so that the human nature of Christ was divinized, but not that the divine nature became flesh or that the human nature became God. Thus, the human nature of Jesus is not God (substantively), but it can be said to be divine (adjectivally). For the Latin text, see Hervé (Westminster, MD: The Newman Bookshop, 1946), 2, 466, 499.

[18] From the back cover of *Jesus Before Christianity* (Maryknoll, NY: Orbis Books, sixth printing, 1997).

PART THREE:

People Jesus Healed

Chapter Six

THE CENTURION'S SERVANT

Action from a Distance

Chapters 8 and 9 in Matthew's Gospel list nine cures by Jesus. Jesus heals a leper, a paralyzed servant, a woman with a fever, two demoniacs, a paralytic on a stretcher, a woman with a flow of blood, a young girl thought to be dead, two blind men, and a man who is mute. The second cure, that of the servant/slave/boy of a Roman centurion appears in two versions. In Matthew, the sick person is a young servant (*pais*) who is paralyzed (Mt 8:5). In Luke, he is a valuable slave (*doulos*) who is near death (Lk 7:2).

Matthew says that the centurion comes in person to ask Jesus to heal the paralyzed boy, or servant. Jesus offers to come down and heal him, but the centurion protests that he is not worthy to have Jesus so much as come under his roof. He is seemingly sensitive to the fact that a Jew was not supposed to enter a Gentile's house. "Only speak the word," he says, "and my servant will be healed" (Mt 8:8). Jesus marvels at such great faith in a Gentile, assures him that the paralyzed servant will be healed in accordance with the centurion's faith, "and the servant was healed at the same hour" (Mt 8:13). Not satisfied with praising the centurion's faith, Matthew's Jesus adds that, while many will come from east and west and eat with Abraham, Isaac, and Jacob in the kingdom, the heirs of the kingdom, namely, the Jews, will be cast out (Mt 8:11–12).

Luke tells the same story, but the circumstances are a bit different and there is no attack on the Jews. Here, the centurion's slave is not just paralyzed, he is also near death. The centurion does not come in person. He sends some Jewish elders to plead for the cure of a slave who is very dear to him. They inform Jesus that this pagan soldier is a friend of the Jews, for he has built a synagogue for them. Jesus is duly impressed and joins the elders as they make their way together to the centurion's house. Upon nearing the house, some friends of the centurion meet Jesus and inform him that the officer does not think himself worthy to come to Jesus in person or worthy enough to have him enter under his roof. The friends convey the message that as far as the centurion is concerned, all Jesus has to do is say the word and his slave will be healed. Jesus marvels at such great faith in a Gentile. He never does enter the centurion's house, but when the friends return there, they find that the slave who was close to death has been restored to health (Lk 7:10).

Healing by Word Alone

How unworthy can one be. In Luke's account, the centurion does not feel worthy to approach Jesus in person but sends intermediaries, first the Jewish elders, and then his friends. In spite of the differences, what the two accounts have in common is that they tell about a cure from a distance. In most cases, Jesus touches the one whom he cures, taking that person by the hand, placing mud on the eyes of a blind man, or placing his finger in the ears of a deaf mute. But here Jesus uses no paraphernalia to enhance the expectations of those he cures. All he has to do is "say the word," like God in the act of creation, and, as with anyone in authority, his orders are carried out promptly.

Matthew and Luke are dealing with the same event: a centurion with a sick servant or slave or boy, his recourse to Jesus, his humility, his unworthiness that Jesus should enter his house, his belief that a word from Jesus is all that is needed, and that Jesus, an authority figure like himself, had only to issue a command and all nature would obey him. But Luke's redaction of the Matthean text introduces several important changes. His slave is not paralyzed and in great distress but is near death. He is no ordinary slave but a favorite of the centurion. There are no intermediaries in Matthew's account, whereas Luke introduces two sets of them, namely, the Jewish elders and the centurion's friends. Luke's Jesus goes to the house of the Roman officer, whereas, in Matthew, he stays where he was when the centurion approached him. Finally, in Matthew, the centurion meets Jesus personally and appeals to him, while according to Luke he neither meets him nor ever talks with him.

Another Healing Story

Either Matthew and Luke are using two different sources for their story, or Luke, coming later, has revised Matthew's story to attribute to the pagan soldier an even more remarkable degree of humility and faith. Whichever happens to be the case, we have also to factor in another miracle story which is similar to the accounts of the healing of the centurion's servant. The reference is to John's account of the cure of the son *(huios)* of a certain *basilikos*. The New Revised Standard Version translates *basilikos* as "royal official," which comes close to the function of the man. He might also be called a courtier or petty official in a royal court. Since the scene takes place in Galilee, the courtier would in all probability be someone connected with the tetrarch Herod Antipas (Jn 4:46–54).

In John's story the Jewish official's son is sick in Capernaum, as in Matthew and Luke, but Jesus works his cure from Cana where the royal official meets him. As a result the cure takes place from a distance, as in the two former accounts. But now the distance is increased to eighteen miles, the distance from Cana to Capernaum. As in Matthew, the father comes in person to see Jesus, begs for a cure, and is told to go home because "your son will live." The man believes, and on his way home he is met by his slaves and is told that the son recovered at precisely the hour when, the day before, Jesus said that his son would live. This is a paradigm story. It follows the same sequence as in the accounts of the healing of the centurion's servant in Matthew and Luke.

Geza Vermes offers other examples of healing from a distance. Hanina ben Dosa, a Jewish charismatic of the first century, is reputed to have cured the son of the famous rabbi Gamaliel.[1] Hanina was in Galilee and Gamaliel's son was in Jerusalem. Philostratus, in his eight-volume *Life of Apollonius of Tyana*, circa 217–220, attributed to Apollonius, a first century contemporary of Jesus', distance healings similar to those performed by Jesus. But, as John P. Meier has pointed out, rumors of such wonders date from a century and a half to two centuries after the events described.[2] The stories about Apollonius were to some degree an attempt by a pagan author to show that Apollonius was at least as great a wonderworker as Jesus.

The Anti-Jewish Slant in Matthew and John

We have seen that Matthew introduces an anti-Jewish note while praising the faith of the centurion. Similarly, John's Jesus, on being asked to heal the Jewish official's son, seems to question gratuitously the quality of the man's faith; for he says, "Unless you see signs and wonders you will not believe" (Jn 4:48). Nothing daunted, the official persists and continues to beg Jesus to "come down before my little boy dies." He does not believe in healing from a distance. But, at least, he meets the test and Jesus tells him that all will be well with the boy.

In Matthew's Gospel, Jesus uses the faith of the Gentile centurion as an occasion for decrying and condemning the lack of faith of the Jews. In John's Gospel, while no Gentile's faith is compared to that of the Jews, the Jews are still condemned. Luke omits the anti-Jewish strain in his account of the cure of the centurion's slave. Writing for Gentiles, he makes the faith and humility of the centurion even greater than in Matthew's account. He also gives us a sense of the character of the centurion. He is not only a man of faith, but he is also a kind and considerate person who dearly loves and cares for one of his slaves. Generous, he has used his own resources to build a synagogue for the Jews. He is truly the very model of the "righteous Gentile." Unlike Matthew and John, Luke here appears to be more pro-Gentile than anti-Jewish. We are also given a glimpse of his kindly nature. In his infancy account, he introduces Mary with great tenderness, gives us a view of tolerance and mercy in the Parables of the Good Samaritan and the Prodigal Son, and has Jesus, while on the cross, forgive his enemies and a reputed outlaw. He even turns the Gentile Pontius Pilate into a paragon of beleaguered kindness. See Chapter 24 of this book.

Excursus on Faith

To sum up, we are dealing in the three above accounts with the importance of faith in relation to healing. Can Jesus cure a sick person by just willing it? In the vast majority of cures Jesus is greatly assisted by the degree of faith the person to be cured can muster. At Nazareth he could work few cures because of the lack of faith on the part of his relatives and townsmen. "And he was amazed at their unbelief" (Mk 6:6). The centurion's faith, grounded on humility and trust, was spontaneous. Can one force oneself to believe? That was what the father of the epileptic boy was trying to do when he found that the disciples of Jesus were unable to cure his son who was suffering from convulsions and foaming at the mouth. The father pleads, "I believe, help my unbelief" (Mk 9:24). Perhaps the desire for faith is already the beginning of faith.

The kind of faith Jesus looked for, the kind he himself had, was a mixture of confidence and singlemindedness: confidence that the cure will take place coupled with a sharp focus on the image of the cure as already achieved. When some people come to Jairus announcing that his daughter is dead, Jesus tells him to ignore the bad news. "Do not fear," he urges, "only believe" (Mk 5:36). In other words, "Let your eye be single *(haplous)*" (Mt 6:22). Envision the girl as already cured and healthy; concentrate on only one, single thing; health.

The words "doubt" and "double" have the same root. Both are concerned with twoness. To doubt means to be double-minded about something to be done. When Peter begins to walk on the water, he is distracted by the fact that he is doing something that is supposed to be impossible. So, when Jesus rescues him, he says to Peter, "You of little faith, why did you doubt?" (Mt 14:31). Instead of focusing on Jesus, he divided his attention between Jesus and the water beneath him. The Greek word used by Matthew for doubt is *distazo*. It includes the prefix di, from the adverb dis, meaning "twice." It turns up in words such as di-polar, meaning two poles, or even in Latinized words such as di-vide and dis-traction, the latter meaning to be drawn or pulled in two or more directions.

Thus, Jesus wants those hoping to be cured to be single-eyed and single-minded. This kind of faith that believes that with God all things are possible should be distinguished from belief as a form of assent to something as true or false. The latter may be concerned either with a fact or a proposition of some kind. If I hold that Lincoln was shot, I am dealing with a fact that is historically well documented. But if I assent to or believe in reincarnation as a fact, not everyone will agree. Then, there are some propositions that I may have to believe when I first hear about them, but which I may later be able to prove as true. For example, the proposition that the square on the hypotenuse of a right triangle is equal to the sum of the squares on the other two sides. Less universally accepted propositions have to do with creedal statements and doctrinal affirmations held to be true in one religion or another. Belief in such matters can be firm or faltering, depending on the degree of confidence the believer can invest in the proposed tenet.

There is, also, belief in a person. This includes the conviction that a particular individual can be trusted, that he or she is knowledgeable and truthful. Sometimes the last two types of belief—belief in a person and belief in a statement as true—coalesce and can be found together. Are there angels? Do they really exist? If Jesus were to assure one of his followers that there are angels, and were that person to assent to Jesus' statement, neither as self-evident nor as true on the basis of rational inquiry, his assent to the statement as fact would depend on his belief in the credibility of the person making it; that is, that he is well informed, honest, and speaks with authority. Here assent to the fact depends on trust or belief in the person.

Finally, there is the kind of faith required for healing. Strictly speaking, the healer does not heal. He is usually a catalyst whose authority in the mind of the one healed is able to activate the immune system or alter brain chemistry. We are familiar today with mind-altering drugs, some good, some dangerous. Lithium can stabilize a person with bipolar disease. Crack cocaine can ruin an individual's ability to function usefully in society. No doubt, many diseases that went by the name of demonic possession in Jesus' day were simply nervous or emotional disorders. They can be alleviated and sometimes cured by medication or extended counseling. As a charismatic person-ality, Jesus was able to cure many disorders of this kind by his author-itative word.

However, not all the illnesses Jesus cured were of a psychogenic nature. Leprosy (Hansen's disease) in its advanced stages is not cured by an encouraging word on the part of an authority figure. Blindness caused by cataracts is not an emotional disorder. The Record Bureau at Lourdes in France contains public records, covering almost a cen-tury and a half, that offer impressive, documented evidence that malignant tumors, shattered bones, and "terminal" cancer patients have been cured, contrary to what professional medical prognosis would have anticipated. What has been done in the broad daylight of our own age would not have been impossible for Jesus to do during the months and days of his short healing ministry.

Healing from a distance is more problematic, especially when the person healed has no knowledge that he is the object intended for the cure. Still, verbal contact may be enough, even by long distance tele-phone or television, though in such cases the healer is in some sense present. He is there visually and orally, and "touches" the one healed by sight or sound.

Nature miracles constitute another category. Honi the Circle-Drawer, was a first-century BCE rainmaker according to the fragmen-tary reports we have about him. He put God on the spot by drawing a circle, standing in it, and declaring that he would not move until God made it rain.[3] (Mt 3:7). The nature miracles of Jesus were not per-formed as a challenge to God nor simply to astonish people and win public acclaim. They resulted from Jesus' compassion for the afflicted. They usually carried a lesson with them. Some may have had natural explanations. Some were erroneously taken to describe deeds done by Jesus when, actually, they had their origin in parables or examples he used as teaching stories. Changing water into wine, multiplying bread, and calming a storm at sea carry with them important lessons and have symbolic overtones that may be of greater instructional value than the works themselves, whether they took place or not.

Altering the molecular structure so that six jars of water are turned into very fine wine is something for chemists to explain. What the phenomenon calls to mind is that God is a generous giver. The same is true when Jesus feeds five thousand people with a few loaves and fishes. After all had eaten, there were twelve baskets of fragments left over. In both accounts what is significant is abundance. The two instances of giving anticipate the Last Supper, when Jesus would give himself to his disciples under the symbols of bread and wine. He had been giving himself to others since the beginning of his ministry. Now he tells the others, "Do this!" Give yourselves to others as I have given myself to you; love others as I have loved you (Jn 15:12). Calming the storm at sea has been meaningful for generations of prayerful people who, in their darkest hours, have envisionned or dreamed of Jesus coming to them to bring peace and calm.

The lesson conveyed by the multiplication of the loaves is that there is enough food for everyone, if we all share what we have. Today, we are confronted with a situation in which we find people in the underdeveloped nations suffering from poverty and starvation, while those in the advanced nations are so well fed that they are overweight and make a fetish of dieting. We can, if we have enough faith and set our minds and wills to it, overcome the problems of transportation and distribution so that there will be enough for all.

Faith and the Fig Tree

One of the more bothersome passages in the Gospels of Mark and Matthew concerns the so-called cursing the barren fig tree. But did Jesus curse it? As told by Mark and Matthew the story states that he did. They indicate that Jesus performed an act of sympathetic magic by symbolically cursing the city of Jerusalem because it had rejected him and his teaching. The barren fig tree that bore no fruit stood for the city that did not know the time of its visitation from on high but turned its back on Jesus. Matthew and Luke say that he lamented over the city and its future fate. It was to be destroyed and left desolate (Mt 23:37–38; Lk 13:34).

However, the Gospels allow for an entirely different interpretation. It has nothing to do with cursing a tree and the destruction of the city of Jerusalem. It concerns, rather, the power of faith. "Truly I tell you, if you have enough faith and do not doubt, not only will you do what has been done to the fig tree [cause it to wither], but even if you say to this mountain, 'Be lifted up and thrown into the sea,' it will be done. Whatever you ask for in prayer with faith, you will receive" (Mt 21:21–22).

Jesus uses hyperbole when he says that with sufficient faith one could move a mountain and cause it to be thrown into the sea. Less spectacular than the idea of hurling mountains into the sea, is the modest example of withering a fig tree. It was sufficient for Jesus to make his point concerning the power of faith. Matthew, incidentally, says that the tree withered "at once" (Mt 21:19). In Mark the tree does not wither immediately. It is only on the next day that the disciples happen to observe that the tree has actually wilted (Mk 11:20). The point of the story in its original form probably had nothing to do with cursing the tree and the faithless city. It was simply proposed as an object lesson to show how firm our faith must be, if we are to expect results.

Three chapters later, Matthew 24:32 offers another parable or adage about the fig tree. When its branches are tender and it begins to put forth leaves, summer is near. The earlier account of the withered tree may also have been spoken as a parable, that is, not describing something Jesus did but something he said. It happens fairly often in the gospels that something Jesus said is converted into something he did. Luke tells the story about the barren fig tree in an entirely different way. In Luke it is clearly a parable, though Jesus may also have had Jerusalem in mind (Lk 13.6). The owner of a vineyard, finding a fig tree barren, orders it to be cut down. The gardener begs him to spare it for another year, and the owner agrees. If the fig tree stands for the city of Jerusalem and its inhabitants, then in this parable they are given a second chance. No cursing is involved. Luke's is a milder version of the fig tree story in Matthew and Mark, and it may be closer to what Jesus actually said. In any case, Luke, having Matthew in hand, elected to leave out anything that might suggest "cursing."

In these various parables about a fig tree, two themes are related: faith and the condition of the fig tree as a sign of the times. The greening of the tree is a sign of spring. The barren one represents the winter of disbelief. Without faith one is fruitless and barren. With it, one can move mountains or cause a tree to wither. That Jesus lamented the city's indifference to his message is credible. That he cursed it via the symbol of a barren fig tree is not a likely reflection of the authentic Jesus.

Whether one chooses to interpret the stories about Jesus—walking on water, calming a storm at sea, multiplying loaves, causing a tree to wither—as physical miracles or simply as teaching stories, one should recognize their meaning and their lessons: When life gets rough we can reach out for Jesus; if we share the earth's resources, there will be enough for everybody; faith can work wonders, provided we believe and do not doubt and become double-minded.

Notes

[1] Geza Vermes reviews a number of stories told about Hanina ben Dosa, including his ability to heal at a distance. See *Jesus the Jew: A Historian's Reading of the Gospels* (Philadelphia: Fortress Press, 1973), 72–78.

[2] See John P. Meier, "Excursus on Parallels to the Gospel Miracles," in *A Marginal Jew: Rethinking the Historical Jesus* (New York: Doubleday, 1994), 2:576–581. Special attention is given to Apollonius of Tyana.

[3] Vermes in *Jesus the Jew*, tells us nearly all we will ever know about Honi the Circle-Drawer, 69–72.

Chapter Seven

THE PARALYZED MAN

Israel Under Roman Rule

The paralyzed man has friends, at least four of them. For it will take four strong men to let him down through the open roof of a house on a pallet or basket suspended on ropes. The friends, if they are to bring the man into the presence of Jesus for a cure, have no alternative. The small house in which Jesus is speaking and the street around it are so crowded that there is no other way for them to gain entry for their charge (Mk 2:1–12).

The four men certainly go to a lot of trouble for the sake of their paralyzed friend. First they have to make an opening in the roof just above the room where Jesus is teaching.[1] Whose house is being dismantled? It is probably Peter's because Jesus stays there whenever he is in Capernaum.[2] Try to imagine the scene. Jesus is sitting on a cushion or on the floor, and as he begins to explain some point in his usual way by telling a story, he looks up and suddenly there is a hole in the roof and he can see daylight. Everyone around him is watching as the sick man is lowered until his litter rests on the ground at the feet of Jesus.

The man does not say anything. He does not ask to be cured. But it is pretty obvious what he and his friends desire. One look at the man and Jesus immediately senses that the paralytic thinks that he is suffering from his ailment because of some sin he committed in the past. Jesus, however, is against that theory, one that has plagued ancient Jewish people for a thousand years of more.[3] Sickness is not a divinely inflicted punishment for sin. Many sinners are not sick and many sick people are not sinners, at least they are not greater sinners than those who enjoy excellent health. Jesus believes in unbrokered forgiveness, so he says to the man, "Son, your sins are forgiven."[4] How does Jesus know that? Because, though we may fall ten times a day, God readily forgives those who repent, up to seventy times seven times, independent of priest or Temple or even John the Baptist's once and for all baptism.[5]

Evidently, a few scribes have come early and managed to get inside the house because we are told, "Some scribes were sitting there, questioning in their hearts, 'Why does this fellow speak this way? It is blasphemy! Who can forgive sins but God alone?'"(Mk 2:7–8). They misunderstood. Jesus did not forgive the man's sins. He merely announced a fact: illness is not a divinely inflicted punishment for sin. He then went on to assure the man that his sins were forgiven.

The scribes who are present at first questioned in their hearts, that is, internally without saying anything. But a moment later they are putting their heads together, "discussing these questions among themselves." Jesus, observing this, knows immediately what they are doing. He does not need divine or arcane knowledge to come to the conclusion that they were debating his words. So he turns to them and asks them which is easier to do, to say to a paralyzed man, "Your sins are forgiven," or tell him to stand up, pick up his pallet and walk?

Both statements are easy to make. Anyone could make them. But in this case when Jesus told the man to get up and walk, he was able to do so, much to the astonishment of those present. What had happened? Assured that he was not a sinner out of God's favor, he no longer needed to be paralyzed. The cause of his paralysis—his thinking that he was in a state of sin and enmity with God—had been removed. Now he could stand up, face the world and walk.[6]

Minority children are all too often given the message that they are the wrong race, the wrong sex, or the wrong color. Told that they cannot make it in the larger world, they remain psychologically paralyzed. Our achievements are so often tied to our expectations. If we are told often enough that we are inferior, without prospects for success, we tend to believe it. A word of encouragement can often release a world of creative energy that has been locked up because of false beliefs.

In one of the "Peanuts" cartoons, Linus has managed to get a splinter in his finger. Lucy says that he is being punished because he has done something wrong. When a moment later the splinter pops out spontaneously, Lucy's theological edifice crumbles to the ground. In Exodus 34:7, God is represented as "visiting the iniquity of the parents upon the children and the children's children, to the third and fourth generation." The same idea is picked up in Numbers 14:18. God punishes not only the sinner but also his or her progeny to the third or fourth generation. This edict was, as it were, repealed at the time of Ezekiel, for he declares in the name of God, that it is only the person who sins who shall die. No longer will the saying be true, "The parents have eaten sour grapes and the children's teeth are on edge" (Ezek 18:2).

Ezekiel still holds that the sinner will die if he does not repent. Repentance, or *teshuvah* ("return"), is the sure avenue of approach for obtaining forgiveness. But we can also forgive one another. Just before the paralyzed man gets up and walks, Jesus declares that the Son of Man has the power to forgive sins (Mk 2:10). Here, the Son of Man can refer to humanity in general, that is, to all of us. Or, the reference may be restricted to Jesus as the divinely appointed redeemer. The evangelist prefers the latter reading, but Jesus also says to his disciples, "If you forgive the sins of many, they are forgiven them" (Jn 20:23).[7] To foregive is to give another person the open future that lies before him. Fully to forgive others is to forget the past, so that each day can become the first day of the rest of their lives.

King David in the fifty-third Psalm laments his past misdeed: "My sin is ever before me" (Ps. 51:3). David had reason to lament. He had committed adultery with Bethsheba, the wife of Uriah, and had Uriah slain in battle, courtesy of Joab, David's chief military officer (2 Sam 11:14–17). There is a healthy kind of regret that sincerely repents for one's past sins, tries mightily to make amends, and resolves never to sin again. With former failures behind the sinner, he looks ahead like St. Paul, leaving behind the dead past (Phil 3:13).

The other kind of regret carries with it "the bird with a broken wing" syndrome. Here the wrongdoer refuses to let go. He grovels and wallows in the memory of what he has done, taking a kind of perverse pleasure in keeping his sin ever before him, thinking that this is somehow virtuous. Such a person does not really believe that God loves and forgives. He identifies with his sin and is confident that he will never fly again. Then, if some accident or misfortune occurs, he is convinced that God is punishing him. To be stuck in some form of sin or addiction is a form of paralysis. Equally paralyzing is the belief, fostered by some "Old Time Religion" preachers, that the stain of guilt remains long after the sin has been forgiven. Not so, declared Isaiah: "Though your sins are like scarlet, they shall be like snow" (Isa 1:18).

The Jews of Jesus' day felt paralyzed because of the imposition of Roman rule on a people who loved freedom, a luxury they have rarely enjoyed over a period of some thirty-five hundred years. They had grown into the habit of thinking that bad fortune was a divinely ordered punishment for the collective sins of the nation. The Romans, by contrast, were as sinful as the Jews, yet they were enjoying extraordinary economic and political success. The Jewish historian Josephus, who had ingratiated himself with the Roman elite, even sees Roman success as a sign of divine favor. Jesus, for his part, turned around the form of fatalism that links success with virtue and sin with suffering when he declares that those who suffer persecution for the sake of justice are blessed (Mt 5:11).

Humans are such impressionable creatures, so easily duped by our own imaginings and educational conditioning. There is no necessary connection between a life of virtue and freedom from suffering. Jesus hanging from a cross ought to be the final refutations of that association. But we do seek causes when things go wrong. If there is an airplane crash, a committee is set up to try to discover why all the failsafe systems failed. No committee will ever be able to demonstrate that the suffering of a terminal cancer patient is the punishment she is now suffering because of some karmic link between what she once did in this life or in a former incarnation. Physical laws and moral rewards and punishments are not necessarily linked to one another. To hold that they are is a category mistake. The best test of virtue is how one handles adversity. One can "rage, rage against the dying light" and refuse to "go gentle into that good night," or adapt oneself to changed circumstances of health and fortune. Most often the source of our inability to cope lies within ourselves.[7]

Human beings are resourceful and need not be paralyzed by the most adverse circumstances. Make a law forbidding some kind of activity, and immediately the criminal element will find a way to circumvent it. The fact that dishonest people are so clever should stimulate law-abiding citizens to use their intelligence in the service of justice and mercy. Jesus wanted his oppressed people to gather together in small groups for common suppers and sharing. There was enough food, clothing, and shelter to meet the simple needs of those willing to cease hoarding and instead pool their resources. This is precisely what members of the early Christian community in Jerusalem did after Jesus had returned to his Father. They were merely following the example Jesus had set as a way to live under difficult circumstances. They did not have to be paralyzed.

Excursus on Dealing with Past Sins and Addictions

Gary Zukav has a chapter in *The Seat of the Soul* that deals helpfully with the kind of paralysis that a long-standing addiction can inflict on a man or woman.[8] As with a twelve-step program, the victim of an injurious bad habit must honestly acknowledge the existence and power of the addiction, and, while recognizing her helplessness, be ready and willing to seek help, both human and divine. Save in cases where substance abuse or compulsive behavior requires chemical treatment, people need not remain helpless and in bondage to their passions. Many overcome and restore order in their lives.

Fortunately, there are techniques for handling addiction, whether the problem is sex, alcohol, or loss of temper. It is useful, of course, to have a counselor in such matters. But if one is not available, a person can perhaps become her own advisor by giving herself, and writing down, the kind of advice she might give to another person in a similar bind. Most people, if they are honest with themselves, know what they should be doing and how to do it. Writing down one's advice for repeated review may be helpful. Still it is not as effective for reform as having to report one's progress to an advisor or spiritual director. One of the advantages of sacramental confession is that the individual sinner or addict has to inform another human being on the state of his soul.[9]

Jesus' program offers an early example of preventive medicine. You forestall instances of murder, theft, and rape by controlling or by not encouraging thoughts of violence, covetousness, or lust. The thought is father to the deed. There is a sign in the private parking space at the back of the Cathedral of St. John the Divine in New York. It reads; "Do not even think of parking here." We have little need to pour large sums of money into expensive investigations to prove that lewd shows on television featuring sex and violence incline viewers to act out what they see. Why do food merchants flood the media with pictures of luscious desserts with glistening chocolate syrup dripping over golden honey cakes? Because they know that the image will induce some viewers to go out and buy the product.

In the Sermon on the Mount Jesus reminds us that it is not enough to abstain from murder; one must banish all vengeful and angry thoughts. It is not enough to avoid adultery; one must not allow the thought to live in one's imagination. Banishing evil or murderous thoughts, however, is only part of the task; they must be replaced by what is positive. One of the most striking and psychologically astute stories told by Jesus has to do with the unclean spirit that has gone out of a person suffering from some kind of sin or addiction. Not finding a resting place, it will return, bringing seven spirits more evil than itself, "and the last state of that person is worse than the first" (Lk 11:26). Just the thought of one's past addictions can encourage them to return sevenfold and in force.

Looking back, the recovered addict (or sinner, to use biblical language) often wonders how he or she could have been attracted by something that now seems so distasteful. Recovered smokers know the feeling. What they have to avoid is pride in their achievement and an attitude of disapproval regarding those who are still in bondage to their habit. They need to remember how helpless and paralyzed they once were. Repentant sinners must give up the habit of believing that they are sinners. "Get up and walk!" says Jesus. You are as free as you think you are. Do not let the past determine your future.

Notes

¹ According to Luke, the roof of the house was made of tiles (*kermai*). This was an accommodation to the experience of Greek and Roman readers (Lk 5:19). In Galilee the roofs of peasant houses were made of planks covered over with brushwood, reeds, and clay. See Joseph H. Fitzmyer, *The Gospel according to Luke* (Garden City, New York: Doubleday/Anchor Bible, 1981) 1:582.

² Jesus is said to be "at home" in the house at Capernaum (Mk 2:1). The house apparently belonged to the brothers Peter and Andrew (Mk 1:29).

³ Exodus 34:7: The prophets blamed the hard luck of the Jews on their collective sins.

⁴ The paralyzed person is man (*anthrōpos*) in Luke's Gospel (Lk 5:20). But in Mark, the earlier gospel, he is called *teknon*, translated as "son." In Greek the word usually means a young person, even a child. In any case, it is a term of endearment. The latest Revised Standard Version translates Luke's *anthrōpos* as "friend." While this is not an ideal rendering of teknon, it is less frigid than "man" and not quite as endearing as "son" or "child."

⁵ Seventy times seven times is 490 times! This is a stellar example of Hebraic hyperbole. Of course, in a lifetime most of us do something blameworthy many times over. But God who is merciful forgives as often as we repent. That seems to be the sense of the saying.

⁶ Jesus' miracles fall into three classes. First, there are those of a psychosomatic nature. This could be the case of the paralyzed man. Secondly, there are the strictly physical cures of blindness from birth or extreme cases of osteoporosis, which appears to have been the affliction of the crippled woman who had been bent over for eighteen years (Lk 13:11). Finally, there are the nature miracles, such as changing water into wine, walking on water, or calming a storm at sea.

⁷ The quotation is from the Dylan Thomas poem, "Do not go gentle into that good night."

⁸ Chapter 10 in Gary Zukav's *The Seat of the Soul* (New York: Simon & Schuster, 1989), 148–160.

[9] St Ignatius Loyola, founder of the Jesuit Order, confessed his sins to another soldier before engaging in the military operation that resulted in a permanent injury to his leg. Having confessed his sins to another human being, although the latter was not a priest, he was prepared to die.

Chapter Eight

THE DAUGHTER OF JAIRUS

Dead or Sleeping?

After Jesus has cured an insane man in the country of the Gerasenes[1] on the east side of the Lake of Galilee, he cross- es the Lake in a boat, and, upon landing, is met by a very large crowd. It is then that the man called Jairus, one of the leading men of the local synagogue, pushes his way through the crowd, falls at the feet of Jesus and begs him to come and heal his twelve-year-old daughter who is at the point of death. Jesus responds immediately and begins the march with the distraught man toward his home where the dying girl lies. The crowd, pushing and shoving, follows the two of them (Mk 5:24).

They do not go very far when a woman who has been suffering from hemorrhages for twelve years manages to worm her way toward Jesus. She has endured much from incompetent physicians and has spent all of her money on cures only to find that she is now worse at the end of the treatments than before. Then, as a last resort, she convinces herself that if she could just succeed in touching the fringe of Jesus' cloak, she will be healed. No sooner does she touch the *zizith* of his garment than she feels a surge of good health coursing through her body, while Jesus in turn feels as though power has gone out from him.

Immediately Jesus knows that someone has tapped into his store of spiritual and psychic energy. Stopping suddenly, he turns around to the crowd and asks who had touched him. His disciples tell Jesus to observe how the crowd is pressing around him. How then can it be possible to single out one particular person as the one who had "touched" him? Nevertheless, Jesus looks around and fixes his eyes on various people in the crowd. He sees a "guilty" expression on the face of one woman. Caught, she stepps forward in fear and trembling, falls at Jesus' feet, and tells him the whole truth. He in turn lifts her up and says, "Daughter, your faith has made you well" (Mk 5:34). Jesus

97

does not scold her for having touched him in spite of her ritually impure condition. He admires her perseverance and determination.

While Jesus is still speaking to the woman with the flow of blood, someone comes running up and bluntly announces to Jairus, "Your daughter is dead." So there is no need for Jesus to go to the man's house. But he, overhearing what has been said to Jairus, counsels him, "Do not fear; only believe" (Mk 5:36). If Jesus is to cure or raise the girl, he needs the faith of Jairus just as surely as he has to have faith himself. If Jairus wavers in his faith, Jesus might not be able to help. Both have to remain single-minded and not think "death."

So, the two of them, followed by Peter, James, and John, make their way to the home of Jairus. In this instance, Jesus does not want a crowd around, although he could make use of the customary faith of his three closest disciples as support. Because they are well acquainted with Jesus' healings in other instances, faith would be easier for them than for those who had never witnessed Jesus' works of power.

Arriving at the house, they hear the wailing of the mourners, which is not very encouraging to Jairus. But Jesus is not discouraged. The mourners laugh at him when he says, "The child is not dead but sleeping." The mourners have seen many children die, and this girl's case is no different from the rest. Yet, if Jesus is to have any success at all, he must exclude from the house all those who believe that the girl is dead and beyond recovery. He allows Jairus and the girl's mother, along with three of his own disciples, to remain in the house because by now the six of them, including Jesus, are striving to hold onto positive thoughts for the sake of the girl.

Entering the room where the child lies, Jesus takes her limp hand and speaks to her. "*Talitha, cum,*" he says, using Aramaic words that mean, "young maiden, rise up." Immediately she stirs, gets up, and begins to walk. But she is still weak, so Jesus instructs the parents to give her something to eat (Mk 5:43).

Dead or Sleeping?

This story is one that has the ring of authenticity, partly because the Aramaic words of Jesus are preserved and partly because the details are so precise. Today we can usually be sure that a person is dead when an encephalograph indicates a cessation of brain activity over a period of some time. Among the ancients, however, it was not uncommon for persons to be pronounced dead after they had apparently ceased breathing and the body had begun to lose heat. That is why it was customary in Palestine to visit the tomb of a deceased person on the third day to make sure he or she was truly dead. By the fourth day it was assumed that resuscitation was unlikely and corruption would have begun.

In the case of the little girl, Jesus declared emphatically that she was not dead but "sleeping." Today we would say she was in a coma. But the evangelists who recount the story want readers to assume that the girl was dead, and that in saying that she was only sleeping, Jesus wanted to give the father reason to believe that all was not lost. When the mourners all scorn Jesus for saying that the child was not dead, this again emphasizes the fact that the people attending her thought she was dead.

Still, if she was dead, her death occurred only a short time before Jesus arrived. The body would still have been warm and supple. Corruption would not have occurred. Suppose she was simply in a state approximating sleep, then her restoration would not have been a case of being raised from the dead but of clairvoyance on the part of Jesus. He felt deep down that the girl was only apparently dead. That, in itself, would have been miracle enough. But the evangelists, writing forty or more years after an event that they themselves did not witness, prefer to treat the raising of the girl as a true return to life on the part of one who was truly dead.

How many people did Jesus raise from the dead? In his reply to the emissaries sent to him by the imprisoned John the Baptist, Jesus told them to go and tell John that "the lepers are cleansed, the deaf hear, the dead are raised" (Mt 11:5; Lk 7:22). There is no indication of how many were raised. In point of fact, aside from the raising of Jairus' daughter, there are only two other instances of raising in the four gospels: one appears in John and the other in Luke.

Lazarus

The most astonishing account of a raising from the dead is in the Fourth Gospel. Lazarus, the brother of Martha and Mary, has been dead for four days, one day beyond the time when resuscitation is thought to be possible. When Jesus comes to Bethany to the gravesite, he orders the stone before the tomb to be rolled aside. Martha, terrified, warns Jesus, saying, "Lord, already there is a stench because he has been dead four days" (Jn 11:49). Jesus ignores Martha's warning and cries out, "Lazarus, come out!" And forthwith the dead man, with hands and feet still bound with strips of cloth and with a napkin covering his head, hobbles out of the tomb alive.[2]

There is another version of the Lazarus story mentioned by Clement of Alexandria (150–215?) in a letter to a certain Theodore.[3] An eighteenth-century copy was tacked onto a seventeenth-century edition of the Letters of Ignatius of Antioch. It is called "Ur-Mark," or "Secret Mark."[4] Here Jesus and his companions come to the village of Bethany, the one mentioned in John's Gospel. It is the home of a woman whose brother has just died. Jesus, approaching the tomb of the deceased man, comes up short because "a great cry is heard from the tomb." Jesus then rolls back the stone before the tomb, takes the man by the hand and raises him to his feet, just as he did with the daughter of Jairus.

Almost everything is the same as in the Lazarus story, save for the fact that the man in the tomb was not dead but very much alive and struggling to get out. Jesus was there, and he "raised him up," taking him by the hand. But he did not raise him from the dead. Still, as in John's version, he was responsible for the removal of the stone before the tomb. It could be the case that the Ur-Mark version of the Bethany affair was a less well-developed, unpolished telling of a story that was current in apostolic circles. Or the Marcan account might be a stripped-down version of John's account. Still, we normally assume that the simpler, shorter, unembellished text is the earlier one, as in the case of Mark's Gospel in relation to the later accounts of Matthew and Luke. The common tendency when marvels are concerned is to embroider an original story.

On the other hand, even assuming that the seventeenth-century, poorly written text is authentic and is an accurate copy of a Letter by Clement, there are a number of suspicious things about the text that indicate some remote dependence on canonical Mark as well as John. The text that Clement cites states that the rich young man whom Jesus raised, "looking upon him, loved him." This is a reversal of the wording in Mark's Gospel. There, it is Jesus who is pleased with the response of the rich man, "looking at him, loved him" (Mk 10:21). Ur-Mark also states that, after six days—the time between the young man being raised and Jesus' arrest in the Garden of Gethsemane—the man came to Jesus, presumably for baptism, wearing only a cloth over his naked body. This again harks back to Mark's description of the flight of the young man at the time Jesus was taken prisoner in the Garden of Gethsemane: "A certain young man was following him, wearing nothing but a linen cloth. They caught hold of him, but he left the linen cloth and ran off naked" (Mk 14:51).

So, Secret Mark depends either on Mark and John or, more probably, its author who, with only a distant and hazy access to the apostolic tradition, managed to patch together on a hearsay basis fragments of words, phrases, and stories found in a more coherent form in the canonical gospels. Perhaps there is a lesson here. Even the canonical Gospels, composed years after the time of Jesus, seem to depend on oral and written traditions that became somewhat blurred in the telling. For example, in Mark's Gospel a man comes to Jesus, saying, "Good Teacher, what must I do to inherit eternal life?" To which Jesus replies, "Why do you call me good? No one is good but God alone" (Mk 10:18). When Matthew describes the same incident, the word 'good' is taken in a quite different context. "Then someone came up to him and asked, 'Teacher, what good deed must I do to have eternal life?'" Here Jesus replies, "Why do you ask me about what is good? There is only one who is good" (Mt 19:16–17). In Matthew, the man did not call Jesus "good"; he asked only what "good deed" he should perform to have eternal life.

What is truly remarkable about the raising of Lazarus is the astonishing fact that this unparalleled miracle is not mentioned in any of the other gospels. Yet, the author of the Fourth Gospel declares that the event was so well known in and around Jerusalem that the high priests feared that on the basis of such a miracle, "everyone will believe in him" (Jn 11:48). John had a habit of turning something that Jesus said into an action that he performed. For example, Jesus said that he came to serve rather than be served, and in Luke's Gospel he speaks of a householder who finds his servants carrying out their duties and remaining alert. What will the master do? "He will fasten his belt and have them sit down to eat, and he will come and serve them" (Lk 12:37). In John's Gospel, Jesus acts this out when he gets up from the table at the Last Supper, girds himself with a towel, and begins to wash the feet of his own disciples, thus performing the work of a servant or slave (Jn 13:4–5).

The suggestion is that John, possibly for dramatic purposes, puts into action ideas that Jesus expressed elsewhere orally. Earlier in the Fourth Gospel, Jesus declares, "Very truly, I tell you, the hour is coming, and is now here, when the dead will hear the voice of the Son of God, and those who hear will live. . . . Do not be astonished at this; for the hour is coming when all who are in their graves will hear his voice and will come out" (Jn 5:25, 28). Jesus is speaking here of the proper response to his spiritual message. Those who presently are indifferent or dead in their sins "will hear his voice and will come out," just as Lazarus did when he heard the voice of Jesus calling, "Lazarus, come out!" However it is interpreted, the raising of Lazarus is also a parable in action. It was meant to concretize the restoration to a spiritual life of grace those who hear "the voice of the Son of God" and respond to his message of Eternal Life.

The Widow's Son

Luke provides the third account of someone being raised from the dead. In this case, the one raised is the only son of a widow and his bier is being carried outside the town of Nain for burial. Jesus touches the bier, tells the young man to rise, and "the dead man sat up and began to speak" (Lk 7:15). The story bears some resemblance to the raising of the only son of the widow of Zarephath by Elijah in the First Book of Kings (17:8–24). The miracle in Luke is a loner. It is not attested in either Mark or Matthew, and, unlike the raising of the daughter of Jairus and of Lazarus, we are provided with few details. The facts of the story are bare: a man on his way to be buried is found to be alive after Jesus touches his bier. A sparsely detailed account does not mean that a miracle did not happen. Luke, no doubt to reassure his readers, says that the miracle was witnessed by the disciples of Jesus and by a large crowd, and that word of it spread all over Judea, although the raising took place up in Galilee. That being the case, one has to wonder why neither Mark nor Matthew, who offer details about thirty or more healing miracles, almost all of them taking place in Galilee, fails to mention the raising of a man from the dead, surely a wonder that surpasses any other healing in the first three gospels.

In reviewing the accounts of the three resurrection miracles performed by Jesus, one cannot escape the uneasy feeling that the widow's son, Lazarus, and the daughter of Jairus were not absolutely and definitively dead, at least by modern standards. From the medical point of view, their bodies might have been "clinically dead" because the usual vital signs or symptoms of life were lacking. But the fact that they regained consciousness would indicate that they were not fully and irretrievably dead. This is not to say the evangelists lied or to question their good faith. People in biblical times did not have the means to distinguish between a stunning resuscitation and a genuine resurrection. In our day, we have reliable reports from a good number of people who recovered consciousness after they were thought to be dead. Most of those who recover have nothing to report about any experience they might have had while "dead." Some, however, tell about traveling to another world where they meet deceased friends and relatives or some religious figure before returning to their bodies. They have had what Raymond Moody has called an NDE, or a "Near-Death-Experience."[5] They have "died" in the sense that their vital symptoms have flattened out for a limited period of time. Meanwhile, some aspect of their consciousness has been engaged in "other-world travels." Among those who recover, some can give an account of what they experienced and whom they met while "out of their bodies."

"Descended into Hell"

According to the Apostles' Creed, between the time when Jesus died and when he rose from the dead, he "descended into hell," or, to the realm of the dead. There, in the words of the First Letter ascribed to Peter, Jesus, still alive in the spirit, proclaims the Good News to the imprisoned deceased spirits, so that "they might live in the spirit as God does" (1 Pet 3:19; 4:6). How was this possible? St. Paul conceived the human being as composed of body (*sōma sarx*), soul (*psychē*), and spirit (*pneûma*). The body is flesh, the soul is its animating principle (something shared with animals), while the spirit is the real person or eternal self. In the context of an Aristotelian body–soul dualism, death takes place when body and soul are separated from one another, or when the soul is simply snuffed out, leaving the body to corrupt. For St. Paul spirit is not identified with soul. Body and soul could remain intact and together, while the spirit visits the realm of the dead.

Excursus on the Resurrection

St. Peter, in his Pentecost speech, quoted the Sixteenth Psalm (the Fifteenth in the Greek Septuagint) to prove that God did not allow the body of Jesus, his Holy One, to see corruption (*idein diaphthoran*) in the tomb. Actually this is a questionable translation of the Hebrew. A better translation is "to see the pit," where "pit" refers to death and the grave. In any case, the evangelist wants us to understand that Peter is declaring that God's Holy One is immortal and that the body of Jesus did not corrupt in the grave (Acts 2:27; Ps 16:10).

For Peter, then, if the spirit of Jesus returned to his body, it would have been to a body that had not begun to rot or decay. He felt it important to stress this fact. In this view, the body of Jesus, sustained by its animating principle (*psychē,*) would not have corrupted because its chemical and biological processes would have remained intact while his spirit engaged in other-world travels, eventually including heaven as well as the region of the dead.

We are engaging in speculation here, but let us suppose that upon returning to his body the spirit of Jesus revitalized the body in such a way as to restart the metabolism, the circulatory system, and the other organic processes so as to rapidly heal the wounds in Jesus' hands, feet, and side, leaving only scars of honor. From this point on we have to try to reconcile two sets of texts in the post-resurrection accounts offered by the evangelists. Luke, especially, is very concrete. For him the risen Jesus walks with two of his disciples on the road to Emmaus, and later appears to the Eleven, showing them the healed marks of the wounds in his hands and feet (Luke does not mention the wound in Jesus' side). He eats with them and apparently digests a portion of broiled fish that they give him. "Touch me and see," he tells them, "for a ghost does not have flesh and bones as you see that I have" (Lk 24:39). Jesus is represented here as alive in his warm body of flesh and blood. It seems to be an ordinary body.

Read another way, the same set of texts accord to Jesus' body properties that defy the ordinary laws of time and space. He seems to be everywhere at once, appearing and disappearing in different places, talking to Mary Magdalene, walking to Emmaus, visiting Peter, then the Eleven (ten of them in John's Gospel when Thomas is absent). Closed doors are no obstacle to a sudden appearance in the midst of his disciples (Jn 20:19). Over a period of forty days Jesus continues to appear to his disciples, "speaking to them about the kingdom" (Acts 1:3). Then he is seen no more because he was lifted up and "a cloud took him out of their sight" (Acts 1:9). How can we reconcile the very lifelike, concrete texts and the more ghostly ones?

The Concrete, Realistic, Flesh and Blood Appearances

The naturalistic explanation would maintain, as some have, that Jesus survived the cross and his burial.[6] On the third day he was found alive in the tomb, nursed back to life only to die some forty days later when he was seen no more. The problem here is with the timing. The risen Jesus was seen on Easter morning near his tomb by Mary Magdalene and "the other Mary" (Mt 28:9) and by Mary Magdalene alone (Jn 20:14). He was standing up and was perfectly healed. That evening he was seen by his chosen apostles with only the scars from the wounds remaining to testify to his identity and to the kind of death he had suffered. In a typical resuscitation scenario, it would have taken weeks, even months, before Jesus could have recovered sufficiently from the beating and his wounds to be able to stand up and make flesh-and-blood appearances.

But let us suppose that when the spirit of Jesus returned to his body, he healed it. He would then have arisen, cast off his burial cloths, opened the tomb by rolling back the stone with the help of one or two angels, and emerged to greet the women. Presumably the angels would have supplied him with some kind of clothing, since the body was buried unclothed. In all the appearances, unless they were only visions, the question of where Jesus got the clothing arises. If the appearances were only subjectively generated visions, there is no problem about clothing.

What scripture scholars have noted in connection with the post-resurrection appearances is that they become increasingly concrete with each successive Gospel. In Mark there are no appearances. In Matthew there are no Upper Room appearances. Near his tomb, Jesus appears to two women who "take hold of his feet," and he is later seen on a mountain, although some doubt (Mt 28:9, 17) it is he. In Luke, as we have seen, Jesus eats, walks, talks, and maintains that he is not a ghost. In John, in the lakeside scene, Jesus himself cooks fish and serves breakfast to seven of his fisherman disciples (Jn 21:9). The later evangelists seem to be answering objections against the Gnostic charge that the apostles only imagined that they had seen Jesus alive after his death and burial. Convinced that he did rise, they add details that help the imagination. We would consider this tampering with the fact, but in antiquity such "aids" were not considered improper.

St. Paul's Solution

St. Paul, partly to explain his own encounter with Christ several years after the ascension of Jesus, introduced the idea of a spiritual or pneumatic body (*sōma pneumatikon*), which was to be distinguished from an animal body of flesh (*sōma psychikon*), a material body animated by a vital principle, or soul (1 Cor 15:44). The spiritual body has properties that transcend all spatial and temporal limitations. It would seem to follow, then, that when the spirit of Jesus returned to his body in the tomb, what rose up was the pneumatic body, leaving behind the somatic body. The pneumatic body, neither gross matter nor pure spirit, could function in two worlds. It could appear in our world and seem utterly real, then withdraw into the transcendent order.[7]

Although there is talk in Luke's and John's Gospels about "touching" the body of the risen savior, no one seems actually to have done so. When Magdalene would have clung to the risen Jesus, he uttered the *"noli me tenere"* warning. And it is unlikely that Thomas dared touch the wounds of Jesus, even though he was invited to do so (Jn 20:17, 20:27). The pneumatic body is entirely real, but not tangible in the way the material somatic body would be.[8]

Because Paul believed that he had seen the risen Christ in his glorified body, he showed little interest in the tomb of Jesus, even when he visited Jerusalem. The pneumatic body does not need the material body in order to exist and act. When it shuffles off its mortal coil, it becomes like an orbiting capsule that has discarded its propulsion rocket. The trouble with this image is that the material body is left behind. But Jesus' tomb was supposed to have been empty. Where did his material body go? Was it transfigured and taken up into another and higher eschatological dimension? In this case, Jesus' resurrection would be the first fruits and beginning of the General Resurrection.

There may be another explanation for the fact that the body of Jesus was never found. It might mean that there never was a tomb and, as suggested by John Dominic Crossan and Bishop John Shelby Spong, the body of Jesus would have been hastily buried in a shallow grave by Roman soldiers—assuming that Roman soldiers were ever assigned to such a detail.[9] However, Paul, who met and knew Peter, John, and James the brother of Jesus, must have discussed the resurrection with them because it was so important to him. He surely believed that there was a tomb; for he says that Jesus was buried (*etaphē*), using a verb that means burial in a *taphos* or *mnēmeion,* a sepulcher, a formal, memorial tomb (*monumentum*) (1 Cor 15:4). In Acts, he says that Jesus, taken down from the cross, *ethekan eis mnēmeion* ("was buried in a tomb") (Acts 13:29).

Let Professor Crossan and Bishop Spong hold out for the "no tomb" theory. The tomb, they say, was a late development, introduced to assure readers that Jesus was given honorable burial. But then one would have to hold that Joseph of Arimathea and Nicodemus, who assisted at the burial of Jesus, were fictional characters—precisely what Crossan claims. So, too, were the women who came to the non-existing tomb to anoint the body of Jesus.[10] But, as has been asked by other scripture scholars, why would the evangelists in that strongly patriarchal age have invented the women, making them heralds of the resurrection? I think we have to restore the tomb and take it from there.

Paul's solution is not without merit. It may be objected that it involves a supernatural intervention on the part of God, something that cannot be allowed, if the commentator is to limit himself to using the strict historical method. But aside from any kind of supernatural intervention, there are spiritual and psychological laws whose work-ings we do not yet understand. It is possible that the deceased in earth-ly terms continue to exist after death in a "spiritual body," for lack of a better name, something that could one day be shown to be perfectly "natural" and in accord with an expanded understanding of nature's laws.

Changed Men

Whatever the chosen witnesses to the resurrection experienced, it changed them from frightened men into firebrands of zeal and con-vinced enthusiasts, ready to suffer imprisonment, beatings, and even death by crucifixion for the sake of what they believed to be true. If Christ has not risen, says Paul, who suffered as much if not more than the others, then "we are of all people the most to be pitied" (1 Cor 15:19).[11]

The apostles' changed behavior and Paul's tireless zeal in preach-ing the resurrection may be the best proof that the tomb, whether empty or not, should not be seen as a symbol of Jesus' absence but a symbol of his enduring presence. Paul was not interested in what hap-pened to the physical, or somatic, body of Jesus. He would no longer relate to Christ according to the flesh. As far as he was concerned, Jesus' body could still be in the tomb, or the desiccated bones of the historical Jesus could have been transferred to a bone box or ossuary after the flesh had wasted away. What was alive, immortal, and indestructible was his Person subsisting in a spiritual body. In any case, it was Jesus in this form that Paul believed he had seen. And he would no doubt maintain that it was this kind of body that the original Eleven had seen when Jesus appeared to them in Jerusalem and Galilee. It was not a ghost but a vehicle that enabled Jesus to be truly present and to communicate with his chosen witnesses.

When Jesus appeared to his disciples, he probably told them what those who have experienced other-world travels and NDEs would report. He had seen the Promised Land and could now assure them that we do survive physical death, that in his Father's house there are many dwelling places (Jn 14:2), that they would all be together once again in the kingdom of God, and that their innermost self is eternal and imperishable. He could heartily agree with what Paul would say later on: "No eye has seen, nor ear heard, nor the human heart conceived, what God has prepared for those who love him" (1 Cor 2:9). Indeed, "the sufferings of this present time are not worth comparing with the glory to be revealed to us [in us, among us, *eis hemas*]" (Rom 8:18).

Words of this kind convey the sort of assurance the risen Jesus could have given his apostles. Death, even a cruel death, was only a rite of passage. Soon they would all be together forever in God's eternal kingdom. That would have been enough to sustain the apostles in their endeavors for the rest of their lives.

Admittedly, we have strayed a long way from Jairus and his twelve-year old daughter. But that is in line with the design of this study. The idea is to take hold of a thread picked up during the treatment of a particular gospel personality, then follow it wherever it leads. In the process we eventually cover most of the important questions and puzzles about Jesus that are of interest to serious Bible students and very much in the minds of contemporary academic scripture scholars.

Notes

[1] The exorcism of the Gerasene demoniac will be treated in the next chapter.

[2] The way Lazarus was prepared for burial, with hands and feet bound with strips of cloth and with a napkin covering his head, indicates the way Jesus was buried. John mentions the napkin, *soudarion*, found by Peter and the Beloved Disciple. It was rolled up in a place apart from the shroud (Jn 20:7).

[3] Ian Wilson provides the text of the Letter of Clement of Alexandria concerning what purports to be an early version of the Lazarus story in Jesus. *The Evidence* (New York: Harper & Row, 1984), 26–27.

[4] The account of finding of "Secret Mark" is told in *The Secret Gospel* by Morton Smith (New York: Harper & Row, 1973). Donald Hansen Akenson offers five reasons for holding that the text that Smith discovered is an 18th Century forgery. See *St. Paul: A Skeleton Key to the Historical Jesus* (New York: Oxford UP, 2000), 87.

[5] Literature on the Near-Death-Experience is now extensive, beginning with Raymond Moody's *Life after Life* (Covington, GA: Mockingbird Books, 1975), and Kenneth Ring's *Life at Death* (New York: Coward, McCann & Geoghegan, 1980). See also Michael B. Sabom, *Recollections of Death* (New York: Harper & Row, 1982), and Ian Wilson, *The After Death Experience* (New York: William Morrow, 1987).

[6] Hugh J. Schonfield's best selling book, *The Passover Plot* (New York: Bernard Getz Associates, 1965; Rockport, MA: Element Books, 1996) was not the first to claim that Jesus did not die on the cross. He cites two novelists who toyed with the idea, namely, George Moore and D.H. Lawrence. Other books supporting the survival hypothesis are Kersten and Gruber, *The Jesus Conspiracy*, 1994; Douglas Lockhart, *Jesus the Heretic*, 1997; and Rodney P. Hoare, *The Shroud Is Genuine*, 1984. All of these authors have trouble explaining what happened to Jesus after he was taken down from the cross. Schonfield says that he died shortly afterward. Who buried him and how?

[7] The ancients, including Aristotle, held that the stars were eternal and that the celestial spheres ("Aristotle calculated that they were fifty-five in number") were composed of indestructible matter. Whether this rubbed off on St. Paul with his indestructible pneumatic body is a question deserving of further examination.

[8] Those who have had NDEs sometimes report that they could see the people around them while out of their body, but these others could not see them. In fact, the "body" of one who was supposedly clinically dead could pass through the fleshly bodies of the surgeons and nurses in the operating room.

[9] The shallow grave theory is supported by John Dominic Crossan in *Who Killed Jesus?* (San Francisco: HarperSanFrancisco, 1995), 188. He says that Jesus was buried "in a necessarily shallow and mounded grave rather than a rock-hewn tomb." For a similar thesis, see John Shelby Spong, *Resurrection: Myth or Reality?* (San Francisco: HarperSanFrancisco, 1993), 225. Crossan and Spong also agree that Joseph of Arimathea and Nicodemus are mythical persons invented by the evangelists. See Spong, *Resurrection*, 226, 236; Crossan, *Who Killed Jesus?*, 172.

[10] Crossan does not deny that women were involved in lamenting the death of Jesus, but "*ritual lament is what changed prophetic exegesis into biographical story.*" (Italics in the original.) All could have taken place without there being a rock-hewn tomb. In *The Birth of Christianity:* (San Francisco: HarperSanFrancisco, 1998), 572, Crossan proposes a strained and not too convincing account of the conduct of the women after the death of Jesus.

[11] Paul lists all of the things he suffered for the sake of the gospel in 2 Cor 11:25–29.

Chapter Nine

THE GERASENE DEMONIAC

The Great Swine Stampede

T he three Synoptic Gospels include the story about Jesus exorcizing a demoniac on the east side of the Lake of Galilee (Mt 8; Mk 5; Lk 8). After crossing the lake in a boat, Jesus lands in the Decapolis, a region of ten Hellenized towns, most of whose inhabitants are Gentiles. Why Jesus goes there is not clear. As far as we know, he has never before visited such Hellenized Jewish cities as Caesarea, Sepphoris, or Tiberias during the time of his ministry; he has also never strayed very far from his native Galilee, except for visits to Jerusalem.[1]

No sooner has Jesus landed in the country of the Gerasenes (Gaderenes according to Matthew) than he is met by a wild man (two wild men in Matthew). The man is wearing no clothing, lives among the tombs, and cannot be restrained. He breaks apart the chains that bind him. The man is possessed by many devils. Upon seeing Jesus, the wretch falls at his feet as the demon in him cries out, "What have you to do with us, Son of God? Have you come here to destroy us before the time?" (Mt 8:29).

Addressing the demons, Jesus askes them for their name. They say that their name is "Legion; for many had entered him" (Lk 8:30). A Roman legion could range from 3,000 to 6,000 foot soldiers. But here the use of the word 'legion' suggests the severity of the infestation and may imply no more than twenty or thirty evil spirits, enough to cause a herd of swine to rush headlong down a slope and drown themselves in the sea.[2] So, when the demons beg Jesus not to drive them back into the abyss (of Hades), he allows them to enter into the swine. "Then the demons came out of the man and entered the swine, and the herd rushed down the steep bank into the lake and all were drowned" (Lk 8:33).

Joseph A. Fitzmyer says that it would be an understatement to say, "This is a strange story."[3] In the first place, why did Jesus enter the

111

region of the Decapolis? Was it because the storm at sea (Lk 8:25) had blown the disciples' boat to the eastern shore of the lake? Immediately after the exorcism, Jesus returns again to his own town of Capernaum (Mt 9:1). Peculiar, too, there is destruction of private property. A herd of swine represents a huge investment for a peasant farmer, there is no indication that Jesus makes reparation for the farmer's loss. And what about cruelty to animals?

Strangest of all is the location of the herd of swine. Mark and Luke say that the exorcism took place in the territory of the Gerasenes. But the town of Gerasa is approximately six miles from the lake in which the swine drowned. Matthew maintains that the cure took place in the territory of the Gadarenes, which creates an even greater problem. Gadara is thirty miles or more from the southeastern end of the lake. If the herd stampeded from Gadara, says Fitzmyer, it was surely, "the most energetic herd in history."[4]

One might justify the location proposed by Mark and Luke because they say that the exorcism took place in the "country" of the Gerasenes. This could include a large area, reaching from the town of Gerasa to the lakeshore. As for Matthew, we might assume that he confused Gadara and Gerasa. Besides, there was another town nearby, tentatively called Gergesa.[5] So, a certain amount of confusion is understandable.

What is harder to comprehend is the miracle itself. The demons did not want to be sent back to the abyss, presumably Hell or Hades. So they all perished by drowning. Does that mean that they became extinct? Was extinction better?

The evangelists' purpose in including this episode lies in their desire to demonstrate that even the demons recognize Jesus as "Son of the Most High God" (Mk 5:7), and that he has power over them. This exorcism is a replay of the very first miracle performed by Jesus in Mark's Gospel. While Jesus was teaching in the synagogue at Capernaum, a man with an unclean spirit cried out, "What have you to do with us, Jesus of Nazareth? Have you come to destroy us? I know who you are, the Holy One of God" (Mk 1:24). The words of these demons are almost identical when compared with the confession of the demons whose name is "Legion" in the Gerasene episode. When challenged to account for the fact that he had power over the demons, Jesus replies, "But if it is by the finger of God that I cast our demons, then the kingdom of God has come to you" (Lk 11:20).

Ousting the Romans

No doubt, the coming of the kingdom of God is what the evangelists had in mind. However, the story can be taken as a kind of allegory about driving the swine-eating, Gentile Roman legions out of Palestine and into the Mediterranean Sea.[6] The basis for the story may not have been original with Mark, who introduced it for his own purposes. It was then copied by Matthew and Luke.

We know that the ancients believed in spirit possession. Some spirits were vicious, while others were benign. On one occasion, Jesus cures a boy who has a spirit "that makes him unable to speak." Jesus addresses the spirit, saying, "You spirit that keeps this boy from speaking and hearing, I command you, come out of him, and never enter again!" (Mk 9:25). From the symptoms provided by the evangelist, it is clear that the boy is an epileptic. But in Jesus' day all diseases were thought to be the work of hostile spirits who had gained entry into an individual because of somebody's sin.

As for the Gerasene demoniac, it would be presumptuous to put a name on his illness. But an extreme case of a man suffering from bipolar disease could in the manic phase result in his being violent. There used to be patients in mental institutions who had to be restrained or confined to a padded cell. Today, however, they can be sedated, at least temporarily. Regarding the question of the enduring nature of Jesus' cures, we are told that Jesus calmed the epileptic boy and that the Gerasene demoniac put his clothes back on and sat calmly at the feet of Jesus. But there is no follow-up mentioned in such cures. The assumption is that the cures were permanent and that there were no relapses. But whether the cures were permanent or not, it does seem to be clear that Jesus, as a charismatic personality, was able to effect remarkable cures. Whether this meant that he was driving out demons in the process is a question most medical people today, whether rightly or wrongly, would be inclined to answer in the negative.

Notes

[1] On at least one occasion Jesus traveled to the region around the Phoenician city of Tyre (Mt 7:24), and somewhat later to the neighborhood of Caesarea Philippi not far from snow-capped Mt Hermon. As for the number of times Jesus went to Jerusalem, a lot depends on whether one credits the Synoptic Gospels, where one trip alone is indicated, or John's Gospel, which mentions at least five occasions when Jesus was reported as having visited Jerusalem. See Chapter 19 of this book for a discussion of the five trips of Jesus to Jerusalem.

[2] The Jews do not eat pork. Mark introduces a story featuring a whole herd of swine. Is he thinking of Palestine, the Promised Land, teeming with Gentile Roman soldiers who have no qualms about eating the flesh of swine?

[3] Joseph A. Fitzmyer, *The Gospel according to Luke* (New York: Doubleday/Anchor Bible, 1982), 1: 734.

[4] Fitzmyer, *op. cit.*

[5] These discrepancies present a problem for inerrantists. How can we reconcile the two different names of the place where the stampede took place and the number of men healed? We noted a similar difficulty regarding the healing of the centurion's servant. No doubt, there are degrees of inerrancy, with some literalists insisting on verbal inerrancy, while others are able to tolerate minor contradictions, as long as the stories are "substantially" in agreement.

[6] Matthew does not mention the name of the demons. Mark and Luke introduce the word "legion," suggesting the Romans. It is hard to believe that this does not have political implications.

PART FOUR:

The Apostles

Chapter Ten

PETER

The Education of a Slow Learner

Peter is introduced twice in the gospels. Jesus first meets Peter at the time of his stay with John the Baptist by the River Jordan. Peter's brother Andrew is one of the two disciples of John who followed Jesus. When they find him they stay with him that day and they are much impressed. After the interview, Andrew fetches his brother Simon—later called Peter (*Cephas* in Aramaic)—and brings him to Jesus. No sooner has Jesus laid eyes on Simon, son of Jonah, than he dubs him Peter, which means "Rock" (Jn 1:40–42).

However, we do not meet Peter until some time later in the Synoptic Gospels. According to Mark, Jesus is walking along the shore of the Lake of Galilee when he sees Simon and his brother Andrew casting a net into the sea. Jesus says to them, "Follow me. . . And immediately they left their nets and followed him" (Mk 1:16–18). It is not as though, sight unseen, Jesus calls on Simon and Andrew to follow him. If the information in John's Gospel is correct, the two future apostles have already been introduced to Jesus and have heard him speak. So they know something about his program for the redemption of Israel. Jesus probably told them, when they were all together by the River Jordan, that when the time was ripe, he would call them. The idea that Simon Peter and Andrew "left their nets" on the spot and abandoned their ship to follow Jesus that very day is unlikely. We learn from later passages in the Gospels that Peter kept his boat and frequently used it to transport Jesus from one side of the lake to the other (Mt 9:1, 14:28 ff.). Luke says that what induced Peter, James, and John to follow Jesus was the unexpected catch of fish. They had been fishing all night and had caught nothing. Jesus, seated in Peter's boat, tells him and his associates to let down their nets again. Whereupon, they haul in a very great multitude of fish. It is this incident that persuades them, according to Luke, "to leave everything and follow [Jesus]" (Lk 5:11).

117

Was Peter a poor man? Probably not. He and his brother Andrew owned a boat on the lake and seem to have shared ownership of a house in Capernaum (Mk 1:29) and possibly another house in Bethsaida, the home town of Peter and Andrew (Jn 1:44). Because of the great demand for salted fish and the abundance of fish in the lake, Peter and Andrew likely make a good living.[1] Their neighboring fishermen, Zebedee and his two sons, James and John, were well off enough to hire men to help with hauling in fish and cleaning their nets (Mk 1:20). According to Luke, Peter says to Jesus, "Look, we have left our homes and followed you" (Lk 18:28). After Jesus' resurrection, Peter, as well as Andrew, James, and John, eventually, left behind their means of livelihood to become evangelists.

We know that Peter was married (Mk 1:30), but we do not know if the other three apostles had children. Jesus said that anyone who leaves family, including children and, in some versions, wives, "for my sake will receive a hundredfold and inherit eternal life" (Mt 19:29; Mk 10:29). In any case, the four apostles eventually abandoned everything, and, one may suppose, with reasonable and not undue haste. It is worth noting that Paul states that Peter and the brothers of Jesus were accompanied by their wives in their missionary travels (1 Cor 9:5). He does not say whether their young children went along with them. Nevertheless, all of them, Peter as well as Jesus' four or more brothers, *hoi adelphoi tou kyriou*, must have had numerous children, something the evangelists do not tell us about. Whether childless or not, we are justified in assuming that family responsibilities did not prevent the apostles from traveling and preaching the gospel.

These are some of the details that slip through the net when one fails to ask some fairly obvious, probing questions.

The Faith of Peter

We know that Peter exercised a leading role in the Church after the death and resurrection of Jesus.[2] Some have felt that this leadership role has been read back into the Gospels, meaning that Peter, during the lifetime of Jesus, was not the commanding figure he later turned out to be in the early Church. Still, his name heads all of the lists of the apostles, and he is usually the spokesman for the other apostles. He is the lead man when the privileged three, Peter, James, and John, accompany Jesus on special occasions; for example, at the raising of the daughter of Jairus, at Jesus' transfiguration, and during

Jesus' agony in the Garden of Olives. There can be little doubt that Jesus was grooming Peter for a leadership role if anything were to happen to Jesus himself.

Because of Peter's strong faith and undoubted loyalty, Jesus trained him in humility, which he needed. There were times when Peter set himself above the others, declaring, "Though all may become deserters because of our association with you, I will never desert you" (Mt 26:33). Peter had cheek or chutzpah; he would take Jesus aside and admonish him on how to conduct his affairs. When it was clear that Jesus intended to go to Jerusalem where his life would be in danger, Peter "took Jesus aside and began to *rebuke* him, saying, 'God forbid, Lord! This must never happen to you.' But Jesus turned and said to Peter, 'Get behind me, Satan! You are a stumbling block to me; for you are setting your mind not on divine things but on human things'" (Mt 16:22–23). This scolding occurred shortly after Jesus had praised Peter and, according to Matthew's Gospel, given him the keys to the kingdom of heaven and juridical power to loose and bind (Mt 16:19–20).

Will Peter ever learn? In the midst of the transfiguration scene when Peter and the other two apostles beheld Jesus speaking with Moses and Elijah in a vision, Peter wanted immediately to build three memento shrines, one for Jesus, one for Moses, and one for Elijah.[3] This was hardly the moment to begin talking about building shrines; it was a time for silence and wonder. And while Peter was thus chattering away, the four of them were engulfed in a luminous cloud and a voice said, "This is my Son, my Beloved; listen to him!"

This brings us up to the time of Peter's final boast at the Last Supper on the night before Jesus died. Jesus says to Peter, "Simon, Simon, listen! Satan has sought to sift you as wheat, but I have prayed for you that your own faith may not fail; and you, when once you have turned back, will strengthen your brothers" (Lk 22:31–32). Sure of his own strength, Peter says to Jesus, "Lord, I am ready to go with you to prison and to death!" We know the sequel. Far from following Jesus to prison and to death, Peter three times denied that he had ever known Jesus after he had been singled out in the yard of the palace of Caiaphas as a disciple of Jesus. Pathetically, Peter wilts before the challenge of a servant girl and other bystanders on that fateful night, as he warms himself before a fire (Jn 18:15–18). Realizing, finally, what he has done, Peter leaves the courtyard and plunges into the night, weeping bitterly. But the fact remains that neither he nor any of the other disciples turned up on Calvary where Jesus was crucified. Only the women were there. I do not identify the Beloved Disciple, who in John's Gospel stood at the foot of the cross, with the apostle John, one of Zebedee's sons.

Peter After the Resurrection

You would think that after such a humiliating experience as his threefold denial of Jesus, Peter would be more reserved. Well, he was in one sense. The final chapter added to the Fourth Gospel has Jesus asking Peter three times whether he loves him. Peter, hardly knowing what to say after having abandoned Jesus before his death, has now encountered the risen Christ. "Simon," asks Jesus, "do you love me more than these?" Jesus is reminding Peter of his boast when he assured Jesus and the rest that, although all might abandon him, he, Peter, would never do so. He would go to prison and to death with him. When Jesus asks Peter for a third time, "Do you love me?" Peter "felt hurt . . . and he says to [Jesus], 'Lord, you know everything; you know that I love you'" (Jn 21:17).

There may be a subtle play here on two Greek words for "love": *agapē* and *philia*. The Latin Vulgate translates *agapas me?* (Do you love me?) as *diligis me?* This is a lofty, intellectual, preferential love, and may go with what Jesus says when he asks Peter, "Do you love me *more* than these?" In other words, is your love more special than that of the others? Peter can only reply by repeating three times that he loves Jesus, "You know that I love (*philō*) you." He uses the verb *philō* in the Greek text. One can only guess what he might have said in Aramaic. *Philō* becomes *amo* in the Vulgate. This latter is not a fancy, superior kind of love but a very down-to-earth, affectionate love. Having pledged his love three times, Jesus finally commissions Peter to be pastor of his sheep (Jn 21:17).[4]

Seeing the so-called Beloved Disciple near him, Peter wants Jesus to tell him what his fate will be. Jesus has just informed Peter that he will be crucified, so Peter is curious about the Beloved Disciple, asking, "Lord, what about him?" Politely but firmly, Jesus tells Peter to mind his own business, replying, "What is that to you? Follow me!" (Jn 21:22). We must remember that the evangelist is writing in hindsight. He believes that Peter was crucified and that the Beloved Disciple died at an advanced age. So we must set the date for the final editing of the Fourth Gospel as relatively late, that is, toward the end of the first century. As often happens in the Gospel according to John, when Peter, representing the Petrine or institutional Church, is paired against the Beloved Disciple, representing the "pneumatic" or charismatic Church, the Beloved Disciple always is a winner and Peter is a loser, invariably saying or doing something inappropriate. See Chapter Fourteen for an extended discussion of the rivalry between Peter and the Beloved Disciple.

Evidently, Peter had a habit of prying into other people's affairs. Later on, he seemd to have become somewhat less self-assertive. This appears very clearly in the case of the conversion of Cornelius, a centurion of the Italian cohort. About noon one day, Peter, who is staying in Joppa, a coastal city in Samaria, has a dream or is in a trance. He seems to see a sheet let down from heaven containing foods that Peter would not eat because they were regarded as unclean by Orthodox Jews.[5] But he hears a voice saying, "Get up, Peter; kill and eat." When Peter demurs, the voice says, "What God has called clean, you must not call profane" (Acts 10:15). When Peter enters the house of the Gentile Cornelius, he says, "You yourselves know that it is unlawful for a Jew to associate with or visit a Gentile; but God has shown me that I should not call anyone profane or unclean" (Acts 10:28). So Peter baptizes Cornelius and his household members and they begin to speak in tongues.

Peter's education was now nearly complete. He was willing to be guided by the spirit rather than depend on his own strength of mind and will. Recovering his courage, as we learn from Acts, Peter is not afraid to say openly to the high priest and his Council, "We must obey God rather than any human authority" (Acts 5:29). Although Peter is present at the so-called Council of Jerusalem, it seems to have been James, the brother of Jesus, who has final say on what should be the nature of the burdens laid on those Gentiles who converted to the new faith. "Therefore," rules James, "I have reached the decision that we should not trouble those gentiles who are turning to God" (Acts 15:19). Thus, it is James, rather than Peter, who makes the final ruling concerning the Gentiles, and Peter accepts his authority.

Peter, with his newfound tolerance and meekness, stands between James and Paul. James would continue to observe the Law of Moses himself while, somewhat reluctantly, allowing converts exemption from circumcision and most of the dietary laws. Meanwhile, Paul has already been baptizing Gentiles without the need of circumcision. At Antioch, Peter is caught between loyalty to the spirit of James and the freedom of Paul. He has been eating with Gentiles, but when a delegation from James arrives, he no longer does so. Paul becomes enraged, and he tells Peter to his face that he is a hypocrite (Gal 2:11–14). Although we have only Paul's account of the incident, Peter seems to have accepted the rebuke meekly and without protest.

The relationship between James, the brother of Jesus, and Peter provides an interesting field for study. Who was head of the Church? James seems to have had last say. People traveled to meet him in order to win his approval. He is clearly the head of the Jerusalem Church. While Peter enjoys great prestige with those in the Jesus movement, he seems to be a minister without portfolio. He moves around, from Jerusalem to Joppa, to Antioch, to Rome. The "keys of the kingdom" passage which appears only in Matthew's Gospel (Mt 16:16–17) has Jesus conferring on Peter the power in the Church to permit and forbid, to loose and bind. This has a juridical ring to it. But two chapters later the same power is conferred by Jesus on all those with authority in the Church. Thus, we read in chapter eighteen of Matthew's Gospel: "Truly I tell you, whatever you bind on earth will be bound in heaven, and whatever you loose on earth will be loosed in heaven" (Mt 18:18). The "you" in whatever you bind (*hósa ean désēte*) is plural, whereas the commission to Peter is pronounced in the singular. It refers to Peter alone.

Is Matthew telling us that Peter's authority is unique and to be distinguished from that conferred on the Church in general? This has been argued back and forth from earliest times between the Roman Church and Eastern Orthodoxy, and between Catholics and Protestants. Catholics hold that Peter was the first Pope and head of the universal Church. The Orthodox allow only that he and his successors were Patriarchs of the West, one Patriarch among several others. Protestants are inclined to hold that Peter was dubbed *Cephas*, or Rock, because of the solidity of his faith, and that jurisdiction had nothing to do with it.

The papacy has experienced days of glory and days of shame, a bit like Peter himself: human, fallible, subject to corruption, sometimes strong, and sometimes lacking in courage. That aside, what we learn from the story of Peter is that he eventually became a truly humble man. More to the point, and for our edification, is the fact that all four evangelists tell about Peter's cowardly denial of Jesus. Even though he was chief of the apostles and highly favored by Jesus, they felt that it was important to provide an account of his weakness and fall, so that others would be encouraged not to despair. Judas betrayed Jesus, regretted his action, and went out and killed himself. Peter denied Jesus and repented, to become a tower of strength. Having "turned around," or converted, he was able to strengthen the faith of others and become a model of prudence and forbearance. Had Judas turned to the risen Christ for forgiveness, he would surely have been forgiven.

Notes

[1] The Sea of Galilee is still well supplied with fish. The fishing business benefitted a few wealthy families but was a lowly and unpleasant occupation for those who were immediately engaged in cleaning and preparing the fish for shipment. Richard A. Horsley and Neil Asher Silberman describe the ancient way of processing fish by pressing, salting, and fermenting them. See *The Message and the Kingdom: How Jesus and Paul Ignited a Revolution that Transformed the Ancient World* (New York: Grosset/Putnam, 1997), 25.

[2] Peter's leadership role is highlighted in all of the gospels, especially in Matthew's where he is given the Keys to the Kingdom. In Acts, he is prominent in the first ten chapters as the major spokesman for the middle position between James and Paul. Even Paul's attack on Peter described in his Letter to the Galatians was in his own eyes a very daring thing to do (Gal 2:11, 14).

[3] Peter wanted to build three monuments or memorial shrines to commemorate the transfiguration of Jesus. Jacob sought to memorialize his dream of a ladder with angels reaching to heaven by marking the spot. "So Jacob rose early in the morning and he took the stone that he put under his head and set it up for a pillar and poured oil on top of it" (Gen 28:18).

[4]
Jesus asks Peter:	Peter replies:	Jesus commissions Peter:
Do you love me	I love you	Feed my
agapas me?	philō se	arnia (lambs)
agapas me?	philō se	probata (sheep)
phileis me?	philō se	probata (sheep)

While Peter's reply is always the same, Jesus links his question to the commission given to Peter in three different ways or combinations: *agapas-arnia, agapas-probata, phileis-probata*. Peter settles for a warm, human kind of love, *philō*, rather than a preferential, almost godlike kind of love, *agapē*. In the end Jesus uses Peter's word, *phileis*, and the commission goes from lambs to sheep and therefore to a more expanded assignment.

[5] Deuteronomy lists the clean and unclean mammals and fowl (Deut 14:4–8). Jesus says, "It is not what goes into the mouth that defiles a person, but it is what comes out of the mouth that defiles" (Mt 15:11). Is this another case of, "You have heard it said, but I say to you:" when Jesus would seem to impose his own authority over that of Moses, as he had done in the case of divorce? (Mk 10:5). Peter's dream in Acts about calling no food unclean (Acts 10:28) may or may not reflect Jesus' own attitude toward clean and unclean foods. It probably represents the view of Luke, the author of the Acts of the Apostles.

Chapter Eleven

THOMAS

Descartes' Precursor

The Apostle Thomas is known as "doubting Thomas" because at first he refuses to believe that Jesus has risen from the dead. He has been absent when Jesus appears to the other ten apostles on Easter Sunday. He says, "Unless I see the marks of the nails in his hands and put my finger in the mark of the nails and my hand in his side, I will not believe" (Jn 20:25).

Seeing was not enough. One can be deceived by appearances. Thomas wants to see and touch. The doubter wants to feel the solid flesh of the man who died on Friday and was buried that evening before sundown. This is not unreasonable. Seeing, as the saying goes, is believing, but touching is knowing.

The purpose of introducing this episode into the Fourth Gospel is indicated in the Gospel itself. After Thomas actually sees Jesus and professes his faith in the resurrection, Jesus speaks to him in words that are destined not just for Thomas but also for the communities of the faithful everywhere. "Have you believed because you have seen me? Blessed are those who have not seen and yet come to believe."

What are those who have not seen to believe? They are to believe (a) that the scriptures are the revealed word of God, (b) that the texts that we have today are accurate reproductions of what the evangelists wrote twenty centuries ago, (c) that, while none of the evangelists was an eyewitness to what he wrote, they all accurately report what others told them, (d) that those others who claimed to be the immediate witnesses to what Jesus did and said sincerely believed that they had seen and heard the risen Jesus, (e) that they were not deceived, and (f) that they told the truth without embroidery concerning what they had experienced.

Can these six interlocking beliefs add up to certitude? In the secular realm, what usually confirms belief in the historicity of some event told to us by others but not actually witnessed by ourselves is multiple attestation by a large number of competent witnesses or scholars. While we have only the four gospels as witnesses to what others witnessed, in religious matters conviction is often aided by an interior grace of God. This is not simple faith, where deception is always possible, but a self-authenticating, living faith, the kind of faith that is like touching and that goes beyond merely seeing.

After Thomas actually sees Jesus and Jesus challenges him—"Put your finger here and see my hands. Reach out your hand and put it in my side. Do not doubt but believe"—Thomas falls on his knees and declared, "My Lord and my God!"

There is no indication that Thomas stretched out his hand and actually touched the wounds in Jesus' hands and side. He did not need that. Experience replaced disbelief, and Thomas fell down and worshipped his Lord. To have reached out and touched the place of the wounds would have seemed like a desecration. When we come face to face with the holy or an object of incomparable beauty, such as a work of art or an arrestingly beautiful person, our instinct is not to reach out and clutch at it, but to stand back and look with awe and admiration. In such moments we do not need to touch externally, but we are touched inwardly by something that is like a revelation of the divine source of all beauty.

The Wound in Jesus' Side

John's is the only Gospel that mentions the wound in Jesus' side. It resulted when the soldier in charge of Jesus' execution, having broken the legs of the two men crucified with him to hasten their deaths, found that Jesus was already dead. But to make sure, the soldier took hold of his fearsome Roman longspear and thrust it into the side of Jesus. Blood and water gushed out. This was offered as proof positive that Jesus actually died on the cross. It would have been easy for the enemies of the followers of Jesus to claim that Jesus did not die on the cross but only lapsed into a comatose state. Several books published over that past few decades support this thesis.[1] They point out that the two miscreants crucified with Jesus were not dead when the Roman soldier came to check on them. So, they say, it was quite possible that Jesus, whose legs were not broken, survived his crucifixion.

The Jewish historian Josephus, who was present at the siege of Jerusalem by the Romans, describes how, upon returning from an assignment given to him by the Roman general and future emperor Titus, he found three of his acquaintances among the men crucified outside the walls of the city of Jerusalem. At Josephus' request, Titus ordered the three men to be taken down from their crosses. Two of the men later died, but one survived.[2] This has been used as an indication that a man could survive crucifixion provided he was removed from the cross soon enough. The Fourth Gospel has Jesus still standing before Pilate at noon (*hōra hektē*) on the day he later died at three o'clock in the afternoon. The Synoptic Gospels, however, say that Jesus was on the cross for six hours, from nine in the morning until three in the afternoon. Difficulties connected with the day on which Jesus died and the length of time he hung on the cross are treated in the excursus at the end of Chapter Twenty-seven.

From an apologetic point of view, it seems clear that the Fourth Gospel introduces the soldier's lethal spear to prove that Jesus really died and that the resurrection was not a case of resuscitation after an apparent death. Through the centuries, the gushing forth of blood and water from the side of Jesus has been given a mystical significance, a symbol of giving birth. What comes forth from the side of the crucified Christ is the Church accompanied by blood and water. For just as Eve is taken from the side of Adam to become his offspring and wife (Gen 2:21–22), so, too, does the Church come into being as the offspring and spouse of Christ through the birthing pains of Jesus.

Paul, too, sees the Church as the Spouse of Christ; for Christ "loved the Church and gave himself up for her" (Eph 5:25). Revelation also refers to the Church as a woman, the "wife of the lamb" (Rev 21:2, 9).

What is the sacramental significance of the blood and water? According to a mystical tradition, water represents the saving water of baptism, and blood, a symbol of life, prefigures the Eucharist, a rite that celebrates the redemptive lifeblood of Christ poured out for sinners. Traditional piety has dwelt on the mystical significance of the wound in the side of Christ as a place of refuge. It also reveals the loving heart of Christ and, like the Temple veil that is rent in two (Mt 27:51), the thrust of the spearman's spear gives those who believe access to the Holy of Holies, the heart of Christ.

Didymus

Thomas is called "Didymus" in three different places in John's Gospel (Jn 11:16, 20:24, 21:2). Thomas means 'twin' in Aramaic. In Greek the word is *didumos*, which has the sense of what is double or twofold, or more properly as *didumaōn,* which means twin brother. The fact that Thomas was called "twin" gave rise to the speculation in the Acts of Thomas, an apocryphal gospel, that Thomas was the twin brother of Jesus. Needless to say that, if this wild surmise were taken seriously, it would mean that Mary, the mother of Jesus, conceived as a virgin and bore twin sons.

As proposed in chapter 6 of this book, to doubt, to "think double," is to entertain two contradictory things in one's mind at the same time. One of them, based on experience, seems sound and secure; the other cannot be fitted into what one has always assumed to be true. If a Christian woman doubts that the Virgin Mary bore twins, it will be because she is convinced of the uniqueness of Jesus as the only child ever virginally conceived. Jesus having a twin is not congruent with that conviction. Or, if an agnostic doubts that Jesus was virginally conceived, it will be because he or she cannot reconcile everyday experience with something so unusual. One doubts when one is asked to believe or do something that seems unsound or impossible, such as walking on water. So Didymus–Thomas was a man given to having strong convictions about what was possible and what was not.

When Jesus repairs with his apostles to the east side of the River Jordan and announces that he will be going to Bethany, near Jerusalem, where his friend Lazarus lies dying, his disciples are appalled that he is actually going to Judea again. "Rabbi," they say, "the Judeans [*hoi Ioudaioi*] were just now trying to stone you, and are you going there again?" (Jn 11:8). Like the others, Didymus doubts that such a trip at this time is advisable. He is of two minds on the subject: he wants at all costs to follow Jesus wherever he goes, but he also feels that death awaits all of them in Judea. Yet, with sublime resignation, Thomas turns to the others and says, "Let us also go, that we may die with him" (Jn 11:16). In point of fact, only Judas dies when Jesus dies; the rest flee when he is arrested (Mt 26:56).[3]

True to his personality, Thomas was skeptical about Jesus' plans and overcame his persistent doubt and negativism only because of his sense of loyalty to his teacher. But how loyal and faithful to his memory was he? What was he doing, where was he hiding on Easter Sunday when the other apostles had gathered together for communal prayer and support in their sorrow over the death of Jesus? Was he so despondent that he preferred to go off by himself and lament in solitude? Or did he refuse to gather with the others because they would not abandon their trust in Jesus, a trust he now felt had been misplaced? At this point we need to go back to the time of the Last Supper, when Jesus speaks to his disciples about leave taking and going away. Thomas cannot fathom what this "going away" and "preparing a place" for them means. We can almost hear the tone of desperation that enters into his voice when he complains, "We do not know where you are going. How can we know the way?" (Jn 14:5). Was Jesus going to Egypt or Damascus or Athens or Rome? If one did not know where he was going, how could one know the way to get there? Of course, Jesus was not talking about earthly journeys, but about a higher state of being in the transcendent order. The way to get there is to follow Jesus who is the Way to the Truth and the Life.

Sometimes one does get the impression that the disciples take on the role of "straight men," playing dumb, in order that the evangelist can highlight Jesus' superior knowledge, and so that we can profit by taking note of their mistakes. At the Last Supper, Philip wants Jesus to "show us the Father." In other words, Jesus is not enough. This gives Jesus the opportunity to declare that he and the Father are one and that anyone who sees him sees the Father (Jn 14:9). "Seeing" here does not mean seeing with the eyes of the body; it means that the mind of Jesus reflects perfectly the mind of God, that in discerning his true mentality one "sees God."

Back in the Fold

Like many, Thomas suffered from his season of doubts. But, as the Buddhists say, before enlightenment comes one's "great doubt." It is the recurring story of darkness before dawn. Once Thomas has been touched and deeply stirred by the visit of the risen Christ, his relief from darkness is all the more exhilarating. He no longer drags his feet. When he hears Peter say, "I am going fishing," he wants to go along. No more standing apart. So, after the resurrection of Jesus, seven of them, including Thomas, go back to their old haunts in Galilee and do what they have always done, awaiting another coming of the Lord. So they fish. Before enlightenment mountains are mountains. After enlightenment mountains are still mountains. But what a difference. Before the resurrection the apostles fished, and after the resurrection they fished, but nothing would ever be the same again. The angel declares to the women, "He is going ahead of you to Galilee; there you will see him, just as he told you" (Mk 16:7). The promise was about to be fulfilled, and the joy of Thomas and the others would be complete. Jesus would "come again," just as he had promised. For the author of the Fourth Gospel the postresurrection appearances of Jesus make up his second coming. John does not espouse the cosmic Second Coming so dear to apocalypticists.

In view of Jesus' promise to meet them all again in Galilee, Peter and the others have good reason to go there, even though Luke maintains that they never left Jerusalem (Lk 24:49).[4] At any rate, when Jesus finally comes, what takes place is a repeat of an episode with which his fishermen apostles are familiar. Before Jesus goes to Jerusalem and dies there, he has told several of his disciples who had fished all night without catching anything, to cast their nets on the other side of the boat. They make a great catch (Lk 5:5–6). Now, back in Galilee, when Peter, Thomas, and their friends are again fishing without results, the risen Jesus standing on the shore tells them to drop their nets down on the right side of the boat. Again there is a great catch of 153 large fish. With the fish safely hauled ashore, the seven disciples share with Jesus a Eucharist of toasted bread and fish. He acts as host, providing the bread and fish from some stock of his own (Jn 21:9).

"Come," says Jesus, "and have breakfast." But "none of them dared ask him 'Who are you?' because they knew it was the Lord." You ask a rabbi questions to test his knowledge and credentials. But the disciples no longer dared do that because they knew who Jesus really was. The two fishing incidents were the same because the men are once again fishing, but they are also different because the mortal Jesus they once knew has become the immortal Christ. Thomas, with the others, ate the breakfast Jesus prepared in silence. When the Lord is nigh, you do not talk because this moment is mystical. It is no longer possible to doubt.

Notes

[1] For authors supporting the hypothesis that Jesus survived the cross, see note 6 in chapter 8.

[2] The horror and scandal of crucifixion, which early Christians would not even represent in drawings or paintings, was outlawed as a form of capital punishment in the fourth century. We no longer crucify criminals. We prefer to hang them, gas them, electrocute them, or kill them by lethal injection. The United States executes more men and women than all other Western nations combined. For the account of the removal of three of Josephus' friends from their crosses, see, "The Life of Flavius Josephus," in *The Complete Works of Josephus* (Peabody, MA: Hendrickson; 1995), 25, #75.

3 The apostles may not have "run away" when Jesus was arrested. That idea was introduced by Mark (Mk 14:50). According to John's Gospel, the apostles may have been
left standing there in the Garden of Olives when Jesus was taken away. This assumes,
of course, that the assignment of the soldiers sent to arrest Jesus had orders to appre-
hend him and no one else. According to John, Jesus' presence so awed his captors that
when he agreed to turn himself over peacefully, the captain of the cohort apparently
let the others go (Jn 18:8). If that was the case, then Jesus was truly their savior that
night. After he had been bound and taken to the palace of Caiaphas, they did not run
away but melted quietly into the darkness.

4 Luke insists that on Jesus' orders the apostles never left Jerusalem after his resurrection and before Pentecost. They were to stay in the city until they would be "clothed
with power from on high" (Lk 24:49). This contradicts what the other gospels say.
Matthew and John describe appearances in Galilee before the Ascension and
Pentecost. As often happens with Luke, he is more interested in symbolism than historical fact. He wants to portray the preaching of the gospel as originating in
Jerusalem and spreading to Rome, the hub of the universe. Jesus tells his apostles to
"be my witnesses in Jerusalem, in all Judea and Samaria (note that Galilee is omitted)
and to the ends of the earth" (Acts 1:8). Luke feels that the mission of the apostles is
accomplished in principle when he has St. Paul brought to Rome, "proclaiming the
kingdom of God" (Acts 28:31).

Chapter Twelve

JAMES AND JOHN

"What's in it for us?"

J esus calls James and John, the two sons of Zebedee, *Boanērges,* Sons of Thunder (Mk 3:17). *Boaō* in Greek means, I roar, thunder, or bellow like a bull. The two brothers are apparently a loud-mouthed pair, given to arguing, boasting, being boisterous, and acting violently. When a town in Samaria refuses Jesus and his disciples hospitality, James and John are indignant. They ask Jesus, "Lord, do you want us to command fire to come down from heaven and consume them?" (Lk 9:54). Needless to say, Jesus rebukes them. Even if it is possible for them to call down fire from heaven, violence and revenge are diametrically opposed to the mind of Jesus.

James and John were not the only violence-prone members of the original twelve. Peter is said to have attacked Malchus, a servant of the high priest, and cut off his ear when he came with others to arrest Jesus in the Garden of Gethsemane. At the Last Supper, when Jesus hinted to his apostles that he would soon be arrested, they produced two swords, *machairai.* Were they long swords or simply daggers? In the latter case, they were ludicrously inadequate weapons to be used in Jesus' defense, should he and his stouthearted men be surrounded by a military detachment or the well-armed temple police. In a rare instance when Jesus calls attention to the humor of a situation, he looks at the two daggers and says with amused irony, "Enough!" The daggers are not enough to enable them to take on the Roman army, and are far too much for a man pledged to nonviolence (Lk 22:38).

Jesus could see where the use of force would lead. It is not clear whether one of Jesus' apostles, Simon the Cananaean, also called Simon the Zealot, was affiliated with some revolutionary group or was simply zealous for the law. Some years later the Zealots would become a military party that would one day join in the rebellion against Rome.[1] Judas may have been a militant activist who eventually soured on Jesus when it became clear that he would neither lead nor encourage an armed rebellion. Those who question whether Jesus actually predicted the War and the destruction of the Temple must close their eyes to the temper of the times. The hills and deserts would soon be alive with bandits and freedom fighters. In their naive enthusiasm they thought they could challenge the Mediterranean's only superpower and wrest the city of Jerusalem and its temple from Roman control. The year 70 proved how wrong they were. Jesus' opposition to an attempted military solution was based to some extent on the futility of using force against Rome. Additionally, of course, the use of violence was also totally in contrast to his idea of a velvet-glove revolution, one based on an economy of universal sharing regardless of who exercised political power.

When Your Kingdom Comes

It was evident, even during Jesus' lifetime, that Peter was his right-hand man. If Jesus was to preside over the New Order, Peter would without doubt play a leading role. Even so, on two different occasions Jesus catches his disciples arguing over which of them is to be regarded as the greatest (Mk 9:34; Lk 22:24). Once more Jesus repeats a principle he has invoked again and again. "Whoever wants to be first must be last and the servant of all" (Mk 10:44). On two different occasions, Jesus says: "The kings of the gentiles lord it over them; and those in authority over them are called benefactors. But not so with you; rather the greatest among you must be like the youngest, and the leader like one who serves" (Mt 20:25–26; Lk 22:25).

Mark points out that John and James failed to get the message, even after Jesus has made it clear that in his commonwealth the greatest, if there is such, should serve the least. Nevertheless, James and John come forward and ask Jesus for the favor of being granted the two places of highest honor when he comes into his kingdom. "Grant us to sit, one at your right hand and one at your left, in your glory" (Mk 10:37). Jesus warns them that anyone who aspires to such positions will have to suffer a great deal, and in the end it is up to God to decide who will be closest to him. In Matthew's Gospel it is the mother of James and John who makes the request (Mt 20:20–21. Clearly those who importuned Jesus in this way, if they were to represent his mind and become authentic disciples, had a lot to learn.

Rivalry was not limited to the ranks of the twelve apostles themselves. They also suffered from the us–and–them syndrome. It is John again, this time by himself, who complains to Jesus, "Teacher, we saw someone casting out demons in your name, and we tried to stop him, because he was not following us" (Mk 9:38). In a contemporary frame of reference this would be like having the Presbyterians complain to God that the Methodists were performing works of charity in Jesus' name, not realizing that the Catholics have a monopoly on good works. Nobody owns the kingdom. Christians in times past, and some even today, berate one another in Jesus' name.

In Later Years

John turns up again, after the ascension of Jesus, in tandem with Peter. They have managed to cure a lame man who has been carried daily to the Temple area at the beautiful gate to beg for alms. After the cure, the people crowd around Peter and John in Solomon's porch in the Temple compound. Peter then makes a long speech about the risen Jesus that eventually attracts the attention of the Temple high priests. They are promptly arrested and forbidden to teach in the name of Jesus. "Impossible," says Peter. "We must obey God rather than any human authority" (Acts 5:29). After being scourged, they are finally let go. We next find the two of them in Samaria preaching and invoking the Holy Spirit (Acts 8:14 ff.).

Of some interest is the fact that Peter does all the talking. Although he and John were anything but scholars like the Scribes (Acts 4:13), Peter had a natural gift of eloquence. John, although one of the noisy *Boanērges*, does not say a word; he is not very articulate as a public speaker. And this brings up the question about whether or not John could have been the author of the Fourth Gospel. An enduring tradition holds that Polycarp (69–155?), an elderly friend of Irenaeus (130–200?), knew John the apostle at Ephesus in his old age. Whether John was the brother of James and author of the Fourth Gospel is open to question.[2]

The Gospel According to John

It is unlikely that the Gospels attributed to Matthew and John were composed by two apostles bearing those names. Their names were assigned to these Gospels after they had been published. No one knows for sure who the "Johns" were who composed the Fourth Gospel, the Letters of John, and Revelation. They seem to have in common some elements besides the name, not the least of which is vocabulary and style. Very likely the Gospel, the Letters, and

Revelation represent the thinking of a particular school of Christian thought with a distinctive approach to Jesus, one that reflects the outlook of the Johannine community, or "The Community of the Beloved Disciple."

In the supplementary chapter added to the main body of the Fourth Gospel, the final editors or redactors refer to someone who was the main source of the information used in the redaction process. If the author, or source of information, was truly the apostle John, this would have been said in unmistakable terms. The Gospel speaks of an eyewitness, and the eyewitness appears to have been the so-called Beloved Disciple, also referred to as "another disciple" or "the other disciple" (Jn 20:2). As we shall see in chapter 14 of this book, this information will have a bearing on who the Beloved Disciple might have been.

The "we" verses in the Fourth Gospel lead one to suspect that the text that has come down to us was pieced together by a committee that based its information on the undisclosed eyewitness. Regarding the witness, the editors declare, "and we know that his testimony is true" (Jn 21:24). This "we" theme runs through the Gospel. Even when Jesus seems to be the speaker, he lapses into the plural and appears to be echoing the views of the community. Thus, after speaking in the first person for the better part of ten verses (Jn 3:3–13), Jesus shifts to the first person plural, saying, "We speak of what we know and testify to what we have seen." Furthermore, a moment later Jesus slips into the impersonal editorial form of speech when he declares, "For God so loved the world that he sent his only son . . ." (Jn 3:16). Here Jesus seems to be talking about himself as though he were somebody else. Such syntactical interruptions can be explained if they are the remarks of the redactor who is speaking for the community.

Finally, Jesus, in three different places, seems to be speaking for the Johannine community when he talks to the Jews (*Hoi Ioudaioi*) about "their law," or "your law," as though "we" know and testify to what is true, while these others are still bound by "their law" (Jn 8:17, 10:34, 15:25). Thus, Jesus is made the mouthpiece for a community that was at odds with the synagogue and, to some degree, the Petrine Church. Whether the Johannine Community was headed by or simply inspired by the apostle John, the Beloved Disciple, or by someone else, will probably never be known for sure.

What happened to John after the fall of Jerusalem is uncertain. Even before that event many Christians had emigrated from Palestine and settled in such places as Pella, Edessa, and Antioch, where the followers of Jesus were first called "Messianists," or Christians. An early tradition that later writers built on, traces a disciple of Jesus named John to Ephesus. The Gospel according to John may have been written at Ephesus or Alexandria or anywhere in between. What we have is an edited version of the recollections of someone who was an eyewitness to the life and times of Jesus. But the theological elaboration for which the Gospel is noted is the product of some other hand other than those of the so-called disciple whom Jesus loved. (Jn 21:7, 20).

Even supposing that the Beloved Disciple was the apostle John, we have to ask again why would those who edited and published the Gospel have concealed the name of their source, if he was one of Jesus' three closest apostles? The eyewitness might have wanted to conceal his identity out of modesty, but his publishers would not have been under that kind of restraint. On the contrary, the publishers would have trumpeted the name. So important was the authority of an apostle in promoting a letter or a pseudo-gospel that the authors of pseudepigrapha put out their compositions under the name of a recognized apostle. This was true of the deutero-Pauline Letters to Timothy and to Titus, of the Second Letter of Peter, and, possibly, the Letter of James. There had to be some reason why the redactor-publishers of the Fourth Gospel refused to give the name of the person who was the source of their information. Was it a woman? I will explore that possibility and offer a tentative explanation later in chapter 14.

James, the Other Son of Zebedee

As with John and Mary, James (really Jacob) was a common name among the Jews of Jesus' day. Along with James, Zebedee's son, there was another apostle, James the son of Alphaeus, together with James the Just, who was the brother of Jesus. Luke tells us in the first chapter of the Acts of the Apostles that after the ascension of Jesus, the apostles, friends, and relatives of Jesus stay together and pray together in Jerusalem, awaiting the coming of the Holy Spirit. Besides the eleven apostles—twelve if Matthias, the substitute for Judas, is counted—one finds Mary the mother of Jesus, other women, and the brothers of Jesus. The latter would have included Jesus' brother James, who was not an apostle, although the former group would have included the apostle James the brother of John (Acts 1:14).

This mention of John's brother James is the last word we hear of him until some time in the forties when he is slain by the sword at the command of King Herod Agrippa I, the grandson of Herod the Great (Acts 12:2). He becomes king in 41 and dies in 44, so we know that James is killed some time between those dates. His death is usually set at 42.

St. Paul never met James, probably because he was away at the time of Paul's first visit to Jerusalem some three years after his conversion experience, when he spent fifteen days with Peter. He says that the other leading figure he met at that time was James the brother of Jesus (Gal 1:18–19). Fourteen years later, he returned to Jerusalem, and this time he met the "acknowledged pillars" of the Church, namely, Peter, James, and John. This can be confusing, because this James is not the James of the triumvirate, Peter, James, and John, about whom we read in the Gospels. He is the brother of Jesus, now risen to high station in the new Jesus movement. As for John's brother James, he proved to be the second apostle to die, following the death of Judas, and the second Christian martyr, after the deacon Stephen.

Notes

[1] Richard A. Horsley with John S. Hanson points out the important distinction to be made between "zealots" committed to a careful observance of the Law of Moses, and members of the anti-Roman movement of the late sixties. The movement included political zealots and the Sicarii. The Sicarii, who specialized in political assassination, are not to be confused with what Josephus calls the Fourth Movement, founded by Judas the Galilean at the start of the century nor with the religious zealots of Jesus' day, among whom we should probably include the apostle Simon the Zealot, also called Simon the Cananaean. See *Bandits Prophets & Messiahs* (Harrisburg: Trinity Press International, 1985, 1999), xxv and 211.

[2] The source of the information about Polycarp's knowing and even being a pupil of the disciple of Jesus named John stems from Irenaeus, Bishop of Lyons, in his book, *Against Heretics, Book III*. But Irenaeus is not a very reliable witness. He says that Papias knew John, but Papias himself admits that he did not know him. And there is always the question concerning the confusion between the John who composed Revelation and John the apostle. According to Eusebius, Clement of Alexandria, among others, erroneously thought they were one and the same. See *The History of the Church from Christ to Constantine* (New York: Dorset, 1984), 128–129, 149–150.

Chapter Thirteen

PHILIP AND ANDREW

The Greek Connection

Among the Apostles, Philip, Peter, and his brother Andrew were from the town of Bethsaida. This was the Bethsaida that belonged to the cluster of three lake towns, Capernaum, Chorazin, and Bethsaida, mentioned together by two of the Synoptic evangelists (Mt 1:21–23; Lk 10:13–15). Bethsaida lay within the territory of the tetrarch Philip, one of the sons and heirs of Herod the Great. It is here that Jesus cures a blind man. He recovers his sight gradually. At first he sees objects only vaguely. "I see people," he says, "but they look like trees walking." Then Jesus places his hands on the man's eyes and looked intently at him. With these two gestures the man's sight is fully restored (Mk 8:25).

Bethsaida–Julias, named for the Emperor's mother, Livia Julia, was a city with a sizable Gentile population. Along with Caesarea Philippi, named for Caesar and Philip, it had been rebuilt by Philip. Jesus did not customarily go to cities where Gentiles were numerous, but because three of his apostles came from Bethsaida, he had some ties to the place. It was also a refuge for Jesus. He could go there whenever he felt the need to get out of the way of Herod Antipas, tetrarch of Perea and his native Galilee.

The Role of Philip and Andrew in the Multiplication of the Loaves

When Jesus is faced with the problem of feeding a very large number of people in the wilderness, Philip and Andrew have a role to play, at least in John's Gospel. To test Philip, Jesus asks him where bread could be bought to feed five thousand people. Looking at the multitude, Philip, a practical man, estimates that it will take six months' wages to buy bread enough to feed so many (Jn 6:7). Andrew notes, however, that there is a boy among them with five loaves and two fish. Presumably a vendor, he will likely be quite happy to sell his bread and fish. "But what are they among so many people?" The sequel is well known. The bread and fish were mysteriously multiplied so that all were fed. When the meal was over, "they took up twelve baskets full of broken pieces and the fish" (Mk 6:43). The number twelve may signify the whole of Israel with its twelve tribes, all of them to be fed by Jesus' teaching.

Various attempts have been made to "get around" the miracle. One of the more venerable reasons has Jesus sharing the bread and fish he had with those around him. His example encouraged those who had brought food into the wilderness to share it with those who had none. As a result, there was enough food for everyone with baskets of scraps left over.

A second alternative interprets this episode as a typical example of something Jesus said rather than something he did. Wanting to instruct people about how important it is for the poor to share with one another, Jesus tells a parable about a man and his servants who are able to feed hundreds of hungry men in a deserted place by encouraging them to share food with one another. Jesus would then have concluded his instruction with the refrain, "Truly, truly, I tell you, if people will share their goods, there will be more than enough food for everyone."

A third "spiritual" interpretation of the story involves the multiplication of the loaves as an example of what takes place when a prophet like Jesus feeds his hungry hearers by nourishing them with his doctrine. By sharing his teaching with others, it is multiplied hundreds and thousands of times. After the people have "eaten," or assimilated his message, with no loss to the speaker, his "food for thought" has been multiplied over and over again. The people are richer, and there is more shared truth at the end than before the teacher began to speak.

Incidentally, the prophetic model for this incident is found in the Second Book of Kings. Elisha, in possession of just twenty small barley loaves, orders his servant to serve a hundred people with only a score of bun-size loaves. Like Andrew, the servant complains, "How can I set this before a hundred people?" But Elisha insists, and after all have eaten, there is still some bread left over (2 Kings 4:42–44).

After this first multiplication of the loaves, Mark says that Jesus "immediately made his disciples get into the boat and go ahead to the other side [of the lake], to Bethsaida. Meanwhile, he dismissed the crowd" (Mk 6:45–46) and fled to the mountains from those who would make him king (Jn 6:15). It is on their way to Bethsaida that a violent storm blows on the lake and Jesus appears to his disciples walking on the water. Oddly enough, after the storm the boat does not land near Bethsaida at the northeast corner of the lake but at Gennesaret (Mk 6:53; Mt 14:34), which is on the west side. Did the storm blow them off their course so that they were forced to land back on the west side?

The Fourth Gospel complicates matters still further by saying that, after the multiplication of the loaves, the disciples get into the boat and head not for Bethsaida but for Capernaum at the north end of the lake. It is there that members of the crowd who have witnessed the multiplication of the loaves finally find Jesus. (Jn 6:17, 24). According to John, the boat party docks neither at Bethsaida nor at Genneserat but at a third location. In another version of the storm at sea, Jesus sleeps in the boat, awakens, and calms the storm, and the entire party lands, as in chapter 9 of this book, on the east side of the lake in the "county of the Gerasenes." These minor discrepancies remind us that the evangelists, writing in distant lands forty to sixty years after the time of Jesus, and without the convenience of modern maps, were a bit vague on the location of the places Jesus visited and the sequence of events in his public ministry.

The Evangelists customarily seek precedents in the Hebrew Scriptures that are fulfilled in the life of Jesus. The four evangelists, along with Paul, constantly remind readers that Jesus said or did something so that the scripture might be fulfilled. According to John, Jesus enters the city of Jerusalem riding on a donkey because it is written, "Look, your king is coming, sitting on a donkey" (Jn 12:14–15; Zech 9:9). When Jesus foresees that his disciples will desert him at the time of his arrest in the Garden of Gethsemane, he cites Zechariah, "For it is written, 'I will strike the shepherd and the sheep will be scattered'" (Mt 26:31; Zech 13:7). Again, Luke sees the betrayal of Jesus as something already determined in the scriptures, "For the Son of Man is going as it has been determined, but woe to the one by whom he is betrayed" (Lk 22:22).

The Gentile Connection

Philip and Andrew are the only members of the apostolic band who bear Greek names. Philip, a contraction for *philos* + *hippos* means a lover of horses. Andrew, based on the Greek word for man, *anēr* (the genitive is *andros*) means manly. The fact that these two apostles came from a somewhat Hellenized town and bear Greek names would lead one to believe that they spoke and understood Greek. This turns out to be the case, for we learn that when some Greeks come to Jerusalem for the festival shortly before Jesus dies, they approach Philip, saying, "We wish to see Jesus" (Jn 12:21). The Greeks choose Philip because he understands Greek. Philip then finds Andrew, and together they tell Jesus that some Greeks want to talk with him.

We have to assume that Jesus grants them an interview and, that in case Jesus is not fluent in Greek, Philip and Andrew will act as interpreters. As often happens in John's Gospel, Jesus offers what L. William Countryman has called an "inappropriate response."[1] Thus, instead of welcoming the Greeks, John has Jesus change the subject and reflect on the significance of his own destiny, saying, "The hour is come for the Son of Man to be glorified. Very truly, unless the grain of wheat falls to the earth and dies, it remains but a single grain; but if it dies, it bears much fruit" (Jn 12:24).

The coming of the Greeks, who were presumably Gentiles or Greek-speaking Jews of the Diaspora, sets off a series of reflections in Jesus' mind, or in the mind of the evangelist. Jesus sees beyond his death when, like a grain of wheat buried in the ground, his death and burial will bear much fruit. Greeks will come from east and west and sit down with Abraham, Isaac, and Jacob at the Lord's table. Jesus goes on to say that his death on the cross will in actuality be his glorification. "And I, when I am lifted up from the earth, will draw all people to myself" (Jn 12:32).

Acting as intermediaries between the Greeks and Jesus, Philip and Andrew play a prophetic role of which they themselves can hardly be aware. We do not know the ultimate fate of Philip and Andrew. Andrew seems to have been a disciple of John the Baptist when he and Philip first meet Jesus (Jn 1:40–43). A medieval tradition holds that he is crucified on an x-shaped cross. We have no further information about Philip, and he should not be confused with the deacon Philip, who is mentioned three times in the Acts of the Apostles (6:5, 8:12, 21:8).

Did Peter Speak Greek?

Given that Andrew, the brother of Peter knew Greek and lived in a Hellenized town, can we say anything for certain about Peter's linguistic skills? It would seem that if Philip and Peter's own brother spoke Greek, Peter must have had at least a smattering of the *lingua franca* of the ancient world. We know from the Acts of the Apostles and from St. Paul's Letter to the Galatians that Peter was able to converse with Gentiles. He addresses Cornelius, a centurion of the Italian cohort together with an assembly of Gentile retainers with sufficient eloquence that he is able to rouse their enthusiasm to the extent that they begin to speak in tongues (Acts 10:46). At Antioch he regularly consorted with Greek-speaking Gentiles and eats with them until emissaries from Jerusalem arrive (Gal 2:12). Eventually, Peter settled in Rome where the language of the poor, common people was Koine Greek. He may have talked with the Jews in Hebrew or Aramaic, but he had to use Greek in conversing with many prospective Gentile converts. It might be too much to assume that Peter also knew Latin.

Excursus on the Lost Sheep of the House of Israel

We are apt to suppose that the Palestine of Jesus' day was solidly Jewish and that Jesus limited his journeys to towns within that area. But he also had occasion to visit the Decapolis, a league of ten Greek cities on the east side of the Jordan River and the Lake of Galilee. It was in that domain that he drove a legion of demons out of a maniac near the city of Gerasa (Mk 5:13), or Gadara (Mt 8:32). Jesus also visited the Gentile area near Sidon and Tyre where he cured a Syro-Phoenician woman's daughter (Mk 7:26). Although all of these Gentile locations were outside of Palestine, we have evidence of a strong Gentile presence in Galilee and even in Jerusalem. For example, archeologists have unearthed at Sepphoris, a city within walking distance of Nazareth, a mosaic featuring a pagan Dionysiac scene, fragments of Roman sarcophagi, and the remains of a large outdoor Greco-Roman amphitheater that could have seated up to 5,000 people. Even Jerusalem had its theater, hippodrome, and, until shortly before Jesus' day, a gymnasium, where naked athletes engaged in Greek-style sports. Interestingly, some Jewish men who participated in the sports activities had undergone an operation to reverse evidence of their circumcision by stretching the foreskin. Jews who became so thoroughly "gentilized" that they ceased for all practical purposes to be Jewish were said, metaphorically, to have reversed their circumcision.

We can gather from such evidence how powerful the dominant Greek culture was and how the primary concern of Jesus was to bring back to their traditional Jewish practices "the lost sheep of the House of Israel" (Mt 15:24). This was the environment in which Philip,

Andrew, and Peter lived. Jesus, too, was aware of the mores of the Gentiles around him. His chosen goal was to purify the Judaism of his own day that suffered from leakage and religious indifference, as many people adopted Greek and Roman ways and names, as well as from an excess of religious ultraconservatism, represented by those few Pharisees who laid intolerable burdens on simple people (Mt 23:4). Philip and Andrew may be taken, then, as symbolizing a monumental clash of cultures, with too many Jews aping their Roman overlords, or conspiring with them against the best interests of their own people. Others preferred "the sweetness and light" of Greece and found it intellectually superior to their highly restrictive ethnic religion.

Notes

[1] L. William Countryman, *The Mystical Way in the Fourth Gospel: Crossing over into God* (Philadelphia: Fortress Press, 1987), 5–6, 48, 95.

Chapter Fourteen

THE BELOVED DISCIPLE

Did Jesus Have Favorites?

T he Fourth Gospel speaks five times of "the disciple whom Jesus loved" (Jn 13:23, 19:26, 20:2, 21:7, 20). Presumably Jesus loved all of his disciples. But, according to the Fourth Gospel, he had a preferential love for one particular unnamed disciple. Can favoritism be harmonized with Jesus' radical egalitarianism? Is it possible to identify the so-called Beloved Disciple? My conclusion, after tracking down various leads, is that the Beloved Disciple, if he existed, was not one of the twelve apostles, but was a close friend and confidante of Jesus.

In his first chapter the evangelist refers cryptically to "two disciples," one of whom is Andrew while the other disciple remains unnamed (Jn 1:40). In chapter eighteen, he refers to "another disciple" and "the other disciple," and in the last chapter we are told about "two other disciples," again without naming the individuals in question (Jn 18:15–16, 21:3). I do not doubt that the author of the Fourth Gospel intends readers to understand that the Beloved Disciple, the one who is described as reclining next to Jesus at the Last Supper (Jn 13:23), is to be identified with "the other disciple," the one who gained access for Peter to the courtyard of the palace of Caiaphas on the night that Jesus was arrested (Jn 18:16)[1]; I also do not doubt that he is one of the "two other disciples" mentioned in the last chapter of the Fourth Gospel. Confirmation of the fact that the Beloved Disciple and "the other disciple" are one and the same appears in the twentieth chapter of John's Gospel, where it is said: "So she [Mary Magdalene] ran and went to Simon Peter and *the other disciple, the one whom Jesus loved* and said to them, 'They have taken the Lord out of the tomb. . . .'" (Jn 20:3).

Rival Communities

Peter and "the other disciple" are paired off against one another on every possible occasion. The two represent, respectively, the mainline

Apostolic Church and the more esoteric, mystical, and faintly Gnostic approach to Jesus. The Fourth Gospel's compilers keep telling us in so many way that the members of their community, represented by the Beloved Disciple, enjoyed a more intimate, intuitive, and loftier insight into Jesus than did the adherents of the more ecclesial, institutional Church, represented by Peter. Their rivalry is exemplified in several situations. At the Last Supper it is the Beloved Disciple rather than Peter who reclines next to Jesus, and Peter has to go through the Beloved Disciple to find out who the traitor is (Jn 13:23–24). It is through the mediation of the Beloved Disciple that Peter, who has been locked out, is able to gain entry to the courtyard of the high priest Caiaphas after Jesus has been arrested (Jn 18:16). It is the Beloved Disciple who stands at the foot of the cross comforting Mary the mother of Jesus when all of the close apostles, including Peter, are conspicuous by their absence. Later, it is the Beloved Disciple who beats Peter in a race to the empty tomb of the risen Christ (Jn 20:4). Arriving at the tomb, the Beloved Disciple not only believes what the women have told them but interiorly also believes in the resurrection, although Peter goes away from the tomb without understanding. After the resurrection, it is once again the Beloved Disciple who first recognizes Jesus standing on the lakeshore and has to inform Peter, "It is the Lord!" (Jn 21:7). In a last pairing of the two, it is Peter who has to pledge his love of Jesus three times to make up for the three times he has denied him, something not required of the Beloved Disciple who is also present. The love and loyalty of the Beloved Disciple are never in doubt. Finally, when Peter asks Jesus about the destiny of the Beloved Disciple, Jesus politely tells him to mind his own business, saying, "What is that to you?" (Jn 21:22).

So whenever Peter and the Beloved Disciple appear in tandem, the Beloved Disciple always appears as the favorite and is more sensitive and perceptive than Peter. It is what Raymond E. Brown calls the game of "one-upmanship."[2]

The Eyewitness

The editors of the Fourth Gospel make it clear that the source of their information about Jesus was an eyewitness, whom they identify as the Beloved Disciple, "and we know that his testimony is true" (Jn 21:2). A possible candidate for the role of the Beloved Disciple is Lazarus, the brother of Martha and Mary. When Lazarus falls sick, his two sisters urge Jesus to come as quickly as possible to heal their brother: "Lord, *he whom you love* is ill" (Jn 11:3). Later, in the same chapter, when Jesus begins to weep over the death of Lazarus, the people say, "See how he loved him" (Jn 11:36). If Lazarus was the Beloved and was present at the Last Supper, we would have to abandon the idea that the original twelve apostles of Jesus were the only ones there. With all of the apostles gathered together, there would have been someone else present who was not an apostle and who is represented as closer to Jesus than any of the others. Could it have been Lazarus? If that were the case, why would the evangelist omit his name at this point in his story when he uses it eleven times in chapters eleven and twelve? The evangelist had no reason to withhold the name of Lazarus.

But was the Beloved Disciple not the apostle John, John the Evangelist, John the Beloved? An early tradition certainly identifies the author of the Fourth Gospel with John, the brother of James and one of the sons of Zebedee. The Last Gospel is even called "The Gospel according to John." The truth of the matter is that no one knows for sure who the authors of any of the four Gospels were. Few scholars hold that the apostle Matthew wrote the First Gospel. We do not know the "Mark" who composed the Second Gospel, and the sophisticated writer of Luke and Acts did not sign his works and is known by name only. The most serious objection to the belief that John the apostle wrote the Fourth Gospel is mentioned in the Preface to this book and elsewhere. In the Acts of the Apostles both Peter and John are said to be *anthrōpoi agrammatoi kai idiōtai*, literally unlettered and ordinary men, possibly even illiterate (Acts 4:13).

This description should not surprise us. Peter and John were sturdy fishermen from Galilee where literacy was probably below ten percent of the population. When Peter denies that he ever knew Jesus in the courtyard of Caiaphas, he is immediately recognized as a common Galilean, "for your accent betrays you" (Mt 26:73). Peter and John were not men of high culture; they belonged to the lower, less privileged classes without formal education. So, it is highly unlikely that John, the brother of James, composed the Fourth Gospel, one of the religious and literary classics of all time. However, some of the information in the Fourth Gospel may have had John as its source. Even so, we are still faced with the enigma: If John, a man so close to Jesus, was the author or at least the source for some of the information in the Fourth Gospel, why did the evangelist not trumpet their relationship instead of choosing to conceal it?

Surely, if Lazarus, Nicodemus, or Joseph of Arimathea was the Beloved Disciple, the evangelist had no reason to withhold the individual's name. The names of the last two men, who were supposed to have shared in the burial of Jesus, were not concealed. Limiting our inquiry, then, to what we learn from the Fourth Gospel, we may conclude that revealing the identity of the Beloved Disciple was a matter of such delicacy and sensitivity to the evangelist that he thought it best to omit that person's name. Furthermore, what if the disciple who ushered Peter into the courtyard of Caiaphas and who reclined next to Jesus at the Last Supper was a woman?

The leading candidate for such a role would have to be Mary of Magdala, not to be confused with the sinful woman who, according to Luke's Gospel, comes from the street, washes the feet of Jesus with her tears, and dries them with her hair (Lk 7:36–38). Nor is she to be identified with Mary of Bethany, the sister of Lazarus and Martha. She was apparently a woman of substance, a native of Magdala, the town made prosperous by the thriving salted fish industry.[3] Prominent in all four Gospels, Mary Magdalene was a close friend and traveling companion of well-placed women, such as Joanna, the wife of no less a person than Chuza, the steward of Herod Antipas. If she was the "the other disciple," she was, according to John's Gospel "known to the high priest" (Jn 18:15) and could exercise enough authority to have the gatekeeper allow Peter, who had been locked out, to enter the palace courtyard.

In any case, this "other disciple," with access to the high priest's palace, does not sound like one of the Twelve, a group composed mostly of Galilean peasant fishermen. If the Beloved Disciple was Magdalene, she had been an eyewitness and could report on the miracles and preaching of Jesus. She is also portrayed as close to Mary the mother of Jesus, standing with her at the foot of the cross. She is also represented as the first to be visited by Jesus after his resurrection (Jn 20:11–18).

Hypothetically and up to this point, it might seem to follow that Mary Magdalene was "the disciple whom Jesus loved." Initially, a suggestion of that nature might seem far-fetched and inappropriate because Jesus was a celibate Hebrew teacher. But before we reject Mary Magdalene as the Beloved Disciple, we have to ask ourselves once more why the identity of the Beloved Disciple was deliberately withheld. Surely the final editors of the Fourth Gospel knew; they declare, "and we know that his testimony is true" (Jn 21:24). One could hardly expect a first-century Jewish evangelist to write, "and we know that *her* testimony is true." The testimony of a woman was of no value in a Jewish court or even in ordinary affairs. So, a case can be constructed to show how and why the Beloved Disciple, although a woman, was portrayed as male.

Could a woman be turned into a man? In the Gospel of Thomas, the Gnostic Jesus opposes Peter who wants Mary to leave the apostolic band, "because women are not worthy of life." He means the higher life of the spirit. Jesus will have none of that kind of talk. "Behold," he says in the idiom of that school. "I shall guide her so as to make her male, that she too may become a living spirit like you men. For every woman who makes herself male will enter the kingdom of heaven."[4] It could very well be the case, then, that in the Fourth Gospel the Beloved Disciple is presented as male, lest the principal witness for what Jesus said and did should turn out to be a woman.[5]

Of course, there would be other fairly obvious reasons for disguising the sex of the Fourth Gospel's star witness and beloved friend of Jesus. In that culture, as in ours, a platonic male–female relationship seemed impossible. More than one author has implied that there must have been a romantic love relationship between Jesus and Mary Magdalene along the lines of *The Last Temptation of Christ* by Nikos Kazantzakis (1951). But one need not follow that tired model. Jesus could have related to Mary Magdalene as an older, prudent, and well-educated woman whose presence balanced the dominantly male composition of the apostolic band. Jesus was not a "tame lion," unable to break with precedent and the prejudices of a patriarchal culture. He offers his unconditional love to all. Anticipating a saying of St. Paul, he seeks to display in his own behavior his conviction that, "There is no longer Jew or Greek, slave or free, there is no longer male or female" (Gal 3:28). All are one and equal as children of God, and all should be treated with that in mind. If Jesus went out of his way to relate to his female disciples with the same degree of love and respect that he conferred on the men, it was partly to show the men that in his kingdom men and women were of equal worth. What is surprising is that he included at least one outstanding woman among his closest disciples. This inclusion was so unusual that the final editor of John's

Gospel may have thought it best to disguise it and turn the Beloved
Disciple into a man.

Three Reasons Against the Idea that
Magdalene Was the Beloved Disciple

There are three episodes that would seem to militate against
Magdalene being the Beloved Disciple. Keeping to John's Gospel, we
are told that Mary Magdalene runs from the tomb to tell Peter and the
Beloved Disciple about what she has discovered: the tomb is empty,
and the body of Jesus is nowhere to be found (Jn 20:2). Were she the
Beloved Disciple, she would hardly be running to tell *herself* about
what had happened. She cannot be both the messenger and the one for
whom the message is intended.

Secondly, when the three Marys stood beneath the cross of Jesus,
one of them was Magdalene. But, according to John's Gospel, there
was also a fourth disciple present, a man. The man is said to be the
Beloved Disciple, or "the disciple whom Jesus loved." (Jn 19:26).
Once again, if John's account is to be credited, Magdalene cannot be
the Beloved Disciple, because the male Beloved Disciple is standing
there beside her.

But independent of whether the Beloved Disciple was male or
female, the author of the Fourth Gospel had a theological reason, concerning Mary the mother of Jesus, for creating the scene at the foot of
the cross. In this passage, Jesus commends his mother to the care of
the Beloved Disciple, saying, "Son, here is your mother." Then, turning to his mother, he asks her to take the Beloved Disciple as her
adopted son (Jn 19:26–27). The Beloved Disciple, as indicated in
Chapter One, stands for all of the faithful, or at least for the members
of the Community of the Beloved Disciple, and Mary the mother of
Jesus becomes their spiritual mother and the mother of all who live by
the teaching of Jesus. In this way she is the embodiment of a renewed
womanhood and, in the eyes of the early Church Fathers, a new and
better Eve. This text, among others, helped provide the basis for devotion to the Blessed Virgin Mary in the Eastern Orthodox and Roman
Catholic Churches.

Thirdly, according to the Appendix to the Fourth Gospel, when
Peter, James, John, Thomas, Nathaniel, and two other disciples return
to Galilee after the resurrection to go fishing, the Beloved Disciples is
listed among them. He is, incidentally, not identified with the apostle

John but is mentioned separately. Presumably he is one of the unnamed "other disciples" (Jn 21:2). It is highly unlikely that, among the seven who went fishing, Mary Magdalene, a woman, would have been among them.

Yet the three texts from John's Gospel outlined above do not definitively disqualify Magdalene as the Beloved Disciple. To begin with, the scene at the foot of the cross is almost certainly a bit of unhistorical midrash, or what John P. Meier calls a *theologoumenon* (a theological insight narrated as historical event.)[6] The three Synoptic Gospels, starting with Mark, make it clear that, although Mary Magdalene and the other women are present at the crucifixion, they stand far off, "looking on from a distance" (Mk 15:40; Mt 27:55–56; Lk 23:49).

Magdalene and the mother of Jesus, if they were there, stood at too great a distance to be able to hold a conversation with the man on the cross. Additionally, there is no mention of a male disciple among the Galilean women who witnessed the crucifixion.

John introduces the episode beneath the cross, along with the theological considerations listed above, in order to show that, in the rivalry between the Community of the Beloved Disciple and the Apostolic Church, between the Johannine and the Petrine approaches to Jesus, the former always prevailed, at least in spirit. When all of the chosen apostles had abandoned Jesus, which of his disciples stood by him and supported his bereaved mother at the foot of the cross? Who was closer than Peter to Jesus and reclined next to him at the Last Supper? Who got Peter into the courtyard of the high priest? Who outran Peter to the tomb? Who understood that Jesus had risen from the dead? Who first recognized Jesus standing on the lakeshore after his resurrection? One would have to be blind not to see what the intention of the Fourth Gospel's author was, and why the Beloved Disciple occupied so prominent a place in that Gospel.

Why Magdalene Might Have Been the Beloved Disciple

Turning now to the absurdity that would have Mary Magdalene running to tell herself and Peter that the tomb was empty, it is worth noting that when Luke describes the same episode, he too has Peter running to the tomb. He says that when Peter learns from the women about the disappearance of the body of Jesus, he "got up and ran to the tomb." Arriving there, "stooping down and looking in, he saw the linen cloths by themselves; then he went home amazed at what had happened" (Lk 24:12). There is no mention in Luke of a second so-called Beloved Disciple running with him; Peter ran solo. This suggests that the inclusion of the Beloved Disciple in the race to the tomb is a midrashic invention of the author of the Fourth Gospel. In addition, the fact that the scene in John's Gospel that has the Beloved Disciple standing with the three Marys at the foot of the cross is almost certainly "a theological insight narrated as historical event." There also is reason to question the literal historicity of both of these incidents in John's account: the one that has a male Beloved Disciple standing with Mary and Magdalene at the foot of the cross and the other that includes the Beloved Disciple in the description of Peter's race to the empty tomb.

Finally, the account of the miraculous catch of fish in the Appendix to John's Gospel is another example of what I have called a "time warp." It is achieved by transposing a story from one period of time to another. Thus, the pre-resurrection account of the unexpected catch in Luke's Gospel (Lk 5:1–11) becomes a post-resurrection scene in John, with Jesus making a fire and cooking fish for seven of his disciples. The scene is almost certainly unhistorical, so that Magdalene's presence or absence is of no consequence.

Alternative Views

There are several other passible interpretations to the mystery of the Beloved Disciple.

(1) Was the Beloved Disciple the apostle John? The Fourth Gospel never states that they are one and the same. In fact, when Peter, James, John, Thomas, Nathaniel, and two other disciples are described as returning to Galilee after the resurrection to go fishing, the Beloved Disciple must be one of the "two other disciples" (Jn 21:3) because in this scene the evangelists have an excellent opportunity to identify John as the Beloved Disciple. Instead, he lists John among the five named disciples and mentions the Beloved Disciple separately. The latter must be, as usual, one of the "two other [unnamed] disciples."

(2) Was the Beloved Disciple an apostle? If he was not John, there are no other candidates among the Twelve to fill the role. Yet, the Beloved Disciple is said to have been present at the Last Supper. This would logically lead one to conclude that the twelve apostles were not the only ones present at Jesus' farewell meal.

(3) Granted that the Beloved Disciple was not one of the Twelve, he or she was at least very close to Jesus, possibly the founder of the so-called Community of the Beloved Disciple, one who, according to the editor of the Fourth Gospel, was especially loved by Jesus, one who was more loyal to him and who had a deeper insight into his divine nature than any of the named apostles, including Peter.

(4) The Beloved Disciple was Mary Magdalene. I do not think this can be ruled out. The three objections to this thesis collapse for the reasons indicated above. The evangelist had a pressing reason to conceal the sex of the primary witness to the words and deeds of Jesus.

(5) Some have hinted that Jesus was homosexual and that the Beloved Disciple was his significant other. There is no real evidence that Jesus played favorites of any kind. Even the idea that the so-called Beloved Disciple was loved by Jesus with a preferential love is probably the way the Community of the Beloved Disciple chose to designate its Founder, not necessarily the way Jesus behaved toward that individual.

(6) The Beloved Disciple stands for and symbolizes all who believe in Jesus' divinity and are faithful to his teaching. They are especially loved by him.

Who, then, was the Beloved Disciple? I am inclined to opt for a combination of (3), (4), and (6) above. The evidence indicates, moreover, that the person John's Gospel identifies as the Beloved Disciple was not one of the twelve apostles, was, nevertheless, present at the Last Supper, and, finally, would have had a vivid recollection of what Jesus said at that final meal, material incorporated in John's Gospel into Jesus' final discourse and prayer on the night before he died (John, Chapters 14–17).

Higher Christology

Independent of the sex of the Beloved Disciple, the evangelist had another reason for introducing such a figure into the Fourth Gospel. It was to demonstrate that the Community of the Beloved Disciple in its superior understanding of Jesus fostered a higher Christology than that of the mainline, Petrine Church. The members and teachers of the more institutional Church honored Jesus as the Jewish Messiah, but the Johannine community believed that Jesus was the Divine Word Incarnate. This is communicated over and over again in the "I AM" (*Egō eimi*) statements that the author has Jesus make about himself:

When the Samaritan woman thinks that Jesus might be the Messiah, he replies, *"Egō eimi, ho lalōn soi."* I AM [is the one] who is even now speaking with you" (Jn 4:26); "Before Abraham was born, I AM [*Egō eimi*]" (Jn 8:58). When Jesus walks on the water during a storm, he tells his apostles not to fear because it is I AM who is with you (Jn 6:20). These I AM sayings are customarily translated as "I am he." For example, as will be pointed out in Chapter Fifteen, when the Samaritan woman thinks that Jesus might be the Messiah, his response is translated as, "I who speak to you am he." This leaves the impression that Jesus is saying, "Yes, I am the Messiah." John, however, intends the I AM to be the Divine Name, as when Jesus declares, "When you have lifted up the Son of Man [on the cross] then you will realize that, *Egō eimi*" (Jn 8:28).

While the Fourth Gospel presents what the evangelist believes is a proper Christology, it is proposed as superior to the view represented, for example, by the Gospel according to Matthew. In Matthew, Peter is seen as chief apostle and he is given "the keys of the kingdom of heaven" with jurisdictional power to bind and loose (Mt 16:19–20). This is more down to earth and legalistic than the outlook of the more pneumatic Johannine community. In any case, the emerging insitutional Church had other rivals besides the community represented by the Fourth Gospel. The highly orthodox Jerusalem community, presided over by James, the brother of Jesus, carefully observed all of the prescriptions of the Law of Moses, although at the other end of the spectrum, the churches founded by St. Paul no longer required circumcision or a strict and literal observance of the dietary laws.

Peter, during his lifetime and before the arrival on the scene of the view represented by the Fourth Gospel, was in the middle, between the two extremes of the Jerusalem Church and the Pauline Church. Although instinctively inclined to be an observant Jew, he eventually relents, enters the house of a Gentile, stays with him for several days, and eats his food (Acts 10:47–48). He believes that Jesus is the Messiah, raised up and "exalted at the right hand of God" (Acts 2:32–33). Lofty as this view was, it did not attribute divinity to Jesus in the full sense of the word, as it is unequivocally proclaimed in the Fourth Gospel. This difference is reflected in the contest between the institutional Apostolic Church and the Community of the Beloved Disciple. Peter's best efforts regularly leave him a step behind the Beloved Disciple, a liability that symbolizes his community's failure to embrace the exalted view of Jesus expressed in the Fourth Gospel.

Scholars have come to realize that much of John's Gospel is simulated reality. The words and deeds of Jesus are almost entirely the creation of the evangelist, a conclusion reached unanimously some ten years ago by the Fellows of the Jesus Seminar.[7] From the beginning to the end of the Fourth Gospel, the Beloved Disciple impersonates the Community of the Beloved Disciple, an individual made to stand for the whole. It was a community that supported a high Christology with its stress on the divinity of Christ.[8] The Gospel was their way of communicating to others what its head and members regarded as a lofty and deeply spiritual insight into who Jesus really was.

Regarding the identity of the Beloved Disciple, I am convinced that he or she was not one of the twelve apostles, and certainly not John. In addition, if the Beloved is to be identified with Mary Magdalene, then, according to the Fourth Gospel, she was present at the Last Supper. Beyond that, "the disciple whom Jesus loved" was a member of, and probably was the inspiration for, the theology of the Johannine Community as it is presented in the Fourth Gospel.

Eventually, after some hesitation, the Fourth Gospel was taken into the canon of the Christian scriptures. There can be little doubt that, historically, the great creeds, including the Nicene Creed (325) and the resounding dogmatic pronouncements of the Council of Chalcedon (451) owe much of their inspiration to the Community of the Beloved Disciple and its manifesto, the Gospel according to John. Without it, the third-generation followers of Jesus may not have introduced him as the Word who, in the beginning was "with God" and "was God" (Jn 1:1).

Notes

1 Raymond E. Brown, in his commentary *The Gospel according to John* (Garden City: Doubleday/Anchor Bible, 1966 and 1970), 1:xcii–xciv; 2:822, 983, hedges on the question of whether the Beloved Disciple and "the other disciple" are to be identified. I think that John 20:2 should be sufficient to settle that matter in the affirmative.

2 "The one-upmanship of the Johannine Christians is centered on Christology; for while the named disciples, representing the Apostolic Christians, have a reasonably high Christology, they do not reach the heights of the Johannine understanding of Jesus." See Raymond E. Brown, *The Community of the Beloved Disciple: The Lives, Loves, and Hates of an Individual Church in the New Testament Times* (New York: The Paulist Press, 1979), 82–84.

3 The salt-fish industry situated at Magdala brought great wealth to some. One spacious villa has been unearthed. In Jesus' day the production of salted fish (*garum*) and stews made of chopped pieces of fish (*salsamentum*) had become a major Magdala

industry. See Richard A. Horsley and Neil Asher Silberman, *The Message and the Kingdom: How Jesus and Paul Ignited a Revolution that Transformed the Ancient World* (New York: Grosset/Putnam, 1997), 24–25.

[4] The put-down of Mary will be found in Saying 113, "The Gospel of Thomas" in *The Secret Teachings of Jesus.* Translated with and Introduction by Marvin W. Meyer (New York: Random House, 1984), 51, Codex II.

[5] Speaking of women in his *De cultu feminarum* 1,12, the Church Father Tertullian writes, "You are the devil's gateway. . . . You are she who persuaded him whom the devil did not dare attack. . . . Do you not know that every one of you is Eve? The sentence of God on your sex lives on in this age: the guilt of necessity, lives on." The outlook of Tertullian on women may be extreme, but even in a more modified form it represents the mentality of many in the ancient world. All the more reason why, they felt, that a woman's testimony in serious matters should be disregarded and of no consequence. The above citation, in quotes, is from *Adam, Eve, and the Serpent* by Elaine Pagels (New York: Random House/Vintage, 1988), 63.

[6] See John P. Meier, *A Marginal Jew*, I, 281.

PART FIVE:

The Women

Chapter Fifteen

THE SAMARITAN WOMAN

Waiting for Number Seven

I f you are in Judea, as Jesus was, and wish to return north to Galilee, you may pass through Samaria or take the Jordan River route and in this way avoid Samaria entirely. On one occasion, Jesus tells his disciples not to enter any Samaritan town (Mt 10:5) because they will not be welcome. Pilgrims from Galilee on their way to Jerusalem usually avoided a march through Samaria because the Samaritans were hostile to Jews.[1] The Jews in turn thought poorly of the Samaritans. The adversaries of Jesus once accused him of being a Samaritan and having a devil, the two liabilities being about equal. On one occasion, when Jesus and his companions were passing through Samaria, they are refused hospitality and turned away because their "face was set toward Jerusalem" (Lk 9:53). Judeans and Samaritans were at odds over whose mountain and whose temple was the more ancient and venerable. The Samaritans held that Mt Gerizim, near Sichar, was to be preferred, while the Jews stoutly defended Mt Zion with its splendid Temple.

John in his Gospel says that Jesus, leaving Judea to return to Galilee "had to go through Samaria" (Jn 4:4). Was it because he was in a hurry or because that season it was too hot and steamy to travel below sea level by way of the torrid Jordan Valley route? As is usual with the Fourth Gospel, the reason is more mysterious. Jesus felt constrained to go through Samaria because he was to meet there a lone woman at noon at Jacob's Well. He would ask her for a drink at High Noon and so begin a remarkable set of verbal exchanges in the course of which the woman would elicit from Jesus some of the most penetrating statements found anywhere in the New Testament.

The sun is directly overhead, and the woman comes to the well where Jesus is resting. He is tired from a long journey on foot, and she comes to the well with her water jar to draw water from the well. Meanwhile, the disciples have gone to the village nearby to buy food.

159

So Jesus and the woman are alone. For a Jewish teacher this situation would already be compromising, because a rabbi should not be seen alone with a woman. This woman would appear to have had a rather checkered past. She has had five husbands and is currently living with a lover not her husband. No matter, Jesus asks her for a drink of water. This surprises her because Jews and Samaritans are not on speaking terms and do not share things with one another (Jn 4:9). She makes a point of this, asking, "How is it that you a Jewish man, ask a drink of me, a woman of Samara?"

Jesus tells her that, if she but knew the kind of water he could give her, she would be asking him for a drink of living water. This statement captures her interest. If he could give her living water, she would no longer have to come each day to the well with her water jug. Jesus, of course, is talking about water as a symbol of life, but she thinks he means spring water. Where can he get such water? The well is deep, and Jesus has no bucket with which to draw water. So he corrects her. He is not talking about ordinary water but about the kind so satisfying one need never thirst again. "The water that I will give becomes . . . a spring of water gushing up to eternal life" (Jn 4:14).[2]

When the woman expresses desire for such water, Jesus changes the subject and tells her to go fetch her husband and come back. Then the women becomes evasive. She says that she has no husband. True enough, replies Jesus, reminding her of her five earlier husbands and her present love. In no way fazed by his knowledge of her past, she remarks with unruffled dignity, "Sir, I see that you are a prophet." If he is really a prophet, she questions him about the rivalry between Mt Gerizim and Jerusalem. Which location is the correct place for proper divine worship? Jesus replies that the time has already come, "when the true worshippers will worship the Father in spirit and truth"; that is, "neither on this mountain nor in Jerusalem" (Jn 4:21). In the future there will be no Gerizim or Jerusalem, no Mecca or Benares.[3] True worship arises in the heart. What the Father wants are not burnt offerings and animal sacrifice, "but to do justice, and love kindness, and walk humbly with your God" (Mic 6:6; Amos 5:22).

Finally, the woman broaches the subject of the Messiah, voicing the opinion that when he comes, he will tell people what to believe. Here, John's Jesus does not deny that he is the Messiah, but, as indicated in Chapter Fourteen, he goes beyond that. He says it is "I AM" who is speaking to you. The I AM is introduced here because it is the divine name, a title that far exceeds being the Messiah (4:25).

Just at this moment the disciples who have gone to buy food return. They are astonished to see Jesus publicly speaking to a lone woman. But Jesus did not hesitate to speak with a polyandrous woman on lofty theological matters. With the return of Jesus' disciples the woman abandons her water jar, goes into town, and tells the men there that she has met the Messiah. The men, after they find Jesus and hear him, are equally impressed, and they persuade him to stay with them for two days.

What Is the Significance of the Five Husbands?

Although movie stars sometimes have had five or more husbands, such a round of marriages seems unlikely for a common woman in ancient Palestine. According to Raymond E. Brown, Jews were allowed not more than three marriages in Jesus' day.[4] This has led Brown and others to suggest that the woman's five husbands symbolize five false gods. After the Assyrians overwhelmed Samaria in 722–721 BCE, they introduced their own religion to the region and brought settlers from various parts of the Empire to replace the leading Israelites, whom they transported elsewhere. In the Second Book of Kings we learn that the new settlers, people from Babylon, Cuth, and Hamath, along with Avviates and Sepharites, brought their gods with them (2 Kings 17:24 ff.). These five foreign groups joined the remaining Israelites and introduced their five pagan gods. Because the Hebrew word for husband is ba'al, and a pagan god is a ba'al, the five "husbands" of the Samaritan woman, who stands for the whole of Samaria, could very well symbolize a nation that had espoused five false gods. Josephus confirms the number five, saying that those who brought their native gods into Samaria and worshipped them "were five in number." Who, or what, then, is the sixth significant "other" to whom the Samaritan woman is attached but not wedded?

A Modern Allegorical Interpretation

We owe to Beatrice Bruteau an original rethinking of the encounter between Jesus and the Samaritan woman.[5] In what she calls "dharma combat," the two engage in a duel of words. A Wisdom figure, the woman gets Jesus to acknowledge that, beyond all possible personal properties or descriptions, he is pure Being, the I AM, or the One Who Is. Having sought fulfillment in one attachment after another, she is now at the stage at which she is not wedded to any of her previous loves. She is free to advance beyond the sixth level, which is already bursting with light because it is High Noon. In the end, she will discover that the significant other she had been seeking was her own true self, her own I am.

In a way this is a temptation story, and it compensates for the fact that, unlike the Synoptic Gospels, there is no temptation in the Fourth Gospel. In the course of the exchanges between Jesus and the woman, she tests him on six different levels: Is he a man, a Jew, a descendent of the patriarch Jacob, a prophet, a revolutionary ("neither on this mountain nor in Jerusalem"), or the Messiah? Jesus meets and rejects all of these suggestions squarely and refuses to be identified with anything less than I AM.

Throughout the discussion, water stands for Wisdom. The woman Sophia asks all of the right questions, and in probing Jesus, she discovers her own true self. Like many seekers, she had been trying to satisfy her deepest needs on various levels. "The first husband," writes Beatrice Bruteau, "represents a lifestyle sometimes spoken of as 'living to eat.'" In Hinduism, this chakra is the first level, where one seeks to satisfy one's primitive instincts and to enjoy the comforts of the good life. Finding this unsatisfactory, one advances to the second husband (the marriage chakra) to take pleasure in the products of one's reproductive energy, in pride of family and in continuing one's bloodline.

The third husband stands for power and creativity. It can mean controlling large assets and other people. But the fourth marriage leaves behind such self-centered concerns; it begins to look out for the welfare of others. What is still lacking is the sense of transcendence and the sacred. So, with the fifth marriage, without abandoning loving one's neighbor as one's self, the quest turns to artistic expression and devotion, to values and causes beyond one's individual surroundings. But even this level of enlightenment and creativity can be transcended; for nothing in the external world can satisfy the soul's hunger and thirst for union with the divine Source of all being. True, the ego-centered self has been dissolved since the fourth marriage, but now one has to free oneself from every possible attachment. The Buddhists say that one is not truly enlightened, or, a Buddha, until he has forgotten that there ever was such a thing as Buddhism, or any other "ism."

So, entering the sixth stage she is no longer married to anyone or anything. It is then that Jesus says to the woman, "You are right in saying, 'I have no husband'; for you have had five husbands, and the one you have now is not your husband" (Jn 4:17–18). She is free. She is nearing enlightenment and the noonday sun is shining brilliantly overhead. In the clarity of her contemplative, metaphysical insight, she knows that only the absolute I AM will satisfy her. She must now transcend every tradition and culture, including nation, sex, and personal description. Bruteau then writes: "This seventh stage is beyond any culture's particular tradition. You've got to go past the 'watchmen of the walls' to find 'the one whom your soul loves' [Song 3:4]."

This is the seventh day, the Great Sabbath. She has found the one whom her soul has loved all along. It is her own true self, her "I am." At this point the woman abandons her water jar (Song 4:28). She will no longer need it because she carries within her the saving waters of eternal life.

Jesus comes to the well. Like the woman, he, too, is thirsty. "The day is at its height. He waits, and then she comes, alone, in the bright light. She comes with her sharp-pointed probing, leading questions that force him to give answers." She is his own Sophia come to meet him at the well. Jacob's well symbolizes tradition, the past, the wisdom of the people. They are both past that stage now, beyond becoming into Being. Fully enlightened regarding who she is, she leaves her water jar and returns to the city. She is like the seeker in the Buddhist Oxherding Pictures. In the last frame the herder, whose lower self has disappeared with the ox, she returns to the city laden with gifts for the people. Likewise, the woman goes back to the village and tells the men about the riches she has discovered in Jesus.[6]

John begins this story by announcing that Jesus "had to go through Samaria" (Jn 4:4). He has to meet his own Wisdom in objective form, and she has to meet him in order to discover her own true nature. When the disciples return from the village with the food, Jesus is no longer hungry or thirsty. He has another kind of food and drink. "My food is to do the will of him who sent me and to complete his work" (Jn 4:34). To complete his Father's work is to help to lead to a richer, fuller life, those who, spiritually, have unfinished business. Everywhere there are opportunities for transmitting to others Jesus' heightened self-awareness. "Look around you," he exclaims, "and see how the fields are ripe for harvesting" (Jn 4:35).

Another Approach to the Story

If Lady Wisdom did not teach Jesus who he is, she strips away every possible predicate, leaving only the unmodified I AM. But even here the "I" and the "AM" are only mentally distinct. They represent God as both personal (I) and impersonal (AM). Those who relate to God as person see him as the Absolute Other, as transcendent but as an object projected before the mind. Others experience God inwardly, as immanent within them, as the subjective wellspring of their being. But the objective, personal "God without" is the same as the subjective, impersonal "God within." The God without is represented as having attributes; the God within has none. It does not have but simply IS.

What the Samaritan woman discovers is that the God she sought is already within her, that in some mysterious way the objective Truth she thirsted for was already an interior subjective presence. Here one cannot avoid thinking of an ancient truth that has its origin in Plato's doctrine of Reminiscence: "You would not now be seeking me, did you not already know me." There is no desire for the totally unknown. The category of the divine, or utter beingness, lies ready within us and is ever on the alert to discover the other mode of Ultimate Reality without. In the Gnostic Gospel of Thomas, Jesus says that his disciples will enter the kingdom only, "when you make the two into one, when you make the inner like the outer and the outer like the inner" (Saying 22).

There are not two Gods, personal and impersonal, sought and seeker. When Jesus asks for water and the woman asks for water, who or what is asking? With a sudden shift of perspective, the seeker becomes the sought and the sought becomes the seeker. Bruteau says, "The mystery figures of the story interchange." The woman has recognized the one who asks her for water and knows him in herself as her own I am. He has to know her in himself as his own Sophia. The asker in us will come to recognize that the asked is actually doing the asking within us. A Vedantist philosopher of India would say that Brahman is the seeker, Brahman is the sought, and Brahman is the seeking. We are all rooted in the one Reality and share in the supreme I AM. We are fashioned in the image of God, and that entails a divine likeness that sets the human far above all other terrestrial creatures and just below the status of angels: "You have made them a little lower than divine beings, and crowned them with glory and honor" (Ps 8:5). This is the good news the story of the Samaritan Woman is trying to impart to us. It is told in the guise of a much-married woman, but, as proposed by the late Raymond E. Brown and Beatrice Bruteau, the story should not be read at its face value. The entire Fourth Gospel is an extended allegory about Divine Wisdom personified in the wisdom and teaching of Jesus.

Notes

[1] For gospel readers, Samaria may almost seem like a foreign land in relation to Judea. But it was part of the united kingdom of Judah and Israel before the Assyrian invasion. Some of the leading Hebrew prophets, such as Elijah and Elisha, carried out their missions in the northern kingdom. The greatest success of the apostles and early Christian missionaries was realized in Samaria, which responded to their preaching more readily than the Jews of Judea and, perhaps, Galilee.

[2] There is river water, rainwater preserved in a cistern, and well water. The best of all and the safest and purest is spring water. It is free from contaminants, cannot be easily poisoned, and is easy to collect.

[3] Nations and tribes have from time immemorial made shrines out of holy places, often because of unusual geological or astrophysical formations. Think of the Kaaba in Saudi-Arabia or the Magic Mountain of folklore or an object once touched by a saint. Jesus rejects the latent materialism in such objects and places of worship. True worship that is pleasing to God is not tied to a place or even, perhaps, a privileged religion. Anyone who in his or her heart recognizes the existence and dominion of a loving and merciful God is worshiping in spirit and truth.

Fundamentalist members of the three Abrahamic religions are especially prone to assume that their way to God is the only acceptable one. The rest are, at best, only faulty ways of approaching God. The Vatican document, *Dominus Iesus* (September 2000), stresses the perils of relativism and pluralism. Other religions, including the religions of the East and even non-Catholic Christian denominations, "are in a gravely deficient situation in comparison with those who, in the Church, have the fullness of the means of salvation." What the Vatican means, say the defenders of the document, is that the Roman Catholic Church and probably the Eastern Orthodox communities have *all* the means.

[4] *The Gospel according to John* (Garden City, New York: Doubleday/Anchor Bible, 1966), 1:171.

[5] "The Seven Husbands of the Samaritan Woman," *Living Prayer* (July–August 1995), 3–8.

[6] The ten Oxherding Pictures, attributed to the Chinese Zen Master Kuo-an Shih-yuan, describes the process leading to the forgetfulness of self. In the eighth frame the self disappears. In the ninth, the herder returns to the source but does not stay there. Filled with abundant light himself, he returns to the marketplace to teach others the way of the Buddha, or enlightenment through forgetfulness of self. See Roshi Philip Kapleau, *The Three Pillars of Zen* (Garden City, New York: Doubleday, 1980), 313–325.

Chapter Sixteen

THE SYRO-PHOENICIAN WOMAN

The Lady With Chutzpah

Ⅰn Mark's Gospel, apparently to escape from the clutches of Herod Antipas, Jesus goes to the coastal district of Sidon and Tyre in the Roman Province of Syria, today's Lebanon.[1] He is desperately in need of rest and has the good fortune of finding a local resident who is kind enough to offer him hospitality. According to Mark, he traveled alone and "did not want anyone to know he was there" (Mk 7:24).[2] Matthew, however, indicates that there are a few disciples with him and that when a woman comes pestering them and Jesus for a cure for her daughter who is afflicted with an evil spirit, or demon, the disciples ask Jesus "to send her away for she keeps shouting after us" (Mt 15:23).

Jesus is perplexed. At first, he puts her off because this woman is a Gentile and he understands that his mission is limited to the Jews: "I was sent only to the lost sheep of the house of Israel" (Mt 15:24). Eventually, the woman manages to come before Jesus, and kneeling down she begs for a cure for her daughter. But Jesus reminds her of an old saw, "It is not fair to take the children's food and throw it to the dogs." In no way daunted, her response is both brilliant and humble. She says, "Even the little pups [*ta kunaria*] eat the crumbs that fall from the master's table.[3] Seeing such faith and humility, Jesus is for a second time amazed to find so much faith in a woman who is not a Jew. She really challenges him and, like the schismatic Samaritan woman he meets at Jacob's well, she contributes to his education.

Could Jesus Learn?

Certainly, Jesus was not born speaking Hebrew or Aramaic. He had to study and master the scriptures. Even as a child he asked the noted rabbis questions when he spent three days in and around the Temple in Jerusalem. Luke says that he grew and increased in wisdom and grace. Was it right, then, to consider Gentiles, as many Jews did, as dogs, or even swine, because of their immorality and failure to worship the one, true God? In saying that it was not right to feed the children's food to dogs, Jesus was, no doubt, repeating an old folk saying. Recalling the adage seemed harsh, but the woman's spirited response challenged his own Jewish assumption about the prerogatives of his own people. He had found faith in the Roman centurion, in the Samaritan woman, and now he finds it again in this poor Phoenician mother. Could his focus be too narrow? True, he saw his countrymen as "harassed and helpless, like sheep without a shepherd" (Mt 9:36), but was he sent for the leaderless Jewish sheep alone?

Perhaps Jesus realized at this moment that there were other worlds to be evangelized. If there was any doubt about what the next step should be, it was St. Paul who provided the answer. As Paul's preaching made fewer and fewer converts among the Jewish communities he spoke to, he turned to the Gentiles with a "reduced" form of Judaism, a package that included sections from the Mosaic law, the prophets, the Hebrew writings, faith in Jesus, and such visible manifestations of the action of the Spirit as speaking in tongues.

We have no way of knowing what Jesus would have thought of the Pauline formula for salvation with its stress on faith in him rather than works. Judaism was supposed to be "a light to the nations" (Isa 42:6). But at what price? Jesus told his disciples that they would not have been able to preach the Gospel in all of the towns of Israel before the Day of the Lord arrived (Mt 10:23). That may have been Jesus' position early on, but as time advanced, he began to have a vision of people, that is Gentiles, coming from east and west, and sitting down with Abraham, Isaac, and Jacob in the kingdom. Whether Jesus also added, "while the heirs of the kingdom [the Jews] will be thrown into outer darkness" (Mt 8:12), is something that should invite serious questioning. It sounds more like something that Matthew or his source added when Jews and Christians were in a state of mutual hostility. I doubt that when Jesus began his drive to bring back home the lost sheep of the House of Israel, he thought that his work for Jewish renewal would ever result in bringing about a schism between his followers and traditional Judaism, a division so radical and irreversible that devout Christians would soon be consigning devout Jews to exterior darkness where there will be weeping and gnashing of teeth.

Hebraic invective can sound very harsh to untutored Western ears. We may easily forget this, and take it literally, which is misleading. The prophets often used minatory language to make sure that their listeners were paying attention. Granted that on occasion Jesus used a mild form of Jewish invective, he would be acting according to the rules of the game of give and take as it was practiced in his day. But that he used the scurrilous language attributed to him by Matthew in his twenty-third chapter (Mt 23:27–36) is hard to believe. See the excursus on this embarrassing passage at the end of this book's chapter 20.

Even when Jesus did attack abuses, he was denouncing them, not renouncing the faith of Abraham and Moses. What he preached was a renewed and less self-righteous form of Judaism. He kept the festivals, observed the dietary laws, and the only occasion when he mentioned circumcision (Jn 7:22–23), he did not disapprove of it, only noting that it dates from the time of Abraham and was later canonized by Moses. But his contact with Gentiles was beginning to convince him that all of the peoples of the earth were children of God and dearly loved by the Father.

A Modern Jewish Problem

Herman Wouk's most recent book, *The Will to Live On*, deals frankly with the problem of assimilation that American Jews face today. They are not reproducing themselves in sufficiently large numbers to replace those who die, and there is an alarming amount of leakage. Jews marry non-Jews, and their children and grandchildren may drift away. Others are nominally Jews but rarely attend synagogue. To their neighbors they might as well be Unitarians or associated with some ethical culture group. Jesus, in his day, wanted to bring such people back into the fold. Many in his day were marrying Gentiles and acting more like Greeks than children of Abraham. Like a good shepherd, Jesus felt that his primary mission was to bring them back home again.

People today, including some scripture scholars, fail to realize the import of Jesus' well-defined goal. It was a mission, to reconvert wandering Jews. The Gospels sometimes leave the impression that Jesus, around midcourse, decided to found a church and a new religion, which is highly debatable, even though a new religion took shape due to the influence of Paul. But the first Jewish followers of Jesus, including Paul himself, started out preaching a messianic form of the traditional Jewish religion, similar in some limited respects to the messianism of the Dead Sea Scroll community. The followers of "The Way," especially those living in Jerusalem, thought they were continuing and implementing the ambition of Jesus, which was to infuse a new spirit of love and compassion into what is sometimes called normative Judaism.[4] They are intent on following exactly the words attributed to Jesus when he insists that he has no intention of abandoning the Judaism of his birth and upbringing: "Do not think that I have come to abolish the law or the prophets; I have come not to abolish but to fulfill. For truly I tell you, until heaven and earth pass away, not one letter, not one stroke of a letter will pass from the law until all is accomplished" (Mt 5:17–18).[5] Members of the Jerusalem Church prayed daily in the Temple and were careful to carry out all of the pre-scriptions of the Torah, as Jesus had commanded. They would hardly have done this, if it were clear that Jesus had intended any kind of relaxation of the law or a break with Judaism.

Nevertheless, the evangelists introduce various kinds of literary and rhetorical devices to justify the situation of the Messianists (Christians) versus Judaism during the decades after the end of the Jewish War with Rome. They attribute to Jesus words that represent a repudiation of, and a separation from, Judaism. It matches the grow-ing Christian anti-Jewish outlook of the last third of the first century.

This is not dishonest if the Gospels are understood to express the way their authors felt about Jews and the persecution Christians had suffered at the hands of Jewish Temple authorities and at the local level.[6] But none of this entered into the attitude of Jesus toward the Torah and the Prophets. Nothing in his outlook suggests that he would have gone as far as Paul did in dispensing with so many Jewish non-negotiables, including circumcision, which was the very seal of the covenant between God and his Chosen People. If Jesus had disap-proved of circumcision, surely at least one of the evangelists would have made a point of emphasizing so radical a departure from an hon-ored tradition.

Jesus would have approved of the Syro-Phoenician woman had she converted and begun to keep a kosher kitchen, attend synagogue, and make sure that all of her male grandchildren were properly cir-cumcised. Had she continued these practices, as did the Jerusalem Jewish Christians during the decades after Jesus' death and resurrec-tion, Jesus would have supported her in spirit as he had supported and cherished those Jews who abandoned their concession to pagan ways and returned to traditional Jewish practice. It is easy to forget that Jesus was not a Christian but a practicing Jew.

But the Jesus Movement drifted away and become the Christian Church. The second- and third-generation churchmen regarded this development as the work of the Holy Spirit. But Pope John Paul II has made it clear that in his mind God never repudiated the covenants he made with Adam, Noah, Abraham, and Moses. They are still valid, salvific ways of relating to God.[7] In August 2002, the Conference of American Bishops approved of John Paul's position and urged mission-minded priests and the laity not to try to convert practicing Jews to Christianity, as though they, in following the precepts of their own religion, were not pleasing to God.

A good question to ask is whether God has not initiated still other covenants with distant peoples who are neither Jews nor Christians. Perhaps covenantal language is not appropriate when speaking of Taoism, Buddhism, or Hinduism. Moslems feel that they share in some kind of preferential contact with Allah that makes Islam special in his eyes. All of the major religions have their lost sheep, people who have drifted away from an age-old tradition to become lost in the secular world with its powerful attractions and distractions. But, yes, you can go home again, *teshuvah*.[8]

Notes

[1] Some friendly Pharisees had informed Jesus that Herod Antipas wanted to kill him as he had killed John the Baptist. No doubt it was because of the danger to his life that he vacated Herod's territory and went to the region of Tyre. In spite of the bad reputation the Pharisees have in the Gospels, Jesus has friends among them, such as Nicodemus (Jn 3:1, 7:51). The Pharisees may have sought to "trap him" in his speech, but the men with truly murderous intentions were those whom the Fourth Gospel identifies as the *Ioudaioi*, the party of the rich and powerful Judeans, specifically, the Sadducees and the Temple hierarchy (Lk 22:2; Jn 5:19, 8:37).

[2] According to Mark's account, Jesus would appear to have traveled to Tyre alone and in secret. He found someone to take him in and give him shelter. Matthew, however, mentions "his disciples" (Mt 15:23). How many of them trekked around with Jesus, especially on a journey outside Palestine? If twelve, they would have had to seek hospitality from the local people. The chances are high that Jesus traveled for the most part with only two or three disciples, such as Peter, James, and John. The rest would have been out doing missionary work.

[3] Unlike today, dogs were not regarded as household pets. They were treated as curs and fed scraps. Both Mark and Matthew soften the apparent harshness of Jesus' reply to the Syro-Phoenician woman by using the diminutive of *kuōn*, puppy dog.

[4] "Normative Judaism" would represent the least common denominator of beliefs and customs generally held among Jews of the first century. But there were too many sects to enable one to determine what was properly normative, beyond adherence to the basic teachings of the Pentateuch. Later, Rabbinic Judaism sought to rein in the apoc-

alyptic sectarians, including the Jesus movement, and restore some kind of order in the Hebrew tradition.

5 To say that "not one stroke of a letter will pass from the law until all is accomplished," could mean, in Matthew's purview, that since Jesus fulfilled the promises of the Law, it could now be discarded. Its whole purpose, then, would have been to identify the future Messiah.

6 Even after the death of Jesus, the Temple authorities remained deeply involved in persecuting his followers. They had Peter and John flogged and commissioned Saul of Tarsus to hunt down disciples of Jesus as far away as Damascus. For his part, King Herod Agrippa I put Peter in prison and had James, the brother of John, slain by the sword (Acts 12:2). Jesus' followers were excluded from the synagogues in many places and, finally, Jesus' own brother James was killed by order of the high priest Ananus (Josephus, *The Antiquities of the Jews* 29,9,1). Paul speaks of being beaten with thirty-nine lashes by the Jews on five occasions and of being stoned on one occasion (2 Cor 11:24–25).

7 See note 3 in chapter 15 concerning *Dominus Iesus*, the document issued by the Vatican's Congregation for the Doctrine of the Faith on the perils of pluralism. The statement has the endorsement of Pope John Paul II. Its return to an older exclusivist form surprised many men and women engaged in ecumenical studies and dialogue with other religions, because John Paul had been so active himself in engaging in friendly dialogue with other faiths, especially with the Jews.

8 *Teshuvah*, literally, "return," it refers to the return to traditional Jewish practice on the part of those who have been lax or strayed from strict observance and regular attendance at the synagogue. *Teshuvah* need not imply that one is being recalled from a sinful life. More often it brings with it inner joy, a renewed sense of the sacred, and closer family ties. The subject is treated thoroughly by Adin Steinsaltz in, *Teshuvah: A Guide for the Newly Observant Jew* (Northvale, NJ: Jason Aroson, 1996).

Chapter Seventeen

MARY MAGDALENE

No, She Wasn't a Prostitute

Mary Magdalene was suffering from some kind of stress that Jesus was able to cure. According to Luke, she is a woman "from whom seven devils had gone out" (Lk 8:2). The number seven probably indicates the severity of her ailment. It does not mean that she is a sinner, although physical and nervous disorders are thought to be the result of sin. The venerable tradition that Magdalene was a prostitute is a misunderstanding. Mary is sometimes confused with the unnamed penitent in Luke's Gospel who bathes the feet of Jesus with her tears and dries them with her hair. She is described as "a woman in the city, who was a sinner" (Lk 7:37). Aside from the fact that we do not know what the woman's name was, there is no indication that it was Mary Magdalene. Secondly, the fact that she was called a sinner does not automatically make her a prostitute. Women in ancient times were capable of committing sins other than engaging in carnal traffic. The woman could have been regarded as a sinner because she was a usurer or married to a Gentile. In any case, there is no episode in the gospels that positively warrants our associating the name of Magdalene with weeping over her sins and drying the feet of Jesus with her hair.

Mary Magdalene is not to be confused with Mary of Bethany, the sister of Martha and Lazarus. That Mary performed an action in some respects similar to the one performed by the sinful city woman in Luke's Gospel. They both poured precious ointment on the feet of Jesus and, according to John, dried them with their hair. Matthew and Mark say Mary of Bethany poured the ointment on Jesus' *head* rather than on his feet, and they make no mention of a woman drying with her hair either the ointment (in John) or her tears (in Luke). The Gospel texts are confusing. We appear to be dealing with separate actions performed by different women in different parts of the land in the homes of two different men. In Luke the action takes place in Galilee. In Matthew, Mark, and John it occurs in Bethany just two miles from the center of Jerusalem. Luke's action takes place in the home of a Pharisee named Simon; John's in the home of Lazarus who, as far as we know, was not a Pharisee. Unlike John, Matthew and Mark further complicate the Bethany scene by failing to mention the name of the woman who poured the ointment. In addition, they say, as indicated above, that the woman poured it on the head of Jesus rather than, as Luke and John hold, on his feet, and that the action took place in the home of Simon the Leper in Bethany rather than in the home of Simon the Pharisee in Galilee (Mt 26:6–7). The following table indicates how the accounts of the four evangelists are the same and how they differ from one another:

Gospel	Where	Whose House	Ointment	Tears	On	Wipes With Hair
Luke 7	Galilee	Simon Pharisee	yes	yes	feet	yes
Mk 14	Bethany	Simon Leper	yes	no	head	no
Mt 26	Bethany	Simon Leper	yes	no	head	no
Jn 12	Bethany	Lazarus	yes	no	feet	yes

Kisses Feet	Who
yes	sinner
no	anonymous
no	anonymous
no	Mary of Bethany

A mix-up like the above should be enough to remind us that the evangelists, viewing the events they describe from afar and up to seven decades after the time of Jesus, do not always get the details straight. The four evangelists may be talking about the same incident, but they are not sure about the place, the persons involved, or the precise nature of the action. Some woman did something memorable somewhere, and Jesus approved what she had done. Did it take place in the home of Simon the Pharisee, Simon the Leper, or Lazarus? After all these differences are taken into consideration, we are left with little choice other than to maintain that we have little justification for identifying Mary Magdalene with any of the previously mentioned women. The standard tradition about Magdalene, that she was a converted prostitute who wept for her sins and on several occasions poured precious ointment on the feet, or head, of Jesus and wiped them with her hair, is a dramatic, sentimental, pious tradition. But the Gospels do not bear it out.

Who then was Mary Magdalene? She was not an impoverished member of the lower class reduced to gaining her livelihood by engaging in the world's oldest profession. On the contrary, she was a woman of substance, an important figure in the life of Jesus before his death, after his resurrection, and, later, during the expansion of the nascent Church. She was a leading member, and possibly the founder, of The Community of the Beloved Disciple. She was by no means poor but was one of those well-placed women who contributed out of their private means to the support of Jesus and his band of apostles. Luke specifically associates her with women of means (Lk 8:3). There is no need to repeat here her family connection and the ties to her relatives engaged in the prosperous fish-packing industry in Magdala. She had, no doubt, been at the court of Herod Antipas with her friend Joanna, the wife of Herod's steward, and could have written a volume on the vanity and luxury of court life. Herod, a client kinglet of Rome—actually, he was only a tetrarch—not only lived lavishly on the taxes he levied against, or extracted from, the peasant farmers of Galilee and Perea, but he used a fair portion of the wealth his tax collectors could squeeze out of his subjects to build pagan shrines and temples in foreign lands in honor of the Emperor Tiberias.[1]

Mary must have found her manner of life intolerable. She could see everywhere the plight of the disinherited poor, while the Herodians and their pampered wives were blind to what was going on all around them. There was little she could do to alleviate the condition of the oppressed poor, as the rich grew richer and the poor all but desperate. She felt trapped and thought of running away, perhaps even ending her life. That temptation may have been one of her seven devils. By the time she came into contact with Jesus she was in desperate need of counseling and what we today would call psychiatric help.

Then she heard Jesus speak. His concerns were identically her own. In addition to his social message that centered on justice for all and the need for the rich to share their resources with the poor, he introduced her to a method of silent prayer that enabled her to become a true contemplative. At a word or glance from him her demons of fear, doubt, and distress vanished forever. In spite of what her Magdala family thought, she became a follower of Jesus and eventually an apostle.

Rabbouni

Truly, one of the more tender scenes in the four gospels is the meeting between Mary Magdalene and the risen Jesus. She has discovered the empty tomb and is greatly distressed. She wonders what could have happened to the body of Jesus. In the midst of her tears she is aware of the presence of someone standing near her. She does not look up, but assumes that this must be the gardener of the burial park. When the stranger asks her, "Woman, why are you weeping?" Mary replies, "Sir, if you have carried him away, tell me where you have laid him, and I will take him away." Then Jesus calls her by name, "Mary!" He no longer addresses her with the polite form, "Woman," or "Lady." She cannot fail to recognize the voice. Suddenly, Mary knows that her savior lives, and she answers him by calling out his name, using the intimate form of endearment, "*Rabbouni*," meaning "My revered and beloved Teacher." It would have been a title of honor in any other circumstance, but here it speaks of the love that Mary holds in her heart for Jesus.

The scene recalls "The Song of Solomon," where the woman says, "I will seek him whom my soul loves. I sought him but found him not. The sentinels found me, as they went about the city. 'Have you seen him whom my soul loves?' Scarcely had I passed them, when I found him whom my soul loves. I held him and would not let him go" (Song 3:2–4). Mary Magdalene, like the bride in the Song of Songs, wants to cling to Jesus. She never wants him to leave him again, but he has to tell her not to keep clinging to him. The Greek verb used here (*haptō*) includes the sense of wanting to clutch or take hold. But Jesus has other work for Mary. She is to become the herald of his resurrection. "Go to my brothers," he tells her. "And say to them, 'I am ascending to my Father and your Father, to my God and your God'" (Jn 20:17). This announcement confirms the message Jesus gives to his apostles on the night before he dies: "It is to your advantage that I go away, for if I do not go away, the Advocate will not come to you, but if I go I will send him to you" (Jn 16:7).

What John's Jesus promises then is an interior presence that will be immeasurably superior to his external flesh and blood presence. This lesson would be hard for his disciples to learn. Luke says that when Jesus departs from his apostles and, symbolically, ascends into heaven on a cloud, they "returned to Jerusalem with great joy" (Lk 24:52). They were joyful and not sorrowful at his departure because when we stop clinging to God as an object, we usually find the divine presence within us, where it has been all the time. "And the end of all our exploring/Will be to arrive where we started/And know the place for the first time."[2] Jesus wants his disciples to be where he is, in the bosom of the Father. "And if I go and prepare a place for you, I will come again and will take you to myself, so that where I am there you may be also" (Jn 14:3). "Place," the "where I am," in this passage refers not to a locality, but to a state of being in God with Christ. It is natural for the disciples to want to cling to Jesus according to the flesh, to make an idol of him. But Magdalene must not do that nor must any of the others. He is returning to his common ground and to theirs, to his God and Father and to theirs, to the One he calls "My God and your God." All that he is and has is theirs also.

Was Magdalene at the Last Supper?

One of the conclusions that ought to follow from what has been said in this chapter and in the preceding chapter is that Mary Magdalene was a close friend and disciple of Jesus. Whether she was the so-called Beloved Disciple or not, it is unlikely that she would have been excluded from the Last Supper. His suppers were not men's club. A second conclusion follows from the first: the twelve apostles were not the only ones present at Jesus' final Passover meal. Were there other women present at this and other earlier meals? The gospels make no mention of women or children, so it has been assumed that only grown men were present in the cenacle that night. We are so used to this assumption that few stop to question it. Years later, the custom arose of having a young boy present to ask the traditional questions about the meaning of Passover.

The fact that neither boys nor women are mentioned does not prove that they were not present at the Last Supper. No doubt, a conclusion based on silence is weaker than one based on positive affirmation or denial. On the other hand, it is nowhere stated in the gospels that there were no women present. They would normally have had a hand in preparing the meal and serving it. Plato assures us that Socrates refused to allow his wife to be present during his last hours because he wanted to discuss philosophical questions of great moment with his male disciples, matters that were not supposed to be the concern of women. But Jesus was not Socrates. To have excluded any and every woman at this most solemn moment was contrary to his deepest insight regarding the dignity, equality, and worth of every human being, whether man, woman, or child. If no women were present, that would have been because Jesus took positive steps to exclude them. If they were present, he would have included them in his Eucharistic plea; "Do this in memory of me."

In any case, it now appears that when a woman was the head of a household during the years immediately following the death of Jesus, she routinely presided at the Eucharist of Christ's body and blood. As late as the end of the fifth century we find Pope Gelasius I (492–496) complaining that female presbytera were officiating at the altar in a role reserved for men. The practice of having a woman preside at the Eucharist was outlawed only when local bishops, all male, decided that spiritual power and the honor of celebrating the Eucharistic should be reserved to men only. Still, the ordination of women as deacons, the lesser of the top two major orders, was a common practice.[3]

Would Jesus have approved the ordaining of women? By the standards of his day, Jesus was unlike most men in his treatment of women, the poor, the diseased, sinners, and member of the underclass. Because he was especially close to Mary Magdalene, if any women were present at the Last Supper, she would have been among those who were asked to "Do this in memory of me."

Had Mary Magdalene been present at the Last Supper, she would have been in a position to have heard, remembered, and later passed on what Jesus had said on that occasion, words largely preserved in chapters fourteen through seventeen in John's Gospel. His farewell address is tender and very different in tone when compared with the lengthy, often contentious speeches attributed to him during his public ministry by the redactors of the Last Gospel. They portray him as a prickly figure engaged in heated and often acrimonious disputes with his adversaries. By way of contrast, the report of Jesus' warm and loving farewell discourse at the Last Supper had to be the contribution of an intimate friend, someone who thoroughly understood his mind and heart. My conjecture is that the recollections of Magdalene, a privileged witness to Jesus' life and times, were included in the Last Gospel. Further, that she was a member, if not the founder, of the Community of the Beloved Disciple, a company of men and women which, based on John 19:27, also included Mary the mother of Jesus.

Notes

[1] "Dedicatory inscriptions mentioning the benefactions of Herod Antipas have been discovered at the healing center at the Temple of Aesclepius on the island of Kos in the Aegean and the Temple of Apollo at Delos." Richard A. Horsely and Neil Asher Silberman, *The Message and the Kingdom* (New York: Grosset/Putnam, 1997), 95.

2 One of T.S. Eliot's most famous lines in "Little Gidding V, Four Quartets."

3 On the concept of ordaining women as deacons, see Elizabeth Schüssler Fiorenza, *Discipleship of Equals: A Critical Ekklesia-logy of Liberation* (New York: Crossroad, 1993). She would not be content with simply opening the deaconate to women, but goes far beyond that when she writes; "Therefore, ordination is not a question of the admission of women to ecclesial ministry. Rather, it is a question of recognition and confirmation of such ministries. Simultaneously, we have to stress women's right to be admitted to all ministerial functions in the Church, including the episcopal and papal offices" (37).

Chapter Eighteen

THE WOMAN TAKEN IN ADULTERY

Where Is the Man?

T he origin of the story about the woman taken in adultery (Jn 8:1–11) is unknown. It is mentioned by Ambrose and Augustine around the year 400 CE. They wanted it to be incorporated into the Bible. But the story does not appear in any of the Greek manuscripts in the Eastern Church for the first 900 years. In spite of that, the story was well known in the West and was included in the Latin Vulgate by St. Jerome. While the text has been inserted into the Gospel according to John at the beginning of the eighth chapter, it occasionally makes an appearance in Luke's Gospel. The early commentators were convinced of its authenticity, as going back to Jesus himself, but they did not know where to put it. It is, in any case, the kind of story that fits in well with Jesus' attitude toward women and sinners.

The scene is a very public one. The woman, caught in the act of adultery, is brought before Jesus in the crowded Temple precincts. An open circle is formed around her and she is made to stand in the middle. Either her hands are tied together or she is bound around the waist by a rope, lest she try to run away. She is not a prostitute but a married woman who, for some reason, has been caught in dalliance with a man who is not her husband. The fact that she has been caught in an adulterous act is no accident. Her husband might have commissioned several trustworthy men to spy on her. In the story, those who accuse her are scribes. They know the law, which requires that an adulteress be stoned to death or pitched off a cliff to perish on the craggy rocks below. The law requires that both the married woman and her male partner be put to death (Lev 20:10).

Where, then, is the man? Did he manage to run away? The reason why the unfortunate woman has been brought before Jesus has to do with his reputation as a teacher who is soft on sinners. He fraternizes with them and even eats with them. On one occasion he tells his very righteous adversaries that publicans and prostitutes are entering the kingdom before them. At least, these despised outcasts of society believe in him (Mt 21:31–32). What does Jesus say, then, about strictly observing the law? "Now in the law Moses commanded us to stone such women. What do you say?" (Jn 8:5).

This is a difficult spot for Jesus to be in. If he adheres to the law, he will be responsible for the woman's death. But he does not know all of the circumstances of the woman's plight. She may have been married to an abusive husband and ran for protection into the arms of another human being. Or the husband may have put her out on the street because she has done something to displeased him. A man may have dismissed a wife for any number of reasons, some of them trivial. If the husband was a vengeful, spiteful man, he might have plotted with an accomplice to seduce the woman, or at least get her into compromising circumstances, so that he could have her executed legally.

Without excusing her for her conduct, Jesus has no intention of being her judge. Mitigating circumstances, if there are any, have to be taken into consideration for the woman to have a fair trial. A public area with curious people gathered around the accused woman is no place to initiate a careful inquiry. Today we would insist on providing the woman with a defense attorney, or advocate (*parakletos*), and witnesses for the defense. Few accused women in Jesus' day would have been granted that luxury. Asked by the woman's accusers, "What do you say?" Jesus remains silent. Instead of answering, he bends down and begins to write with his finger on the ground. Although the Gospel says that he writes something, it does not tell us exactly what it is. Does he spell out something that would have been meaningful to the woman's accusers? Perhaps he is just stalling for time. Could he have written in Aramaic, "Where is the man?" The law is clear: "If a man is caught lying with the wife of another man, both of them shall die, the man as well as the woman" (Deut 22:22).

Today, we in the West do not execute a man or a woman for adultery. Jesus, who had some reservations about the Mosaic law, may have felt that such punishment was excessive and cruel, especially when, in practice, the male partner to the sin usually escaped punishment. It seems not to have occurred to the men who brought the woman to Jesus for judgment that they should have brought the man along with her. If Jesus was outraged by the unevenness of justice, he may have bent down to trace some figures on the ground to give him some time to rein in his anger. We should not think of Jesus as incapable of righteous anger.

When Jesus finally rises and stands facing the woman's accusers, he eyes them coldly and challenges them by extending his open hand saying, "Let anyone among you who is without sin be the first to throw a stone at her" (Jn 8:7). None of the accusers would be so self-righteous as to step forward and declare, "I have never sinned. Give me a stone." Because no one steps forward and the crowd starts to break up, the woman's accusers drift away, leaving the frightened woman still standing before Jesus. How could Jesus send her away? She cannot not go back to her husband and should not go back to her lover. She needs protection, some safe place to go. Looking around, Jesus sees several of his female disciples, Martha, Mary, Joanna, Magdalene, or any one of a number of Galilean women who travel around with Jesus and his apostles. One of them should take this other woman home with her. She should give her wine, food, warm clothing, loving kindness, and time to rest.

As the woman is about to depart, Jesus remarks that her present accusers have all gone away. Then he asks whether anyone else has condemned her. She answers, "No one, Sir." Because he and no one else condemns her, she is free. Jesus says, "Go forth! [*poreuou!*], and sin no more" (Jn 8:11). He is giving her a future to live in abundance and service.

Her gratitude to Jesus would have been inexpressible. Like so many others whom he had healed, she must surely have joined with the other women who were followers of Jesus. Together they lived through his crucifixion, death, and resurrection.

Excursus on Women in the Early Church

St. Paul, in his First Letter to the Corinthians, makes a list of the post-resurrection appearances of Jesus. These include appearances to Peter, James, the Twelve, five hundred brothers, *adelphoi*, to all of the apostles, and, finally, to Paul himself (1 Cor 15:5–8). He never mentions any appearances to women, even though women were the first to discover the empty tomb in all four Gospels and the first to be visited by the risen Christ (Mt 28:9; Jn 20:14). Why does Paul omit any mention of the role of women in the resurrection story? Partly because in the ancient world, the testimony of women was regarded as worthless, not only among Jews but also in the Gentile world. Nevertheless, the four evangelists had no choice about presenting the women as the first witnesses to Jesus' resurrection, and this is one of the factors that lends credibility to the story of the empty tomb and the resurrection itself. The male evangelists, presuming they were all men, had no alternative but to tell it the way it was. Before any of the men had any inkling about what had taken place, a number of women had been informed by angelic figures about the resurrection, and when they ran to tell the hiding apostles, the men refused to believe what they were told.

Does this make Paul a male chauvinist because he ignores the fact of the women's witness? Paul was a man of sharp contrasts and contradictions. We first hear of him in the role of the archenemy of the Church, one who presided over the murder of Stephen. After his conversion, he became "The Apostle," whose efforts and sufferings for the sake of the gospel outstripped all others.[1] This conflicted man seemed to enjoy excellent relations with the women he knew. He has high praise for Phoebe, a deacon–minister, of the church at Cenchreae, whom he calls his patron. She is greatly trusted and carries Paul's message to Rome. There is Prisca, named ahead of her husband Aquila, in whose home Christians meet. A certain Mary, who works among the Romans, is praised in Paul's Letter to the Romans, along with other female coworkers who are greeted, some of them by name: Tryphaena, Tryphosa, Persis, the much-loved mother of Rufus, and the unnamed sister of Nereus. Foremost among "the apostles" is Junia, apparently a woman and either a relative or close friend of Paul (Rom 16:1–13). Lydia is outstanding among the new converts in Philippi. A wealthy dealer in purple, she owns a house with a large retinue of servants. It becomes a center for the new movement when she and her entire household embrace the faith.[2] Less commendable are two other women, Euodia and Syntyche, whose disagreements are upsetting others (Phil 4:2).

In all of these instances, including the disturbance by the last two women, it is fairly clear that women in the very early Church played an important role as teachers, missionaries, co-workers with Paul, and hosts who served Paul and the Christian communities.

On the other hand, we have to face texts, rightly or wrongly attributed to Paul, that reflect a very dark view of women. An often-cited passage appears in the First Letter to the Corinthians: "As in all the churches of the saints, women should be silent in the churches. For they are not permitted to speak, but should be subordinate, as the law also says. If there is anything they desire to know, let them ask their

husbands at home. For it is shameful for a woman to speak in church"
(1 Cor 14:33–35).

The editors of *The New Oxford Annotated Bible* put this passage
in brackets with the suggestion that "these culturally conditioned verses [are] an editorial insertion" (Note on 14:33–35). The reader is
referred to the pseudonymous First Letter of St. Paul to Timothy. It has
a similar, even more negative passage dealing with women. The Letter
is called 'pseudonymous' because, as was customary among the
ancients, it was published in the name of a highly respected person in
order to lend the document greater authority. Paul did not write the
Letters to Timothy or Titus, although they reflect some of his ideas in
a style different from his own. We know they were composed long
after Paul's death because they are no longer concerned about the
proximity of the end of the age and the second coming of Christ. The
time is long past for that. Because Paul thought the end was near, he
counseled people not to marry but to prepare for the "rapture," when
the dead would rise and those still alive would be taken up to reign
with Christ (1 Tim 4:16–17).

The later "Pauline" Letters urge church members to marry and
roundly condemn those who teach otherwise (1 Tim 4:3). Since the
second coming is long past due, it is clear that the two Letters to
Timothy date from a period when marriage was no longer regarded as
an inferior state, when the parousia had been indefinitely postponed,
and when the suppression of women and their leadership role in the
Church was all but complete; all spiritual authority rested with members of the gradually forming male hierarchy. Thus, we read in the
Letter to Timothy: "Let a woman learn in silence with full submission.
I permit no woman to teach or to have authority over a man; she is to
keep silent. For Adam was formed first, then Eve; and Adam was not
deceived, but the woman was deceived and became a transgressor. Yet
she will be saved by childbearing, provided they [sic] continue in faith
and love and holiness, with modesty" (1 Tim 2:11–15).

This sounds very much like the passage in Corinthians, with addi-
tional severity to boot. Does it really reflect the mind of Paul and
other men in the early Church, or was the gist of the passage in
Timothy inserted into Corinthians by a hand other than Paul's? One
would like to believe so, but then we have to explain what a seemingly genuine passage has Paul say in the eleventh chapter of the First
Letter to the Corinthians. The text holds that women and not men
should wear a veil when they pray in church or prophesy. If a woman

disgraces her head when she prays or prophesies without a veil, a husband, who is the head of his wife, should not cover his head. Orthodox Jewish men today wear a head covering when they pray. Does Paul's community know nothing of such a custom? People in other cultures, for example, India, wear prayer shawls. But here Paul wants men to pray bare headed, without so much as a yarmulke covering the head (1 Cor 11:4).

Such anomalies make this passage suspect. The reason why a man should pray with an uncovered head is because he is the image of God, whereas the woman is only the reflection of a man. Whoever wrote this is intent on keeping women in their place. They have no glory of their own, not even as images of God, but live only in reflected glory which they borrow from a man. If Paul, or the author of this strange passage, had been content with saying that women who pray or prophesy in church should be veiled, he would have been honoring tradition. But then the text goes on to say that the reason why a woman should pray veiled is because "man was not made from woman, but woman from man" (Gen 2:22). But "neither was man created for the sake of woman, but woman for the sake of man. Therefore, "a women ought to have a symbol of authority [*exousia*] on her head, because of the angels" (verse 10). The Latin Vulgate uses *potestas*, 'power,' to translate *exousia*. However we choose to interpret this passage, the veil indicates that a woman must always live in a state of subservience, whether to a man or to an angel.

The author tempers his statement about woman coming from man a few verses further on, when he admits what is obvious, namely, that men come from women. But both the questionable Corinthian passages and Timothy look upon women's inferior condition and subjection to men as a punishment for the sin of Eve. Added to her inferiority, powerlessness, and subordination, the pains of child-bearing are also viewed as punishment, which have, however, a redeeming feature, provided she "continues in faith and love and holiness, with modesty."

Paul takes and Paul gives. He also seems to contradict himself. At the start of the eleventh chapter in First Corinthians, he says that when women speak in church to pray aloud or prophesy, they should have their heads covered. But in chapter fifteen and in the Letter to Timothy the rule is that women should keep silent and not talk in church. This means that they should not ask questions during the liturgical service or in a teaching session, but should reserve their questions until they get home. Then a woman is allowed to ask her husband about the meaning of some particular point, and he will provide her with as much information as befits her limited ability to understand.

Paul used common sense. When he found women useful as patrons or helpers, he respected them. But then his theology got in the way. He apparently took the story of the Fall and Eve's part in it as history, and he regarded the Genesis passage, which holds that women were to be ruled by men and suffer the pangs of childbirth, as expressive of the divine will to punish all women for all time because of the sin of Eve (Gen 3:16).

Still, Paul was not yet the type of male chauvinist who would rule in the Church shortly after his day. His preference for celibacy attracted young women and widows. Being unmarried they were in a position to be free from subordination to a men, whether a father, a husband, or a son. Women of ample means were apt to be more free than their poorer sisters, but women in ancient times rarely had a choice regarding marriage, which were arranged. If a young woman refused to to marry, as some of the followers of Paul might have done, this would have caused great turmoil in pagan and Jewish households.[3] A woman was supposed to have the authority of her father over her head, and to disobey him was a sign of inexcusable impiety. So what did Jesus think or teach about women and their right of self-determination.

The Teaching of Jesus

As far as we can determine, Jesus offered no specific teaching, as did Paul, on relations between the sexes. We have to glean what he might have thought by examining the way he related to women. When Jesus is asked, after he lays down the only condition for divorce, whether it is better for a man not to marry, he says, in effect, that celibacy is not for everyone. "Let anyone accept this [celibacy for the sake of the kingdom of heaven] who can" (Mt 19:12). Because Jesus was talking here about "eunuchs," he was referring primarily to men, without necessarily excluding women. The three women who were close to Jesus—Martha, her sister Mary, and Mary Magdalene—do not seem to have had husbands, or they might even have left them "for the sake of the kingdom." Jesus says that those who wanted to be his disciples should be ready to leave "father, mother, wife, and children" (Lk 14:26). If a man can leave his wife to follow Jesus, may not a woman leave her husband or parents for this higher calling? Jesus does not say explicitly that wives can leave their husbands to join his little band. But if they did, it is not hard to imagine how the woman's withdrawal from conventional social bonds would be received.

Law and custom required that a woman always be under the supervision of some male figure. This man could be her older brother, if her father and husband were deceased, or even her eldest son. This is not as bizarre as it might appear in the eyes of contemporary men and women. It was a practice that meant that a woman would always be protected. Caring for the female orphan or the widow was primarily a male responsibility. Even the women who joined the Jesus Movement acquired the protection of the men in the group.

What Jesus had to say about divorce was said largely in defense of women. As indicated earlier, a man could dismiss his wife because "he finds something objectionable about her" (Deut 24:1). Jesus said that Moses allowed divorce because people in those days were so hardhearted. But it was not like that from the beginning. Then Jesus continues: "And I say to you, whoever divorces his wife, except for unchastity, and marries another, commits adultery" (Mt 19:9). The phrase "except for unchastity" does not appear in many early manuscripts or in Mark 10:2–12. What was the divorced wife to do? She was now "used" and, if her own family refused to take her back, she was without protection. Such women were often reduced to prostitution as their sole means of survival in that culture. Clearly seeing the injustice in many such divorces, Jesus added that the husband who divorces a woman and marries another also commits adultery.

Because of radically changed social conditions, our attitude toward divorce has also changed. In "no fault" divorces, where the partners agree to separate and there is no injustice to either party or to any children involved, most people are inclined to wish the divorcés well. A more difficult situation arises when the personal relations between the married couple are so dreadful that they cannot live together in peace. Battered wives whose lives are often in danger will sometimes return to their bludgeoning husbands because there is no place else to go or for the sake of the children. But there comes a time when there is no marriage of minds or hearts.

Jesus did not take this latter kind of situation into account, but he may have suspected it in the case of the woman taken in adultery. If the husband committed adultery with another woman, no one would have cared because the woman literally belonged to the husband who owned her, as Abraham or any Arab sheik could own cattle and wives. A wife was an incubator for producing, preferably male, babies. The offspring was the product of the man's seed. He did not want any of the fruit his wife might bear not to be of his bloodline.

Stoning the woman taken in adultery would not only kill her but it also made sure that, if she had been pregnant, the other man's offspring would die with her. When they brought to Jesus the terrified woman who had been found guilty of adultery, he did not blame her or ask any questions. He would not permit the scribes to endanger the life of an unfortunate woman in order to try to trap him into saying or doing something that would, on the one hand, violate the Mosaic law and, on the other hand, show callousness regarding the sacredness of human life. According to Matthew, Jesus would allow divorce and remarriage on the part of the husband, if the wife were unfaithful. Even that condition seems to be lacking in Mark. His Gospel leaves one to conclude that Jesus was against divorce in any circumstances, although not necessarily against separation from bed and board. The main thrust of Mark's position is that there must be no injustice to women. It was in their defense that Jesus goes so far as to challenge the law that allowed divorce at the whim of the man.

If a man is not held to the same standard as a woman, there is inequality and injustice. Or, is it all right for a man to be unfaithful, as long as he provides for his wife and children? After all, many important men in history have had paramours. While such conduct is unacceptable in the case of a woman and wife, it was, and still is, a standard behavioral pattern for successful and powerful men. Where divorce was concerned, Jesus would ask only one question, "Is there any injustice involved?" In his day, women were treated unjustly in the area of marriage and sex. His ideal was that both the married and the unmarried were to be perfectly faithful and chaste. Beyond that, when a marriage had broken down beyond repair, would he still insist, even today, on condemning divorce, now that social conditions are so changed? Of one thing we can be sure, Jesus would want the same rules to apply for both men and women.

Notes

1 Paul disapproves of those who compare their achievements with the achievements of others (2 Cor 10:12). "Not that we venture to class or compare ourselves with some of those who commend themselves. But when they measure themselves by one another, and compare themselves with one another, they are without understanding." But

then, in the next chapter (2 Cor 11:21–29), Paul's list of all of the things he has suffered for the sake of the gospel runs to 31 lines, covering nine verses. Not being one
of the original apostles who knew Jesus in the flesh, Paul needs to assure others that
he has not only seen the risen Christ but has suffered more than the rest

2 After Paul baptized Lydia and her whole household, he was imprisoned in Philippi,
beaten, locked in a dungeon, and finally let go with apologies because he was a
Roman citizen. Paul made use of his citizenship here and later in Jerusalem (Acts
16:37; 22:26). Freed, he returned to Lydia's home.

3 The apocalyptic Acts of Paul and Thecla offer a titillating account of the adventures
of Thecla, a young virgin who scorns marriage to her suitor Thamyris after listening
to the preaching of St. Paul. Needless to say, her suitor and family are upset. Escaping,
she is imprisoned, almost burned to death at the stake, and lives to the age of ninety
years, having preserved her virginity to the end, in spite of some close calls. See *The
Lost Books of the Bible*, with an introduction by Frank Crane (New York: Gramercy
Books, 1979), 99–111. The original translations are by Jeremiah Jones (1693–1724)
and William Wake (1657–1727).

Chapter Nineteen

MARTHA AND MARY

Two Sides of the Same Coin

M artha and Mary appear three times in the Gospels, once in the Gospel according to Luke and twice in John's Gospel (Lk 10:38–42; Jn 11:1, 12: 2–3). The two women behave in characteristic ways in the three loci. In Luke, Mary sits at the feet of Jesus listening to his words, while Martha is busy around the house, "worried and distracted about many things." She is a busybody of a practical turn. Mary, however, is contemplative.

In the style of her devotion to Jesus, Mary of Bethany is like Mary of Magdala. However, while both represent the contemplative attitude toward him, they are different women from different cities. As indicated earlier in chapter seventeen, popular piety has collapsed into one The Galilean Magdalene, the Judean Mary of Bethany, the sinful woman who came in from the street in Luke's Gospel, and even the woman taken in adultery thrown in for good measure.

True to form, in the scene describing the raising of Lazarus in John's Gospel, it is Martha who is immediately up and doing the moment she hears that Jesus is nearby. After meeting Jesus, she hastens home to tell Mary that Jesus was present and was asking for her. Then Mary, who has been nursing her private grief over the death of Lazarus, rises up and comes running to Jesus. Finding him, she takes her usual place and casts herself at his feet where she belongs, just as Martha is busy going and coming.

Later, after Lazarus has been restored to life and health, the Bethany family prepares a dinner for Jesus. Mary, as usual, is anointing the feet of Jesus with expensive perfumed ointment and wiping them with her hair. And, of course, "Martha served" (Jn 12:2).

Martha and Mary symbolize two aspects of the spiritual life, the contemplative and the active; or, in Hindu terminology, *bhakti* yoga and *karma* yoga, the yoga of devotion and the yoga of action. Although Jesus is reported to have said that Mary had chosen the better part (Lk 10:42), neither aspect can be neglected in an integrated

191

spiritual life. Jesus himself was both a contemplative and a social activist.[1]

The Bethany Family

Martha, Mary, and their brother Lazarus lived in Bethany, a village in Judea, near Jerusalem. From the account in the Fourth Gospel, one would assume that Martha, Mary, and their brother Lazarus all lived together. But in Luke's Gospel, Martha and Mary seem to be living together alone, just the two of them, and when Jesus visits them, Martha is said to have entertained him in *her* home (Lk 10:38), not their home. Also, from Luke, one gets the impression that the two women lived in Galilee, since Jesus' visit to their home took place early in his ministry, that is, before Jesus made his final trip to Jerusalem.

But John's Gospel corrects this when it situates the village of Martha and Mary just two miles from Jerusalem (Jn 11:1). It is clear that Jesus' visit to Martha and Mary took place not in Galilee, but in Bethany, a suburb of Jerusalem. It also means that Jesus visited the two women fairly early in his ministry of preaching, and that he had visited Jerusalem at least once before his final trip to the Holy City. All of this is significant in connection with the dispute over how long the ministry of Jesus lasted. According to the Synoptic Gospels, it would appear to have lasted less than a year. According to John, it could have lasted from three to four years. The Fourth Gospel mentions three Passovers—all of them occurring between the start of Jesus' public ministry and his death in Jerusalem—as well as three other festivals when Jesus seems to have been in Jerusalem: Tabernacles, Dedication, and possibly Pentecost.[2]

We can be fairly certain that Jesus was a close friend of the Bethany family and that he probably stayed with them on his various visits to Jerusalem. It could have been in their home that Nicodemus, a Pharisee and a leader among the Jews, visited Jesus by night. Jesus had other friends and disciples in the Jerusalem area, not the least among them would have been Joseph of Arimathea.

The Gospels offer no indication that Lazarus and his sisters Martha and Mary were married and had children. To be unmarried well past the marrying age was something of a disgrace in the Jewish culture of Jesus' day. We tend to think of Martha and Mary as young. Suppose they were elderly women, widows even, whose children were grown. That is less romantic than the image many people have of

Mary removing her head covering, kneeling at the feet of Jesus, and drying his anointed feet with her hair (Jn 12:3). She would have wound up bearing as much of the ointment and its perfume on her hair as she lavished on Jesus' feet. Gospel readers rarely think through the consequences of some of the actions described in the Bible. If it seems unlikely that the two women were consecrated virgins, the fact remains that a short time later Luke in Acts writes of Philip the evangelist and his four virgin (*parthenoi*) daughters (Acts 21:9). Could it be that even in Jesus' day, and at his behest, some women were already choosing the celibate state? One would expect Jewish men and women of that period to be married, unless they had some affiliation with the Dead Sea Scroll community. Celibacy was mandatory for the monastic community of men and may not have been entirely discouraged for the townspeople. Josephus says that community members are not isolated in any single city but "dwell in every city," not excluding, one might suppose, Bethany?[3]

Simon the Leper

Mark and Matthew give an account of Jesus' visit to the house of Simon the leper (Mk 14:3–9; Mt 26:6–13). The visit took place in Bethany, and a woman anoints Jesus' head with precious ointment as he sits at a table. The disciples complain about the waste of precious ointment (John says it was Judas who complained). The name of the man in whose house all this took place was Lazarus, the brother of Martha and Mary. So it is clear that Simon the leper and Lazarus are one and the same person, and the woman who anoints Jesus (unnamed in Mark and Matthew) is Mary, the sister of Lazarus and Martha (Jn 12:3).[4]

What we learn from the three accounts is that the brother of Martha and Mary was known as a leper. If Lazarus had been suffering from his ailment before he reached marriageable age, he may not have been able to find a marriage partner belonging to his social caste. People knew that the disease was contagious. And even though a man was declared cured by a priest, maybe his children could inherit the disease. So Lazarus, even if he had been cured by Jesus, was still a *vitandus* (a person to be shunned and avoided.) Perhaps the entire Bethany family were social outcasts; all the more reason why Jesus would have favored them and stayed with them when he visited Jerusalem.

We need not be surprised then that Jesus dines with a leper and even sleeps in his house. One of his first miracles is described in Mark's Gospel: "A leper came to him begging him, and kneeling he said to him, 'If you choose, you can make me clean.' Moved with pity Jesus stretched out his hand and touched him, . . ." (Mk 1:40–41). The leper is cured. But Jesus has become ritually unclean for having touched a leper. It can be doubted whether this weighed very heavily on his conscience, because he did not hesitate to eat with Publicans and other sinners and he refused to condemn a woman taken in adultery (Jn 8:1–11).

Luke's Lazarus

Lazarus, an alternate form of Eliezar, is a name associated with a skin disease in Luke's parable of the Rich Man and Lazarus. The parable contrasts the lot of Lazarus and the rich man. Covered with sores, Lazarus lies at the gate of the rich man. With the dogs that lick his sores, he would gladly feed on the crumbs that fell from the rich man's table. But the rich man pays him no heed. After death, the rich man is in Hades, while Lazarus is at peace in the Bosom of Abraham (Lk 19:23). Over the centuries the name Lazarus has become associated with leprosy, also called Hansen's disease. An asylum for lepers, called a leprosarium, is also sometimes called a lazarium. Father Peter Damien, a Catholic priest, spent his life tending the lepers confined to an area on Molokai, an island in Hawaii. Eventually he caught the disease himself and rejoiced that now he was truly one of them, one with them. He was beatified in 1995 by Pope John Paul II.[5]

Not every sort of offensive skin disease can qualify as true leprosy which was widespread in biblical times. So, if Lazarus, the brother of Martha and Mary, was a true leper, he would have been forced to live apart from others. Yet, when the Bethany family hosted the dinner for Jesus, Lazarus seems to have been cured. Had Jesus healed him earlier, called him back from a condition of living death, so that the first resurrection of Lazarus would have been his restoration to health and the second his return from the grave? Or did the tradition about his miraculous cure turn into a story about his being raised from the dead?

The Friends of Jesus

We commonly think of Jesus as being closely associated with his twelve apostles, and we learn of their names. Four of them, however,

are only names. Thus, James son of Alphaeus, Thaddeus, Bartholo-
mew, and Simon the Cananaean are listed as apostles, but unlike the
other eight they neither say nor do anything. This may mean that the
number twelve is more symbolic than descriptive of a close relationship with Jesus. Three of the men listed as apostles, Peter, James, and
John, seemed to travel with Jesus on a regular basis. Occasionally, we
hear of Philip or Andrew or Thomas. Did all twelve of the apostles go
about with Jesus wherever he went? We know that some were sent out
to do preaching and missionary work (Mt 10:5), so that only rarely did
all twelve come together.

On the other hand, we learn that Jesus had many intimate friends
who were not listed among the Twelve. One thinks of Nathaniel,
Nicodemus, Joseph of Arimathea, Mary Magdalene, and the members
of the Bethany family. The two sisters of Lazarus and Mary
Magdalene were women, and there were many other women—a
Joanna the wife of Chuza, a Salome, and several Marys—who were
close to Jesus. A number of these people were Judeans, something that
should alert us to the fact that Jesus did not restrict his ministry to
Galilee. He was known to a number of influential friends and disciples
in and around Jerusalem months, possibly years, before he died there.

The Gospels give us only the bare bones of the many things Jesus
said and did. The first ending of John's Gospel warns us about this by
declaring, "Now Jesus did many other signs in the presence of his disciples that are not written in this book" (Jn 20:30). We should respond
in an interactive way with what is explicitly said. Jews regularly read
their scriptures in this creative way. We can become far too needle-
nosed when we take a purely positivistic approach and refuse to pon-
der what might have, could have, or should have happened in any
given instance. When a text leaves us with a problem unresolved, as
many texts do, we are invited to communicate with a passage until the
dead text comes alive and we are back in the first century with Jesus
and his friends.

Notes

[1] An indication that the Martha and Mary incident is a teaching story is the fact that
Jesus seems to be their only guest in a very domestic kind of scene, with Jesus alone
in the home of two women. The story is an icon portraying the contemplative and the
active life according to the traditional interpretation.

[2] The three Passovers mentioned in John's Gospel will be found at Jn 2:13, 6:4. and 13:1. Tabernacles (Booths) is mentioned at Jn 7:2, and dedication at Jn 10:22. A sixth festival is referred to at Jn 5:1. It may have been Pentecost, the Festival of Weeks.

[3] Josephus, *The Wars of the Jews* 2,8,4 in *The Works of Josephus*. The William Whiston translation (Peabody, MA: Hendrickson Publishers; tenth printing), 605.

[4] As indicated in chapter 17, there are three episodes when a woman anoints Jesus. We do not have, to my knowledge, any other instances outside of the gospels of women uncovering and taking down their hair to wipe the feet of a teacher or prince. Hindus speak of bowing before "The Lotus Feet" of Krishna, or a teacher. It is an example of supreme respect. The Mary of Bethany mentioned in John's Gospel is neither the sinful woman of Luke's Gospel nor Mary of Magdala.

[5] A short biography of St. Peter Damien of Molokai will be found in *All Saints: Daily Reflections on Saints, Prophets, and Witnesses of Our Time* by Robert Ellsberg (New York: Crossroad Publishing Co., 1997). Ellsberg draws his "witnesses" from different faiths and various professions. Along with standard Catholic saints he also includes Dante, Galileo, Mozart, Jonathan Edwards, Albert Camus, and "The Anointer of Bethany."

PART SIX:

The Passion

Chapter Twenty

PHARISEES AND SADDUCEES

Piety and Power

The Pharisees loom large in the Gospels as the persistent adversaries of Jesus. They are portrayed as mean-spirited, hypocritical, self-righteous, and sanctimonious. This portrayal has given rise to the adjective "pharisaical." The Jewish historian Josephus gives us an entirely different picture of the Pharisees. In his eyes they were kind, flexible, humane, and studious.[1] They fostered holiness in the home, the kind that high priests should have been practicing if they were true to the Torah. They thought of themselves as a sort of lay priesthood. Holiness should be the vocation of every true Israelite.

In the Gospels, Jesus disagreed with the Pharisees on several issues, including tithing, Sabbath rest, fasting, and the purity laws. Hillel, the leading Pharisee who lived a generation before Jesus, would have agreed with Jesus on the need to adapt *middôt*, rules for interpreting the Torah, to new and changed circumstances.[2]

Both Hillel and Shammai were known as *hasidim*, pious and especially observant Jews. But, although Shammai withdrew from the common people and from those who might be sinners, Hillel deliberately lived among the poor, rejecting the chance to live comfortably and go into business with his brother. He remained poor and earned his living partly as a day laborer.[3] The word "Pharisee," as it has come into our vocabulary, was especially applicable to Shammai. He was among the *perushim*, those who separated themselves from the world to avoid contamination. As a consequence, his form of observance tended to multiply "rules" in order to build, as it were, a fence around the Torah. Hillel was certainly not lax, but he believed in treating the body well, without undue austerity. As for the inviolability of the Sabbath, he held that, if the preparation for Passover requiring "work" fell on the Sabbath, the needs of the Passover overrode Sabbath restrictions.[4] Like Jesus, Hillel used parables to teach. Unfortunately, most of his stories have been lost or reduced to simple proverbs.

199

It is very important, then, to distinguish the two main varieties of *perushim* (Pharisees). Jesus' teachings and practice were closer to the way of the Hillel Pharisees than to any other Jewish sect. Hyam Maccoby goes so far as to maintain that Jesus speaks and acts like a Pharisee, not only because he believed in survival of death, immortality, and the general resurrection, but also because his teaching, for example in the Sermon on the Mount, is not far removed from what many Pharisees would have applauded.[5] So there is a problem. Granted that Jesus may not have agreed with the *gevurah* (sternness) of Shammai, why is he portrayed in the Gospels as railing against all Pharisees without distinction (Mt 23:25–32)?

The standard reason given for the portrayal of Jesus as vigorously opposed to the Pharisees is probably the correct one. After the fall of Jerusalem, the people who truly saved Judaism and were responsible for the survival of the synagogue following such a disaster were to a great extent the Pharisees. Under Jonathan ben Zakkai, the survivors of the catastrophe met at Jamnia, reinvented Judaism, settled the canon of the scriptures, and began to train rabbis in a form of their religion that would manage to prosper without the Temple, animal sacrifice, and the priesthood. This new outlook became known as Rabbinic Judaism. It proved to be a staunch adversary of all forms of sectarian Judaism, among which it grouped both native Jewish apocalyptic messianism and the Jesus Movement as it evolved under the influence of Paul of Tarsus.

Paul and his followers were eventually excluded from the synagogues of the Diaspora, and when several of the leaders of the new Christian sect were slain under Jewish auspices, any hope of reconciliation between the new Judaism and what eventually became the Church was out of the question.[6] Even before the Roman persecution of the followers of Jesus became common, Rabbinic, that is Pharisaic, Judaism, became the enemy. As a consequence, we witness the phenomenon of retrojection, the reading back into history the enmities that existed at the time the Gospels were written.

In *Gospel Truth*, Russell Shorto's chapter entitled, "Murder Mystery"[7] is another version of John Dominic Crossan's *Who Killed Jesus?* According to the Gospels, Pilate, the Roman prefect, did everything in his power to save Jesus from the cross. It was only when the bloodthirsty Jews, crying "Crucify him!" were on the point of rioting that Pilate reluctantly delivered up Jesus according to their will (Lk 23:24).[8] The Fourth Gospel is even more explicit. There we read,

"Then [Pilate] handed [Jesus] over to them [the Jews who were calling for his death] to be crucified" (Jn 19:16). But, of course, Pilate did
not hand Jesus over to the Jews but to his Roman soldiers. The wording of John's sentence readily conveys the idea that those who killed
Jesus were the Jews.

The evangelists did not bother to make a distinction between
Caiaphas along with other Temple authorities and the millions of
Jews, living, dead, and yet to be born, who knew nothing about Jesus,
even during his lifetime. For the Synoptic Gospels the enemies
became the Pharisees. In John's Gospel, those responsible for the actual condemnation of Jesus were the *Ioudaioi* (Judeans), a term that
refers especially to the Sadducees and the Judean Temple hierarchy.
Unfortunately, the word in italics has been traditionally translated as
"the Jews."9 If the principal author of the Fourth Gospel was a
Samaritan or a Galilean, he may be laying blame for the death of Jesus
on *"those Judeans."* Upon consulting Strong's *The New Concordance
of the Bible*, I find that while the Fourth Gospel refers to "The Jews"
just short of seventy times, almost always with disparaging intent, the
three Synoptic Gospels use the words sparingly and never in a con-
demnatory or negative sense. For them the principal enemies of Jesus
are the Pharisees.

Although there were Pharisees who were friendly to Jesus (Lk
13:31, 14:1), there were some who merited Jesus' complaints about
their pettiness and pretentiousness. We find similar complaints in the
Talmud. In Jesus' day the Pharisees probably numbered around six
thousand, just as at the time of Herod the Great, but of that number
very few were enemies of Jesus.10 St. Paul in his preconversion days
represented the more rabid type of Pharisee. He was by no means typical.

There are a number of passages in the Gospels where the
Pharisees are represented as trying to catch Jesus in his words.
However, it was customary for established masters of the law to test
the knowledge and wisdom of a newcomer by asking him difficult
questions. Although Jesus was not a textual scholar like the Scribes,
on several occasions the Scribes, many of whom were Pharisees, con-
gratulated him for answering one of their probing questions well (Mk
12:32; Lk 20:39).

Among those Jews who were hostile to Jesus, he had much more
to fear from the Sadducees than from the Pharisees. After all, the high
priests, most of whom were Sadducees, were the ones who brought

Jesus to trial and sent him to the Romans to be crucified. Even on doctrinal matters the Pharisees were much closer to Jesus than the Sadducees. Aside from denying the existence of angels and the resurrection, the Sadducees also rejected all books of the Hebrew Scriptures except for the five books of the Pentateuch. Jesus, on the other hand, accepted not only the Torah but quoted the words of the Prophets (*Nevi'im*) and the other Writings (*Ketuvim*).[11] So, Jesus in his teaching and beliefs was closer to the Pharisees than to any other persuasion of his day.

Excursus on Matthew 23:13–35; Luke 11:39–52

If a complete stranger were introduced to the Gospels and if he or she were guided entirely by what the evangelists tell us about the personality of Jesus, Jesus would have come across as a paradoxical and conflicted figure. Andrew Vogel Ettin indicates how a case can be made to show that Jesus was antagonistic, overbearing, and, at least in the Fourth Gospel, self-promoting.[12]

On the one hand, Jesus is presented in the Synoptic Gospels as "gentle and humble of heart" (Mt 11:29), as loving and kindly, as ready to forgive seventy times seven times (Mt 18:22). If insulted, he would turn the other cheek, love his enemies and pray for those who persecuted him (Mt 5:44). On the other hand, Matthew, followed by Luke, has Jesus comparing the Scribes and Pharisees to whitewashed sepulchers, full of corruption and dead men's bones. They are blind fools, hypocrites, a brood of vipers, descendents of those who shed the blood of the prophets.

Finally, Matthew has Jesus utter a blood-curdling curse against the Pharisees as murderers of the prophets, "so that upon you may come all the righteous blood shed on earth from the blood of the righteous Abel to the blood of Zechariah son of Barachiah, whom you murdered between the sanctuary and the altar" (Mt 23:13.35; Lk 11:39–52). Luke's version is shorter and does not include the unsubstantiated charge that accuses the Pharisees of "crucifying" God's prophets. If Matthew is referring retrospectively to the crucifixion of Jesus, the Jews who had a hand in it were the high priests, most of whom were Sadducees, not the Pharisees. How could the present-day Scribes and Pharisees murder and crucify prophets (plural) who lived centuries before there were any Pharisees? Luke, incidentally, was careful not to identify Zechariah as the son of Barachiah (Zech 1:11); he was, in fact, the son of Johaida (2 Chr 24:20–21).[13]

Later on, in his twenty-seventh chapter, Matthew has a mob standing before Pilate calling down on their heads and on the heads of their children the blood of Jesus. But, as indicated above, he has Jesus anticipate them by calling down on the heads of the Pharisees all the righteous blood shed on earth since the time of Abel.

What are we to do with these less than edifying passages?[14] The first thing to remember is that the evangelists mix history with politics. Matthew found it hard to excuse those unbelieving Jews who refused to join the Jesus movement. Instead, Jewish authorities were among those who persecuted its members. Writing at a time when there was little love lost between Christians and the new Jewish leaders, most of whom were Pharisees, Matthew attributes to the Jesus of history the hostility the evangelist's community felt toward the Pharisees and other Jews. The author of the Gospel according to Matthew was almost certainly an ethic Jew himself.

Predictably, the Jews gave back in kind. During the forties, differences between Jews and Christians appear to have resulted in clashes, usually initiated by conservative Jews. In the year 49, the Emperor Claudius (41–54) expelled the Jews from the city of Rome for rioting. Rightly or wrongly, Suetonius blamed "Chrestos" (Christ) or his followers as responsible for the disturbances. Claudius made no distinction between Jews and Jewish Christians. When the Gospels were written some twenty or more years later, the enmity had, if anything, worsened. The evangelists were not writing from a neutral position. So we have to try to discriminate between what the Gospels attribute to Jesus in the light of a situation when they were composed and what Jesus actually said and did.

Although Paul is often angry and frustrated with Judaizers, those Jewish–Christians who wanted to impose on Gentiles all the restrictions and obligations of the Law of Moses, he never portrays Jesus as anti-Jewish. As for himself, he sees his fellow Jews as "beloved for the sake of their ancestors; for the gifts and the calling of God are irrevocable" (Rom 11:18–19).[15]

The Gospels, along with a good measure of otherwise valuable historical reporting, reveal the outlook of each individual writer. One has to allow for the human element entering into even the most sacred documents. We can be sure that Jesus was not timid, that he was forthright in challenging his adversaries where abuses were concerned. But that he deluged them as a group with ugly and insulting names and called down on their heads the blood of all the righteous men since human time began is hard to believe.

It will not do to say that the type of name calling attributed to Jesus in Matthew's Gospel was typical of the invective used by Hebrew prophets and that Jesus was simply speaking and acting in accord with the accepted tradition, that unless he pounded the table and used strong language people would not listen. Mark, the earliest of the four Gospels, does not include the kind of violent language Matthew attributes to Jesus in attacking the Pharisees. It makes one wonder whether such language really comes from the earliest stratum among the sayings of Jesus, that is, from Q^1 or even from Q^3. (Q stands for *Quelle*. It refers to the more or less parallel passages in Matthew and Luke that do not appear in Mark. Scholars speculate that the two evangelists were using an early collection of Jesus' sayings composed before his death.) The fact is that the shorter passage in Mark (Mk 12:38–40; Mt 23:6–7) does not go on to include the outrageous and basically untrue accusations put into the mouth of Jesus by Matthew and copied by Luke with important modifications. What if the source of Jesus' diatribe against the Pharisees is not the hypothetical early, preresurrection saying Gospel represented by Q, but is the creation of Matthew who wrote some fifty years after the time of Jesus? By then Matthew found reason to "improve" on the observations of Jesus about the pettiness and pomp of some Pharisees, minor foibles later substantially confirmed in the Babylonian Talmud? What Matthew was actually attacking, when he pilloried the Pharisees, were their latter-day heirs, the Rabbinic Jews of his own day.

It is Matthew, copied again by Luke, who has Jesus condemn to Hell the three Lake towns that failed to respond suitably to his message:

> Woe to You, Chorazin! Woe to you, Bethsaida! For if the deeds of power done in you had been done in Tyre and Sidon, they would have repented long ago in sackcloth and ashes. But I tell you, on the day of judgment it will be more tolerable for Tyre and Sidon than for you. And you, Capernaum, will you be exalted to heaven? No, you will be brought down to Hell. (Mt 11:21; Lk 10:13–15).

Again, it is Matthew who has Jesus, as Son of Man and final judge, seated on his throne of gold on judgment day, damning as "accursed" those guilty of sins of omission, such as failing to visit those in prison or welcome strangers. The guilty ones will burn forever in "the eternal fire prepared for the devil and his angels" (Mt 25:41). Granted that this is only a parable, one of the three parables that are included in chapter twenty-five of Matthew's Gospel, it is Matthew who has added this dire theme of draconian punishment to what is otherwise a typical Jesus story. Leaving aside the appalling punishment Matthew would have Jesus inflict on those who commit sins of omission—they are not guilty of murder, child abuse, grand larceny, or genocide—what Jesus is actually teaching is that whatever you do for or against a neighbor as a member of the human race you actually do to Jesus and to your own greater self. No wonder the Fellows of the Jesus Seminar dismissed the preceding three instances in which Jesus is portrayed as putting a curse on others as unhistorical.

It is not Jesus but the author of the Gospel according to Matthew who is the conflicted and paradoxical figure. It is in this Gospel that we find the elevating and exquisitely beautiful Sermon on the Mount, and it is at the very start of the Sermon that Jesus declares, "If you insult a brother or sister, you will be liable to the council, and if you say 'You fool!' [*rakah*], you will be liable to hellfire" (Mt 5:22). It is inconceivable that the Jesus who so roundly condemned such behavior could have turned around and violated his own principles by addressing the Pharisees as "You blind fools!" (Mt 23:23). Matthew's jeremiad goes on for 37 verses (23:1–36). The earlier Markan parallel covers only three verses. If Jesus was to be a model for others, it does him no honor to have him savage an entire class of respected men without distinction.

What kind of person, then, was Jesus? Was he so self-contradictory internally and in his teaching that he could counsel meekness, gentleness, and love of one's enemies and then do the exact opposite in practice. No doubt, there are some who can feel comfortable with that kind of confrontational, hell-raising Jesus. If he had been that sort of person, it is no wonder that he made enemies who wanted nothing more than to destroy him.

However, we know that the Pharisees, whom Jesus is represented as attacking so fiercely, came in all shapes and sizes, from the austere and ultra-conservative Shammai to the genial and open Hillel, from the nonjudgmental Gamaliel to the lax Josephus. There undoubtedly were censorious Scribes and Pharisees, some of whom accused Jesus of being an agent of Beelzebul, the Prince of Devils, but there were others who praised him (Mk 12:32), invited him to eat in their homes

(Lk 7:36), warned him when his life was in danger (Lk 13:31), and even helped bury him (Jn 19:39). So, faced with having to choose between Matthew's Jesus and a Jesus who was closer in spirit to the Pharisees than to any other Jewish group, I would have to choose the latter. Although he may not have been a Pharisee himself, as some have held,[16] Jesus was in basic agreement with the beliefs of the general run of Pharisees. He stood for a discriminating and judicious interpretation of Torah that would have pleased and been approved by his recent Pharisee predecessor, the universally respected Hillel.

I felt obliged to introduce this Excursus because, historically, there have been times when it has become necessary to rescue Jesus from his friends, not to mention his evangelists.

Looking Down the Well

As with so many others, "My Jesus" is undoubtedly a reflection of how I want him to be. In other words, I recreate him after the image of my ideal. What is revealed in that image is the set of preferences I select out of what the Gospels tell me about Jesus, coupled with the ones I superimpose upon him. Most approaches to the Jesus of history reveal as much about the writer as about Jesus. In that sense, they are, if not autobiographical, at least self-revelatory. This applies to the evangelists themselves as well as to St. Paul. So we all find, in our various approaches to Jesus, the Jesus we need in line with our own character, personality, politics, and cultural conditioning.

A particular person's reading of the Gospel is a synthesis of what a literal reading of a text might *propose* and what is *imposed* by individuals living in various parts of the world and in different time frames. What we get out of a text is partly what we bring to it. Well aware of the danger of applying scientific notions to religious material, I still think there is a kind of analogy between the way the observer affects the observed in quantum mechanics and the way each person's approach to the Gospels enters into and affects the meaning one draws out of them. The result is a combination of objective and subjective factors. So, "My Jesus" is as much my creation as he is the Jesus the evangelists intended to portray following the rules of their craft. Jaroslaw Pelikan, in his introduction to *Jesus Through the Centuries,* agrees with Albert Schweitzer:

Each successive epoch," Schweitzer said, "found its own
thoughts in Jesus, which was indeed, the only way in which
it could make him live"; for, typically, one "created him in
accordance with one's own character." There is," he concluded, "no historical task which so reveals someone's true
self as the writing of a Life of Jesus."[17]

Notes

[1] Joephus speaks eloquently of the virtues of the Pharisees in *The Antiquities of the Jews* 18,1,3. But he does tend to exaggerate, and it is always good to remember that he became a Pharisee himself at the age of nineteen.

[2] *Middôt* were Hillel's seven norms for interpreting the Torah. See Yitzhak Buxbaum, *The Life and Teachings of Hillel* (Northvale, NJ: Jason Aronson, 1994), 23–27.

[3] On Hillel's poverty, see Buxbaum, 12–15.

[4] On Passover superseding the Sabbath, see Buxbaum, 23 and note 5, 307–308.

[5] Hyam Maccoby, *The Myth-maker: Paul and the Invention of Christianity* (San Francisco: Harper & Row, 1987), xi and 29–44.

[6] The early victims of Jewish persecution were Stephen, James the apostle, and James the brother of Jesus. Luke says that after the stoning of Stephen, "A severe persecu-tion began against the Church in Jerusalem, and all except the apostles were scattered throughout the countryside of Judea and Samaria" (Acts 8:1).

[7] Russell Shorto, *Gospel Truth: The Image of Jesus Emerging from Science and History, and Why It Matters* (New York: Riverhead/Putnam, 1997).

[8] See chapter 24 for an evaluation of Pilate's role in the condemnation of Jesus.

[9] The Fourth Gospel uses the words *Hoi Ioudaioi*. They are usually translated as "The Jews," but the same word may also be rendered as "The Judeans," as distinguished from the Samaritans or Galileans. One senses a Galilean bias in the use of a word that is subtly trying to make a statement about the distinction between Judeans and other Jews, including Jesus, the apostles, and the evangelists. After all, the Judean high priests are the ones who collaborated in the arrest and execution of Jesus. After the resurrection of Jesus the disciples had more success in converting Samaritans than Judeans. That is reflected in the parable of The Good Samaritan and in the fact that of the ten lepers whom Jesus cured, only one returned to offer thanks, and he was a Samaritan.

[10] We owe the figure 6,000 to Josephus, *The Antiquities of the Jews*, 17,2,4.

[11] The *Tanakh*, or Hebrew Bible, is divided into three parts: the Torah (the first five books, or Pentateuch), the *Nevi'im* (prophets), and the *Kethuvim* (writings, including such books as the Psalms, Job, Esther, etc.). *Tanakh* is an acronym composed of the first letters of the three parts, TNK.

[12] See Andrew Vogel Ettin, "That Troublesome Cousin," in *Seeing Jesus Through Jewish Eyes: Rabbis and Scholars Engage an Ancient Brother in a New Conversation*, by Beatrice Bruteau (Maryknoll, NY: Orbis Books, 2001), 63–73.

[13] The Zechariah Matthew was referring to was the son of the priest Johaida. He was stoned to death in the house of the Lord (2 Chr 24:20–12). Since Chronicles is the last book of the Hebrew Bible and the murder of Abel was the first one mentioned in

Genesis, Matthew implies that the Pharisees are somehow responsible for shedding the blood of all the just men from Abel to Zechariah. The reasoning here is not unlike that of those who harbor anti-Jewish prejudices today. They feel that contemporary Jews are guilty of the death of Jesus because Caiaphas who turned Jesus over to the Romans was a Jew.

14 Warren Carter, echoing L. Johnson's article in *Journal of Biblical Literature* 108 (1989), 419–441, points out how this kind of invective is a stylized version of a typical sectarian attack on an adversary. It may represent the mind of the evangelist but not that of Jesus. See Carter, *Matthew and the Margins* (Maryknoll, NY: Orbis Books, 2000), chapter 23.

15 This view of St. Paul was reinforced in the *Declaration on the Relationship of the Church to Non-Christian Religions* issued by the bishops who met during the Second Vatican Council and approved by Pope Paul VI. Speaking of the Jews and the Covenant of the Chosen People with God, the Church declares, ". . . the Jews still remain most dear to God because of their fathers, for He does not repent of His gifts." More recently (August 12, 2002), the Conference of American Bishops and the National Council of Synagogues (representing Reform and Conservative Judaism) issued a statement which declares that "Judaism is a religion that springs from divine revelation" and that the Church has no divine mission to convert the Jews "who believe in the true and one God" (p.7). http://www.catholicbook.org/comm./archives/2002/02–154.htm.

16 On Maccoby's theory that Jesus might have been a Pharisee, see note 5 above.

17 *Jesus Through the Centuries: His Place in the History of Culture* (New Haven: Yale University Press, 1985), 2.

Chapter Twenty-one

HEROD ANTIPAS

Marrying Your Brother's Wife Can Be Risky

Herod Antipas, King Herod's son by his wife Malthace, and brother of Archelaus, could never forget that in his father's next-to-last will, he was to have succeeded his father as king of all of his father's territory. Only days before his death, Herod changed his will and split his kingdom into three major portions, leaving Antipas with only the arid and rocky Perea and the fertile Galilee.[1] When his brother Archelaus was finally deposed and sent into exile, Antipas did not regain Idumea, Judea, and Samaria. Instead, these provinces became a single imperial province to be governed in the future by Roman prefects appointed by the emperor.

Throughout his long reign of forty-three years, Antipas never gave up hope of one day becoming ruler of the whole of what had been Herod the Great's kingdom. It is one of the ironies of history that it was Antipas' own Nephew, Agrippa I, the grandson of Herod the Great who, for three years before his sudden death, ruled as king over most of his grandfather's territory. But Agrippa did not become king until 41 CE, two years after Antipas had been deposed. Meanwhile, Antipas was busy building fences and trying to ingratiate himself with the people. At festival time he would enter Jerusalem with great pomp and make a show of his respect for the Torah, the Temple, and Jewish traditions.[2] At the same time, he was using the tax money and produce he squeezed out of his Galilean subjects to build new cities, such as Sepphoris and Tiberias, while also endowing pagan shrines to honor Asclepius and Apollo on the island of Kos and at Delos.[3]

As indicated briefly in chapter 4 of this book, Herod Antipas was the monarch who was responsible for the beheading of John the Baptist. The Baptist had dared to criticize Antipas for having married his half-brother Philip's wife Herodias, who was also his niece. After John's arrest, he was kept for a time in prison, but when Salome, the daughter of Herodias by Philip, danced in such a way as to please Herod, he promised to grant her any request she might choose to make. Prompted by her mother, she asked for the head of John the Baptist. Josephus also records the execution of John but does not tie it directly to Salome's request for the head of the Baptist. He says that John had won such favor with the people that Antipas feared they were ready to do anything he might incite them to do, including participating in a rebellion. To anticipate such an outcome, he had John executed as a precautionary measure.[4]

However, there is an indirect connection between the marriage of Antipas to Herodias and his fall from favor in Rome. In order to marry Herodias, Antipas was prepared to dismiss or assassinate his present wife, daughter of King Aretas IV of Nabataea. She wisely fled; but a war ensued between Aretas and Antipas in which Antipas' army was badly defeated.[5] Rome refused to help, and Antipas lost respect in Rome. Then, when Caligula made Lysanius "king" over Philip's territory after the latter's death in 34 CE, Herod Antipas, urged on by Herodias, went to Rome to seek a similar title. The trip proved to be their undoing, for Agrippa, Herodias' own brother and also a nephew of Antipas, accused the tetrarch of assorted crimes, including posturing as a king without Roman permission. As a result, Antipas not only failed to win the title of king, but both he and his controversial wife Herodias were sent into exile to Lyons in Gaul. Thus, Herodias proved to be Antipas' nemesis.

Herod and Jesus

After he had beheaded John the Baptist, Herod Antipas began to hear rumors about the teaching and physical cures performed by Jesus. Joanna, the wife of his steward Chuza,[6] had become a follower and supporter of Jesus and the movement he had set in motion. No doubt, Herod learned something about Jesus through this indirect contact. But he was puzzled. No sooner had he disposed of John the Baptist than another even more popular crowd pleaser arose. From Antipas' point of view this spelled danger. Who was this Nazarean who suddenly made his appearance in the towns around the Sea of Galilee? Had he inherited the spirit of John the Baptist, as Elisha had inherited the mantle of Elijah (2 Kings 2:13)? Herod was not thinking here of a mere delegation of authority but of a real indwelling of the spirit of the deceased John. It meant that Jesus had become possessed with John's spirit and had come back to haunt Herod (Lk 9:7–9). When Jesus asks his disciples who the crowds say that he is, they answer that some think he is John the Baptist or Elijah or one of the prophets (Lk 9:18–19). This again assumed that the spirit of a dead person could take over and act through the body and spirit of a living person.

When Jesus is warned that Herod wants to kill him, he tells his informers that he is destined to go to Jerusalem and die there in the Holy City, where Herod has no jurisdiction (Lk 13:32–33). In Mark's Gospel, Jesus tells his disciples to "beware of the yeast of the Pharisees and the yeast of Herod" (Mk 8:15). "Yeast" here means the characteristic vice of the Pharisees which was hypocrisy, and of Herod which was the lust for power.

Eventually, according to Luke, Herod Antipas met Jesus in Jerusalem at the Passover season. Herod usually made an ostentatious pilgrimage to the city at festival time. It was a way to remind the people that his father had rebuilt and furnished the Temple, and that he, too, was a patron who supported it. So, during the trial of Jesus before Pilate, the Roman prefect learning that Jesus was a Galilean, sent him to Herod for judgment. Since Herod had been eager to meet Jesus for some time, he appreciated the favor and proceeded to interrogate Jesus. Jesus, however, refused to answer the question put to him. So Herod and his soldiers treated him as a fool and sent him back in a fool's garment to Pilate. Pilate's gesture of seeming to cede jurisdiction over Jesus to Herod, even though Herod had no true authority in Judea, served to lessen the tension between the two men. Luke says that, whereas Pilate and Herod had been enemies, they became friends on that day (Lk 23:12).

Maybe they became friends. But as long as Pilate remained as governor of Samaria, Judea, and the holy city of Jerusalem, he stood in the way of Herod's one ambition, to be ruler of the whole of Palestine and several adjacent territories. Beginning with Herod the Great, the Herodians had powerful connections in Rome. The younger sons, including Antipas, had spent their adolescent years there studying and learning Roman ways. Pontius Pilate, on the other hand, although a Roman, was not of senatorial or consular rank. As an equestrian, he would in most cases rank below favored client kings. While Lucius Aelius Sejanus was in power as the confidante of the Emperor Tiberias and in command of the Praetorian Guard, Pilate had as his patron and protector a man of equestrian rank like himself, which was to be the upper limit of his ambition. When Sejanus fell from favor in 31 CE Pilate's chance of becoming procurator–governor of the whole of Palestine was greatly reduced.[7] But he was not above pulling strings in Rome to make sure that Antipas did not become king.

When Pilate was recalled to Rome in 36 CE, there was a chance that Antipas might then be given rule over Judea, Samaria, and Idumea. But this was the very year in which his army had suffered such a crushing defeat at the hands of King Aretas IV of Nabataea, a defeat intimately connected with his marriage to Herodias and the flight of the daughter of Aretas. Three years later, Antipas and Herodias were on their way to exile and oblivion in Gaul.[8] We do not know whether they learned about Agrippa's accession to the title of King of the Jews and rule over the Kingdom of Israel. If they did, it must have pained them greatly. One tradition has it that Pilate, like Herod Antipas, was exiled to Gaul. If the two of them met there, they would have had many interesting reminiscences during the enforced leisure that exile usually inflicted on those whose careers ended in something short of execution.

Notes

[1] Josephus says that Herod the Great was acting like a madman at the end of his life. He tells about changing his will at the last moment and awarding his kingdom to Archelaus rather than to Antipas. *The Antiquities of the Jews* 17,8,1.

[2] Horsely and Silberman mention in passing the pomp and circumstance with which Herod Antipas surrounded himself when visiting Jerusalem at festival time, *The Message and the Kingdom* (New York: Grosset/Putnam, 1997), 80.

[3] Horsely and Silberman, 95.

[4] Josephus, *Antiquities* 18,5,2.

[5] Josephus, *Antiquities*, 18,5,1, describes the flight of the daughter of King Aretus and his defeat of Herod's army.

[6] Luke 8:3.

[7] Sejanus was involved in a plot against Tiberius and was summarily executed. See Josephus, *Antiquities* 18,6,6.

[8] Josephus (*Antiquities* 18,7,1) blames Herodias for egging on Herod Antipas to seek the Kingship. The trip to Rome ended in disaster and exile, an unhappy ending for a reign that had lasted for forty-three years.

Chapter Twenty-two

CAIAPHAS

The "Yes, Man's" Dilemma

In 142 BCE, Judas Maccabeus established an independent Jewish state. His successors became the Hasmonean dynasty of kings who were also high priests. They held office for life and combined both political and religious powers. When Herod the Great became king and decided to diminish the power of the high priests, he abolished life tenure by limiting their term of office. He appointed and deposed high priests at will. After his death the Roman governors followed the same policy. The length of time any high priest remained in office depended entirely on how well he served Roman interests. Annas, the father-in-law of Joseph ben Caiaphas, had five sons. All had been high priests for limited periods of time. His son-in-law, however, remained as a high priest from 18 CE to the year 37, an astonishingly long period.

What accounted for the success of Caiaphas was that he served the Roman prefect, and did whatever Pilate told him. When the procurator Gessius Florus ordered the high priests to round up eighteen disturbers of the peace and bring them to him, they promptly did so.[1] As an indication of how subservient high priests were to their Roman overlords, they were not even allowed to possess their own ceremonial robes; those needed, for example, for the Day of Atonement when the high priest would enter the Holy of Holies alone in full regalia. It was the Roman governor who kept the vestments in the Tower of Antonia, allowing the high priest to have them only seven days before a major feast.

The relationship between Pilate and Caiaphas, while not cordial, was successful enough. During the ten-year period between 26 and 36, that Pilate was prefect, he retained Caiaphas as high priest. Both were relieved of office within a few months of one another, Pilate in disgrace and Caiaphas because he had probably outlived his usefulness.[2]

All of this history needs to be considered when dealing with the relationship between Jesus and Caiaphas. In the Gospels we hear noth-

ing about Caiaphas until a short time before the arrest and condemnation of Jesus. The high priest must have worried about Jesus' popular-
ity and the large crowds who followed him. He did not need Pilate
telling him to move against Jesus after Jesus' entry into Jerusalem
when a crowd hailed him as the royal Son of David and King of the
Jews. The Synoptic evangelists say Jesus planned his triumphal entry
into Jerusalem (Mk 11; Mt 21; Lk 19). John indicates that he did not
arrange in advance to procure a donkey on which to ride. One was
found during one of his routine trips from Bethania to the city of
Jerusalem (Jn 12:14).

Jesus may have attacked Caiaphas indirectly by calling the
Temple "a den of thieves" (Mt 21:13). Questionable, however, is the
account that has him single-handedly upset the tables of the money-
changers, drive out the animals, and then walk away under the noses
of the Temple police. It is surely significant that this act of violence,
so offensive to the high priests, was not the charge brought against
Jesus during his trial before Caiaphas. Rather, he was accused of having spoken, or prophesied, against the Temple, saying that it would be
destroyed or that he would destroy it (Mk 13:2 and par.). Thus, we
have one more instance of having something Jesus said turned into
something Jesus did. Jesus was not naïve. Unless he was deliberately
planning actions that would assuredly result in his being arrested and
killed, he would not have staged a triumphal entry into Jerusalem.
When and if he had been hailed as King on what we celebrate as Palm
Sunday, he would have regarded it as a liability and an embarrassment. He had fled to the mountains when the people tried to take him
by force and make him king after the multiplication of the loaves and
fishes (Jn 6:15).

The arrest of Jesus had little to do with his physically attacking
Temple property or planning a triumphal entry into the city. John's
Gospel is almost certainly correct when it portrays the Jewish Council,
headed by Caiaphas, as warning: "This man [Jesus] is performing
many signs. If we let it go on like this everyone will believe in him,
and the Romans will come and destroy both our holy place and our
nation." Caiaphas says that there is an easy solution: simply do away
with Jesus. The evangelist turns this advice into a prophecy, making
Jesus inadvertently the savior of the nation. Thus, Caiphas prophesies,
"It is better for you to have one man die for the people than to have
the whole nation destroyed" (Jn 11:50).

So, Jesus was to be taken out, one way or another. The safest course was to wait until after dark and, after finding out where Jesus customarily stayed at night, send out a well-armed band of soldiers to arrest him. The population of Jerusalem had been estimated at around thirty thousand people. But during festival time, at Passover, there could have been two or three times as many with pilgrims from out of town, who had to stay somewhere in the surrounding area. But how could they find Jesus and his husky band of Galilean disciples among sixty or ninety thousand visitors with no set address? Judas was the answer. He knew that Jesus and his apostles stayed on the Mount of Olives near Bethany, possibly on the property of Lazarus, whose sisters were the Martha and Mary in the Gospels of Luke and John.

Judas came with a sizable number of soldiers. Mark gave one the impression that Jesus was arrested by a crowd equipped with swords and clubs (Mk 14:43). The Greek word οχλος (crowd) signifies an unruly mob sent by the high priests to arrest Jesus. As indicated in the Preface to this book, those who came to arrest Jesus in John's Gospel were anything but an unruly mob. They were Roman soldiers, members of a speira, a maniple or cohort, headed by a chiliarch, a Roman military officer who could command as many as a thousand men: "So the band of soldiers (σπεῖρα), their officer (χιλιαρχος), and the Jewish police arrested Jesus and bound him" (Jn 18:3, 12). The people sent by the Temple authorities played a minor role in the arrest. Clearly, if Jesus was arrested by Roman soldiers, Pontius Pilate played a major role, something that the Synoptic evangelists are at pains to downplay. Although Jesus was arrested and executed by Romans, three of the Gospel writers, living at a time when it was expedient to show that Jesus and Christians were loyal Roman subjects, cast the blame for the arrest and execution of Jesus not on the Romans, but on the Jews.

The Roman and Jewish military personnel were well prepared for any resistance on the part of Jesus' followers. Of course, there was no resistance, save for a futile and impetuous attempt on the part of Peter to attack one of the servants of the high priest. Jesus chided him and told him to put up his weapon. Jesus went quietly with his captors, having asked only that his apostles be released. So, by this request, he became their savior, for he saved them from what was to be his own fate.

The Synoptic Gospels say that Jesus was brought before Caiaphas and at least a rump session of the Sanhedrin. The Fourth Gospel mentions only an informal interrogation before Annas, the father-in-law of

Caiaphas and a former high priest. What authority Annas would have had in questioning Jesus is problematic. After his brief session with Annas, the Fourth Gospel indicates that Jesus was sent to Caiaphas. By that time it was well past midnight and there is no indication in John's Gospel that a formal trial presided over by Caiaphas ever took place.

The Trial

The Synoptic Gospels hold that there was a formal trial before the Sanhedrin late at night on the day beginning at sundown after the day on which the lambs were slain. This would have been at the start of the day of Passover itself. Asked if he is the Messiah, in Luke's Gospel Jesus simply refuses to answer (Lk 22:67). However, when the same question is put to him in Matthew's Gospel, he gives an ambiguous reply, on the basis of which he is accused of blasphemy. But even if Jesus had claimed to be the Messiah, this would not be blasphemy. So Luke has Caiaphas ask Jesus two questions: "Are you the Messiah?" which Jesus does not answer, and "Are you the Son of God?" to which Jesus replies, "You say that I am," which is hardly a direct "yes." Only Mark has Jesus answer in the affirmative to the question of his being the Messiah. (Cf. Mk 14:62; Mt 26:64; Lk 22:70.)

What Luke has done is turn one question into two. In Mark and Matthew the high priest asks Jesus, "Are you the Messiah the Son of God?" Because the king or any pious Jew or even the whole nation was regularly called God's Son, clearly the Messiah, if he came, would be Son of God.[3] So the formula, "Messiah-the-Son-of-God," is still not the same as identifying the Messiah with the divine name. But Luke breaks the question into two, so that the second question seems to be asking Jesus whether he is somehow a divine person. To claim to be God or God's Son in this latter sense would be blasphemy according to the Jewish understanding in Jesus' day.

Luke, for reasons of his own, omits all reference to the charge that Jesus said he could or would destroy the Temple, which might be regarded as a form of blasphemy, because to speak against the Temple by foretelling its destruction would be to "bad talk" blaspheme the House of God and indirectly God Himself. Luke prefers to have Jesus condemned for not denying that he was "Son of God" in some special sense.

What we are not sure of is whether the trial before Caiaphas took place as it is described in the Synoptic Gospels. What many scripture scholars question is whether the trial was a formal one conducted before the assembled members of the Sanhedrin at night, and, indeed, whether such a trial would have been legal.[4] Who among Jesus' disciples witnessed the private hearing and was able to pass on that information that would be written in the Gospels forty to sixty years later? Was Jesus condemned because he spoke against the Temple, or because he claimed to be the Messiah, or because he claimed to be Son of God? The trouble is that the Gospels were composed at a time when the thinking about Jesus and his identity had evolved to a considerable degree. It is only in the Last Gospel that the divinity of Christ is unmistakably proclaimed, but the Synoptic Gospels were also moving in that direction. For that reason, they anticipate John's Gospel by, so to speak, moving the question.

Actually Caiaphas was minimally interested in whether Jesus was the Messiah. He was thinking primarily of his own and Pilate's interests. He wanted credit, because this would have seemed to be in the national interest. Caiaphas, with Pilate, thought that if the Jesus Movement got out of control, there would be no telling where it might go.

Why was a detachment of Roman soldiers sent to arrest Jesus when the Temple police should have been sufficient? Pilate and Caiaphas did not know how many armed men made up Jesus' "bodyguard" and his company of retainers. Therefore, Pilate, sent an overwhelming array of military personnel, so that any attempt at resistance would be immediately crushed. Yet Pilate included the Temple police because he wanted to involve the religious authorities in the arrest and later Jewish trial of Jesus to indicate that the leading Jews were in agreement with the Roman governor that Jesus was a threat to law and order.

Notes

[1] According to Josephus, the procurator Gessius Florus outdid Pontius Pilate as an unscrupulous murderer of defenseless Jews. Because some hoodlums in the crowd had used unbecoming language when Festus spoke, he ordered the high priests to arrest the guilty parties under threat of their own lives, if they failed to do so. Angered by their pleas for mercy, he allowed his soldiers to plunder the upper marketplace with the loss of several thousand lives. This, according to Josephus in *The Wars of the Jews* 2,14,8.

[2] In 1990 the tomb of the Caiaphas family was discovered. It contained twelve ossuaries, one of them belonging to *yhwsp br qyp*, that is, Joseph son of Caiaphas. From Michael D. Coogan, *The Oxford Companion to the Bible*, edited by Bruce M. Metzger and Michael D. Coogan (New York: Oxford University Press, 1993), 97.

[3] Even the whole nation is called Son of God (Hosea 11:1; Mt 2:15).

[4] Based on legality and the rules of order found in the Mishna in 200 CE, a trial for a capital offense should not be held at night, and the decision to condemn and carry out punishment should not take place on the same day. Certainly, no criminal should be publicly executed on the eve of a Sabbath or on a festival such as Passover. This is the judgment of Paul Winter (On the Trial of Jesus) cited by Gaalyah Cornfield, ed., in *The Historical Jesus: A Scholarly View of the Man and His World* (New York: Macmillan, 1982), 163. Assuming that the trial of Jesus took place as described in the gospels, Winter concludes that "in one single session, the Sanhedrin managed to break every rule in the book."

But was there a formal trial? How could the Sanhedrin's seventy members be assembled at a moment's notice in the middle of the night, when they lived all over the city and in the distant suburbs at a time when almost all would have gone to bed three or four hours earlier? See H. Cohen, *The Trial and Death of Jesus* (New York: Harper & Row, 1971).

Chapter Twenty-three

JUDAS THE TRAITOR

If Jesus Knew, Why Did He Choose Him?

O f one thing we can be sure, Jesus did not choose Judas in order to have a disciple who would betray him, someone who would be an instrument in bringing about his death for the salvation of the world. It is unthinkable that Jesus would "use" another human being in that way. When he chose Judas, he had every reason to believe that he would be an asset in his mission to the disinherited. I do not believe that Judas was "fated" to turn traitor, although the Gospel writers may give that impression.

Historically, speculation has been rife concerning the reasons why Judas betrayed Jesus. The lesson to be learned from the turnaround in Judas is that good men occasionally turn bad, that the promise of youth is no guarantee of a virtuous later life. Aristotle said that no life should be called happy until it is over, when that person could no longer sin or suffer. It is only when we look back from the end viewpoint that we can we say that an individual's life has been tragic or blessed with good fortune. After one is safely dead, the worst is presumably over, unless there are postmortem sanctions. The life of Judas ended in a violent death. Overall, his was not a happy successful life; and was the kind of life Jesus wanted desperately to save.

Judas the Outsider

Just as Peter is listed first in the catalogue of the apostles' names, the man Judas appears last. The evangelists could not deny that one of the twelve had betrayed Jesus, so they list Judas Iscariot ('Ισκαριωθ in Greek) at the end of the list. Iskariot was not the man's surname; it probably refers to his place of origin. He is called Son of Simon Iskariot, or Simon from Kariot, provided the genitive, 'Ισκαριωτου, is taken to refer to his place of origin, rather than simply stand in apposition to the father's given name (Jn 6:71). Later, Judas is called "*the* Iskariot" (Jn 12:4), much as we would speak of Zorba the Greek. The

219

root of the name is *kariot*, so that Judas would be referred to as "the man from Kariot."

If kariot is a place-name, where is the place? There were three villages that bear a similar name south and east of Jerusalem. There was kiriath-Arba in Judea. On the far side of the Jordan River and the Dead Sea we find Keriathaim and Kerioth. The latter is in Moab and comes closest to Iskariot, or Is-karioth, spelled with a Greek theta.

Was Judas a Moabite, that is, from a land that was at times an enemy of the Jews, or was he a Judean?[1] In either case, he would have been the only one among the Twelve who was not a Galilean. This, conceivably, could have contributed to Judas' feeling that he was an outsider, a "stranger." The fact that he carried the purse also may be significant. Perhaps the other apostles did not care to carry around with them coins with the graven image of Caesar stamped on them, because the Emperor was held to be a deity. But there were times and places when it was important to have the coin of tribute available. Under Roman rule everything in Judea and Samaria was taxed. So Judas may have become purse-bearer by default, especially if he was less sensitive than others to the significance of the coin. He was certainly more calculating than the rest of the apostles.

Apparently, carrying the purse proved to be a source of temptation. John in his Gospel remarks that Judas used to steal from the money that was put in the purse (Jn 12:6). Judas is said to have protested vigorously on the occasion when Mary, the sister of Martha and Lazarus, poured extremely costly ointment on the feet of Jesus. "Why," asks Judas, "was this perfume not sold for three hundred denarii and the money given to the poor?" (Jn 12:5). John adds that he said this not because he cared about the poor, but because he was a thief. Judas' criticism brings a sharp rejoinder from Jesus. "Leave her alone," he says, noting that she is anticipating his burial when his body would be anointed with myrrh and aloes. Taking the words out of Judas' mouth, he continues. "The poor you always have with you, but you do not always have me" (Jn 12:7–9).

Interestingly, neither Mark nor Matthew identifies the disciple who complained. In fact, they hold that several were involved in murmuring and using angry words, and they do not hesitate to scold the woman for her extravagance (Mk 14:5). Only John identifies the culprit and names Judas as the one who complained and was reproached by Jesus. Shortly after this incident Judas goes to the chief priests and asks them what they would give him if he delivers Jesus into their hands. Having been awarded thirty pieces of silver, he looks for an opportunity to betray him (Mt 26:14–16).

The Last Supper

John's account of Judas' behavior at the Last Supper is the most complete. He begins by declaring that "the devil had already put it into the heart of Judas, son of Simon the Iskariot, to betray him" (Jn 13:2). This does not prevent Judas from allowing Jesus to wash his feet in the symbolic action whereby Jesus seeks to teach his disciples that there should be no distinction between masters and servants. Those in authority should be ready and willing to serve other members of the community. Peter, as we know, stands up and at first does not allow his esteemed teacher to wash his feet. Judas remains silent. Still, one cannot help wondering what may have gone through the mind of Judas, knowing that he would soon betray Jesus, while watching him act as a servant. Maybe he despised Jesus for lowering himself.

Later, in the course of the Last Supper, Jesus remarks ominously, "Truly I tell you, one of you will betray me, one who is eating with me. For the Son of Man goes as it is written, but woe to him by whom the Son of Man is betrayed" (Mk 14:21). The apostles, hearing these words, look dubiously at one another, wondering who it is that Jesus means. He says that the traitor is one, among others, "who is dipping bread into the bowl with me" (Mk 14:20). This could have been any-one of the twelve. But it is not enough to satisfy Peter. He motions to the Beloved Disciple who is reclining next to Jesus, wanting him to find out to whom Jesus is referring. In John's account it is Jesus him-self who dips a piece of bread into the sauce in the bowl and hands it to Judas. The Beloved Disciple understands the significance of the gesture but the others, including Peter, do not understand. Peter three times denies that he has ever known Jesus before the night is over. But for the moment he is confident that he is not the traitor. Indeed, were he to find out that it was Judas, he might have been tempted to attack and throttle him. Peter was a man capable of violence, as the evening's events would soon prove, when, in the Garden of Gethsemane, he attacks the high priest's servant with a sword (Jn 18:10).

To eliminate the chance of violence during his last meal on earth, Jesus tells Judas, when he gets up to leave, to carry out his chore as quickly as possible. This gives Peter and the others the impression that

Judas, because he holds the purse, is being told to buy some bread or give something to the poor.

Judas the Stranger Buys a Field

Judas must hurry. He must get back to the palace of Caiaphas, join a company of Roman and Jewish soldiers and lead them to the place in the country where Jesus and his disciples will be staying for Passover season. But why did Judas decide to betray Jesus? Was it just for the bounty money that he would receive, thirty pieces of silver, the price of a slave? There must have been other reasons, and several come to mind. First, Judas could see that the actions of Jesus were apt to lead to his undoing. He had affronted the high priests by his attack on the Temple, whether physical or merely verbal, and his entry into Jerusalem on Palm Sunday, when he was hailed as "King of the Jews," was enough to alarm Pilate. The worldly wisdom of Judas the stranger, the non-Galilean, told him to save himself when the opportunity offered itself. He did not want to be caught in the company of Jesus when disaster struck. By offering to help arrest him, he would prove that he was no Galilean.

Secondly, not all of Jesus' close disciples were natural-born pacifists including Judas. He lost face in Galilee when it became clear to many that he was not going to lead an insurrection against Rome and Roman rule.[2] Judas may have been among those awaiting the call to action, only to learn that Jesus would have no part in any kind of armed rebellion. "All who take the sword," warns Jesus, "will perish by the sword" (Mt 26:52). That was a disappointment and reason enough to make the more eager fighters feel frustrated. Finally, Jesus had publicly chided Judas when the apostle complained about the waste of good money on an anointing when an equivalent amount could have been given to the poor. Judas was a practical man who felt that pouring ointment on a man's feet whose perfume could not last for more than a day was wasteful, lavish, and improvident. He was convinced that he was right and that Jesus was wrong in defending the woman.

The role of an informer or traitor is not a comfortable one. When Judas approaches Jesus in the Garden of Gethsemane at the head of a contingent of armed men, it will not be easy to kiss him, for that was the sign agreed upon for identifying him in the dark among his disciples. Judas says, "The one I will kiss is the man" (Mk 14:44). Jesus does not resist, but wonders that one of his close disciples would stoop to betray him with a kiss, the symbol of love and friendship (Lk 22:48). John in his Gospel does not allow Jesus to be betrayed with a kiss. Instead, when the would-be captors announce that they are seeking Jesus of Nazareth, Jesus identifies himself, declaring, "*Eγω eiμi.*" This is usually translated as, "It is I," or "I am he." In John's Gospel it is the divine name. God is the supreme I AM. Thus, when Moses asks the Lord who he should tell the people of Israel sent him to lead them out of Egypt, he is to say to the Israelites, "I AM sent me" (Ex 3:14). As he does elsewhere in John's Gospel, Jesus here identifies himself as the One Who Is, as I AM (Cf. Ex 4:25, 8:28, 8:62, 10:7). The moment Jesus says this all the soldiers fall to the ground immobilized by the awesome presence of Jesus.[3] Once recovered, they bind him and lead him to the quarters of the high priests Annas and Caiaphas.

Perhaps Judas thinks Jesus will find a way to save himself, as he has done on so many other occasions. But this time it does not happen. Jesus is condemned to the cross. It is only then that Judas realizes the enormity of what he has done. Matthew says that he takes the thirty pieces of silver back to the Temple. Wringing his hands and declaring that he has betrayed innocent blood, he throws the silver pieces down in the Temple and, departing, "he went and hanged himself" (Mt 27:5). Matthew then goes on to indicate what is done with the money. "But the chief priests, taking the pieces of silver said, 'It is not lawful for us to put them in the treasury, since they are blood money.'" After conferring together, they use it to buy the potter's field as a place to bury strangers.[4] "Then was fulfilled what had been spoken through the prophet Jeremiah, 'And they took the thirty pieces of silver, the price of one on whom a price had been set, on whom some of the people of Israel had set a price, and gave them for the potter's field, as the Lord commanded me'" (Mt 27:9–10).

Curiously, there is no mention of thirty pieces of silver in Jeremiah, although he mentions seventeen pieces in one place (Jer 32:9). The potter's field makes its appearance in Jeremiah, and there is mention of a purchase. The prophet is described as going down to a potter's house and watching the potter at his wheel (Jer 18:2–4). Fourteen chapters later, the prophet devotes eleven verses describing how he acquires a field by purchase from his cousin Hanimal (Jer 32:6–16). Zechariah, not mentioned by Matthew, refers to thirty shekels of silver, the price of a slave. No longer willing to work for his overlords, Zechariah demands his just wages. "So they weighed out as my wages thirty shekels of silver. Then the Lord said to me, 'Throw it into the treasury'—this lordly price at which I was valued by them. So I took the thirty shekels of silver and threw them into the treasury, in the house of the Lord" (Zech 11:12–13).

By carefully rereading all of the above quotes, one can sort out all the key words and phrases used by Matthew, drawn equally from Jeremiah and Zechariah. They are potter, purchase, field, thirty pieces of silver, the worth of one on whom a price had been set, the Temple or house of the Lord, and throw them down in the treasury. It may be that all any of the evangelists knew about a man called Judas was that he betrayed Jesus for a price and later committed suicide. Matthew says that he hanged himself. Luke in Acts writes of Judas, "Now this man acquired a field with the reward of his wickedness; and falling headlong, he burst open in the middle and all his bowels gushed out" (Acts 1:18). Unlike Matthew's Judas who hangs himself, Luke says that his entrails gush out when he falls upon rocks. Casting a man from a precipice and hurling him headlong, letting gravity do the job, exonerates to some extent those who have stoned a sinner.[5] Did Judas "stone" himself, or was he perhaps murdered by being pushed from a high place and sent headlong to his death? David Flusser thinks the latter may have happened.[6]

So Judas, a stranger among Galileans, dies. With his bounty money he indirectly purchases the potter's field for burying strangers. Peter, in Acts, points to the irony of the situation when he says of Judas, "now this man *purchased a field* with the reward of his wickedness" (Acts 1:18). Indeed, Judas may have been buried in his own field; for after his suicide, or murder, his body must have been buried somewhere. For the evangelists, all of this happened to fulfill the word of the prophets. John has Jesus apply to Judas the forty-first Psalm where David laments, "Even my bosom friend in whom I trusted, who ate my bread, has lifted his heel against me" (Jn 13:18; Ps 41:9). The suicide of Judas is prefigured in the death of Ahitophel. He betrays King David and hangs himself (2 Sam 17:23).

Luke, in Acts, using scripture as predictive of the future, says that, after the defection of Judas, Matthias is chosen by lot to replace him among the Twelve; for it is written in the Book of Psalms, "Let another take his position" (Acts 1:20; Ps 109:8). As elsewhere in the New Testament, events, passages, and personages in the Hebrew Scriptures serve as prophetic models, or types, anticipating future events. There is supposed to be an organic continuity between the new and the old. Jesus, referring to Judas, says, "I know whom I have chosen" (Jn 13:18) and then John cites the forty-first Psalm to indicate that the defection of Judas was foreknown (Ps 41:9).

Excursus on the Role of the Prophetic Model in Apologetics

To ask whether the betrayal by Judas and other events in the life of Jesus were predestined in the strict sense of the word would be to enter on an unhealthy discussion of something like Greek fate in a Christian context, along with the question of God's foreknowledge. Does God foresee the future and let it happen, or does God pull strings and predetermine the future and arrange for events to happen? In the latter case, one would have to assume that, because Jesus had to die for the sins of the world, several people—Judas, Caiaphas, Pilate— had to play their part in bringing about his death.

The fact that the evangelists, early Christians, and some fundamentalists once believed or even now believe that events in the life of Jesus were foreknown and predetermined does not make it so. The Hebrew Scriptures constitute a large pond in which to fish. Parallels between what happened in the past and in the career of Jesus are not hard to find. Homilists today regularly cite scriptural passages that seem to bear on contemporary events. Revivalists love to dwell on the Book of Revelation in which they claim that they find mystical numbers and names that predict the present and the future.

The evangelists relied heavily on the prophetic dimension of scripture. It was not sufficient for them to proclaim the Gospel and assert that Jesus wrought miracles, died, and rose again. Something more "objective" than their private, sectarian convictions was needed. What could be more factual and objective than scripture texts penned in black and white and written hundreds of years before the first century CE? Did they not foretell in type and figure the coming of Christ and did they not outline in advance the main elements ultimately realized in his conception, birth, life, and death? Surely, the principal reason why the Christian Bible contains the Hebrew Scriptures is because they are thought to prove that Jesus was the Expected One. After all, is God not the Lord of History? Would he not have seeded the older Scriptures with prophetic texts that certify Jesus as Messiah? Past events are often pregnant with the future; they cast their shadows before them. Such was the mind of the evangelists, and perhaps to some extent of Jesus too. Judas' betrayal was, in a perverse way, the carrying out of the will of God, for so it had been written.

Today we are less inclined than the ancients to see the course of history as written in advance by the hand of God. Mark, as indicated earlier, has Jesus declare, "For the Son of Man goes as it is written of him, but woe to that one by whom the Son of Man is betrayed" (Mk 14:21). Can a text from the past legislate for the future free acts of man? Is anyone ever caught in the web of circumstances with no way out because "it is written"? A similarity between a past event and the present does not mean that the present one was inevitable.

Are we dealing, then, with prophecy historicized? I do not doubt that someone betrayed Jesus, perhaps even with a kiss; that he was scourged and mocked by cruel soldiers because of the rumor that he had claimed, or that his followers claimed for him, the title, "King of the Jews." Such a false pretender deserved to be crowned with laurel or some other mock makeshift wreath. The branches of a thorn bush nearby might have to do. No doubt, Jesus was forced to carry the crossbeam that would be lifted up onto the scaffold on which he would be crucified. On the trek to Calvary, someone would carry before him the titulus that would be placed at the top of the cross, indicating the nature of the charge against him. That others were crucified with Jesus is not surprising. Though none of the apostles was present at the scene of Jesus' crucifixion, some of his many friends and followers must have witnessed and reported it to one or more of the apostles, which became an oral tradition.

But the fact remains that the evangelists used scriptural models to flesh out what they knew about a typical Roman execution. Putting these two sources together, they could in all probability create a likely account of what might have taken place on Calvary. Even the "last words" of Jesus, such as forgiving his executioners and commending his spirit to his Father before expiring, could appropriately be placed in the mouth of Jesus because they are in harmony with the overall thrust of his teaching. Professor Crossan has steadily maintained that, where the passion narrative is concerned, we are dealing with prophecy historicized.[7] But it could very well be the case that history remembered, by way of an oral tradition based on the testimony of eyewitnesses, might turn out to be not too far removed from what the Gospels tell us actually took place on the occasion of Jesus' crucifixion, except for the astrophysical phenomena, such as the sun being darkened, the earth quaking, the tombs being opened, and the veil of the Temple being rent in two. These are standard symbolic props for describing a historically important event.

Getting back to Judas, there is a "Greek streak"[8] in the way the evangelists play on the inevitability of his defection. After the event, they go back and search the scriptures to find something that nearly matches what took place. Sometimes the parallel is striking; oftentimes it is strained. The texts dealing with the betrayal of Judas are more contrived than usual.

But before we put Judas to rest, may it not be that his self-slaughter was but a pitiful way of punishing himself for what he had done? Was it an act of repentance? Why should he kill himself, unless his self-hatred for his betrayal drove him to it? Once Jesus was dead, Judas did not know how to bring him back to life again. All he could do was to offer his own life as a feeble way of saying, "I'm sorry." The Jesus who forgave all of his enemies would not have excluded the distraught Judas after the deed. Jesus loved Judas as only God can love even his most wayward children. Perhaps Judas was so ashamed that he despaired of forgiveness because his sin was so great. In his favor is the fact that he at least recognized his crime. I am among those who believe that he was forgiven and that in the night of his despair, he would one day awaken to find himself in the arms of the Jesus he had betrayed.

Notes

[1] There were on-and-off wars between Moab and the kings of Judah and Israel. In 2 Kings 3:25, it is said that the kings of Judah, Israel, and Edom thoroughly destroyed Moab. They leveled everything, even stopping up the springs. On the other hand, the fragmented Moabite stele found in 1868 celebrates King Mescha of Moab and his wresting territory from Omri, the king of Israel. See *The Bible as History* by Werner Keller (New York: William Morrow and Co.; second revised edition, 1980), 234–235.

[2] The so-callerd impenitent towns, Chorazin, Bethsaida, and Capernaum, may have turned against Jesus when it became evident that he had no intention of leading a rebellion against Rome (Mt 11:20–22).

[3] The fact that the soldiers who came to arrest Jesus fell to the ground when Jesus announced who he was, is John's way of indicating that Jesus was in complete control of the situation, and that he allowed himself to be arrested because he had freely chosen to do so.

[4] "A place to bury strangers": Because many thousands of people came to Jerusalem three times a year or more, it was inevitable that someone would die while there, far from home. Because it was necessary to bury a deceased person on the day he or she died, there was need for a place to bury visitors.

5 James the brother of Jesus was "stoned" by being hurled from a high place, then clubbed to death, according to Eusebius. Jesus himself was led to a precipice to be cast down when he offended the townspeople of Nazareth (Lk 4:29).

6 David Flusser writes, "There were plenty of people at that time who would have repaid Judas in blood for having handed over a Jew to the Romans." See *Jesus, in collaboration with R. Stephen Notley* (Jerusalem: The Magnes Press, The Hebrew University; corrected and augmented, 1998), 143. A hanged man would not burst open in the middle. Judas may have been stoned, that is, cast headlong from a cliff, not voluntarily but forcibly by assassins.

7 Are we dealing with prophecy historicized or history remembered? John Dominic Crossan finds this a valid principle of discernment to be kept in mind, especially when one is dealing with the Passion narrative in the four gospels. See *The Historical Jesus: The Life of a Mediterranean Jewish Peasant* (1991), 375; also *Who Killed Jesus?* (1995), 1–38, and *The Birth of Christianity: Discovering What Happened in the Years Immediately after the Execution of Jesus* (1998), 521. The three books are published by HarperSanFrancisco in San Francisco.

8 "Greek streak":We see the cruel hand of ineluctable fate in the tragedies of Sophocles. People in the audience know that Oedipus will one day discover that he has killed his father and married his mother, for so had the fates decreed. Moira, one's portion in life, cannot be altered, not even by the gods. In the gospels and in the writings of St. Paul we are told that one event after another took place, "that the scripture might be fulfilled." For an analysis of the Greek concept of fate, see E.R. Dodds, *The Greeks and the Irrational* (Boston: Beacon Press, 1957), 6, 8, 38.

Chapter Twenty-four

PONTIUS PILATE

How a Rascal Became a Saint

The Jewish philosopher Philo, in the first part of his *Treatise on Virtue*, included the text of a letter sent earlier to the Emperor Gaius Caesar (Caligula, 37–41). The letter was composed by Herod Agrippa who, later, under the Emperor Claudius, became king of the whole of ancient Palestine, including Judea and Samaria. Philo's *Treatise*, which includes, "On the Embassy to Gaius," has Agrippa berating Pontius Pilate as "a man of very inflexible disposition, and very merciless as well as very obstinate."[1] Turning to his relation with people, Agrippa speaks of Pilate's "corruption, and his acts of insolence, and his rapine, and his habit of insulting people, and his cruelty, and his continual murders of people untried and uncondemned, and his never ending, and gratuitous, and most grievous inhumanity."[2]

Josephus' evaluation of Pilate was no better than Agrippa's. He recounts how, at a signal from Pilate, he had his soldiers disguised as laymen club to death many of those in the crowd who came to protest Pilate's impounding the Temple's money (*corban*) to build an aqueduct. Later, he had his soldiers and horsemen fall upon a group of Samaritans who were preparing to climb Mt Gerizim in search of some sacred vessels. He killed many of them in a pitched battle, and the rest who had tried to flee he slew in cold blood. As a result Vitellius, the Emperor's legate in Syria, compelled Pilate to go to Rome and answer charges of misconduct in office. We do not know what happened to Pilate after that. By the time he reached Rome, the Emperor Tiberias was dead.[3]

In spite of these unfavorable reports, Pilate, as previously indicated in chapter 22 held office for ten years over the High Priest Caiaphas. While there can be little doubt that Caiaphas had his own reasons for wanting to get rid of Jesus of Nazareth, according to John's Gospel it was Pilate who took the initiative and was the principal agent in the arrest and execution of Jesus.

If we turn now to the account of the trial of Jesus before Pilate, what could easily escape notice is the fact that, while Pilate makes no effort to save Jesus from the cross in the earliest Gospel, that of Mark, in both Luke and John, far from wanting to condemn Jesus, the prefect repeatedly tries to spare him. In Mark, Pilate poses three businesslike questions. He asks Jesus, "Are you the King of the Jews?" He next asks the bystanders whether he should release Jesus or Barabbas. When they cry "Barabbas," Pilate then asks the people what he should do with Jesus. They cry, "Crucify him!" (Mk 15:13).

Pilate does not argue or raise a finger to save Jesus. But in Luke's Gospel he tries ten maneuvers to have Jesus released (The numbers at the right refer to the verses in Luke's twenty-third chapter.):

1. "I find no basis for an accusation against this man." (4)

2. Pilate sends Jesus to Herod to avoid having to condemn him. (6)

3. When Jesus is returned from Herod, Pilate says again, "I have not found this man guilty of your charges against him." (14)

4. "Neither has Herod found him guilty." (15)

5. "He has done nothing to deserve death." (15)

6. "I will flog him [a lesser punishment] and release him." (16)

7. When the question of releasing Barabbas or Jesus was brought up, Luke says, "Pilate, wanting to release Jesus, addressed them again." (20)

8. When the crowd yells, "Crucify him!" Pilate again resists, saying, "Why,what evil has he done?" (22)

9. "I have found no grounds for the sentence of death." (22)

10. Pilate for a second times offers to flog Jesus and let him go. (22)

Pilate used one ploy after another, but the voices of the crowd prevailed, and Pilate reluctantly sent Jesus to the cross. Because Pilate had engineered the arrest of Jesus in collaboration with the servants of Caiaphas, it is most unlikely that he would suddenly have reversed himself and tried to save Jesus, once he had him in his power. But because Luke and John represent Pilate as valiantly trying to save

Jesus, even at the risk of his own career, he was subsequently raised to the altar in the Coptic Church and honored as a saint and martyr.

The Jews Did It

Because Pilate, who stands for the power of Rome, tried to release Jesus, responsibility for his arrest and crucifixion must lie with the Jews, an impression that all four Gospels communicate. In Matthew's Gospel, when Pilate washes his hands and declares, "I am innocent of this man's blood" (Mt 27:24), a frenzied mob of Jews cries out, "His blood be on us and on our children!" If this seems unlikely, because Jesus was so popular with the masses that his enemies were afraid of openly arresting him for fear of the people (Lk 22:2), still less plausible is the spectacle of a truly representative crowd of Jews, who were ground down under the heel of Rome, crying out, "We have no king but Caesar!" (Jn 19:15).

One must view with reserve the idea that an angry crowd of Jews bullied Pontius Pilate into crucifying a member of their own nation and a holy man in the bargain. And even if those who are represented as crying out for the crucifixion of Jesus actually did so, they would have been among the retainers (*hyperētai*) of Caiaphas and in no sense representative of the vast majority of Jews living at that time. Aside from the people who, with enthusiasm, hailed Jesus as king on Palm Sunday, Jesus had many Jewish friends and supporters, including members of the lower clergy (Acts 6:7), a number of Pharisees, certain wealthy and well-placed men and women, and, of course, his own very numerous and loyal supporters.[4]

Why blame the Jews, without distinction, for the death of Jesus? It is a libelous accusation that is rooted in certain Gospel texts and has persisted for the better part of twenty centuries, and has caused untold anguish for Jewish men, women, and children.[5] Even if the entire population of Jerusalem stood before Pilate at six o'clock in the morning on Good Friday and cried out for the blood of Jesus, the next generation of Jews would still not be guilty of his death, nor would the Jews living in Galilee or in the distant cities of the Roman Empire be a party to his execution. But these prejudices have long lives and they can be enormously destructive. No doubt, the Jewish high priests cooperated with Pilate in the arrest and execution of Jesus, but the members of the Sadducean high priestly family were anything but representative Jews. They were roundly hated for being tools of Rome and, not being of Zadokite lineage, they were seen as usurpers of the office of high priest and without legitimacy.[6]

The Gentiles Are Coming

The first Christians were overwhelmingly Jews. But after the fall of Jerusalem, more converts were made among the Gentiles than among Jews. Soon the Church, with the influx of Greek-speaking members became rapidly Hellenized. It is no accident that all four Gospels were written in Greek, the lingua franca of the Greco-Roman world. St. Paul was a Roman citizen and was not above taking comfort in that fact. Other Greeks and Romans who were loyal to the Empire would have been repelled when they learned that Jesus was executed as a criminal with two other troublemakers in accordance with Roman law. To reassure potential converts, it was imperative to indicate that the Roman governor of Judea, who stood for Roman justice, did everything in his power to save Jesus from the bloodthirsty Jewish mob that cried out for his death. According to Matthew, Pontius Pilate, eventually recognizing that "he could do nothing, rather that a riot was about to break out, took a basin of water and washed his hands before the crowd, saying, 'I am innocent of this man's blood; see to it yourselves'" (Mt 27:24). Lest potential Gentile converts think that Jesus might have been an enemy of the State, Pilate, one of Rome's most unsavory operatives, is represented as putting his own career on the line in an effort to save Jesus, "for he knew that it was out of jealousy that they [the Jewish hierarchy] had handed him over" (Mt 27:18).

Luke, the evangelist who favors Pilate the most, was probably a Gentile convert. Clearly well educated, he may have been a Roman citizen like Paul. This could have influenced him in a desire to exonerate Rome and its leading official in Judea from the charge of having killed Jesus. So the blame must lie elsewhere, that is, with the Jews.

A second consideration in the effort to shift responsibility for the death of Jesus away from Rome and onto the Jews was the precarious state of the first Christians in the Roman Empire. After they had ceased to be Jews in the eyes of both Jews and Gentiles, they lost their exemption from the requirement to honor the Roman gods and acknowledge the deity of the Emperor. Christians could not do this. So, very early, they were looked on as enemies of the genius of Rome, and persecution followed. So it behooved the evangelists to make sure that, if any of the Gospels fell into hostile hands, Jesus would be seen as friendly to Rome and a victim of Jewish intolerance at a time when Jews were already under a cloud in the Empire because of the Jewish War of Rebellion against Rome. Lest anyone forget what the Jews had done, Titus, the victorious Roman general who presided over the destruction of the city and the Temple, took to Rome for his triumph the sacred vessels from the Temple, a large number of slaves, and some seven hundred handsome youths, who were to be exhibited before the people of Rome.[7]

The Christians' Dilemma

Christians might cling to their Jewish allegiance and be safe from persecution, although few synagogues welcomed them, or they could definitively separate themselves from the Jews in order to be in no way associated with the rebellion against Rome. In the latter case, they lost their exemption from emperor worship. To counter this liability, it was important for Christians to be seen as loyal subjects of Rome. A superficial pro-Roman face can even be put on Jesus' statement, "Render to Caesar the things that are Caesar's" (Mt 22:21). To a Roman official this could sound very loyal. Paul urged Christians to "pay taxes to whom taxes are due" (Rom 13:7). But to a pious Jew that could only mean, "Render to Caesar nothing whatsoever," because Rome had no right to tribute money.

The Gospel writers had good reason to want to distance themselves and Jesus from "the Jews" to demonstrate the loyalty of Christians in the Empire at a time when Jews were in disfavor in Rome and many potential converts were Gentiles. Thus, it was necessary to shift the blame for the execution of Jesus from Roman authority to "the perfidious Jews."[8] Because it could not be denied that Jesus had been crucified "under Pontius Pilate," the best thing to do was to portray Pilate in the best light possible, as a man who courageously resisted the demands of the Jews for the blood of Jesus, a ruler who sent him to the cross with the greatest reluctance, and only to avoid a riot among the people.

On balance, it is hard to deny that Jewish hierarchy cooperated in bringing about the death of Jesus, and that Pilate had the final say in deciding whether he would live or die. A Roman of lower rank, he was probably no better or worse than many another Roman official sent out to govern sternly in remote parts of the Empire. It is unfortunate that the effort to redefine Pilate as an official of high integrity, a man known for cruelty, corruption, and "his continual murders of people untried and uncondemned," has resulted in bringing down on the heads of the Jewish people nearly seventeen hundred years of persecution and obloquy as Christ-killers and even deicides. I say seventeen hundred years, more or less, because the Jews fared fairly well in the Roman Empire until after the time of the Christian Emperor Constantine. Under him Christianity became a licit religion (*religio licita*) and, under later Emperors, the State Religion. At that point, the Jews lost many of their civil rights, and their situation became progressively worse with the succeeding centuries. The mass slaughter of Jews during the time of the Crusades culminated in Hitler's "Final Solution" with the goal of total extermination. Within the past few years leading Christian Churches have extended the hand of friendship to the Jewish people, acknowledging past injustices, and working toward better relations in the future. What they cannot do is alter the Christian scriptures with their historically and culturally conditioned anti-Jewish bias. The best that one can do for the future of Christianity is to tell people the unvarnished truth, that the Gospels are biased against the Jews. It will take courage on the part of pastors and preachers to explain the origin of this bias to their congregations. But it is important for the sake of truth that all Christians understand this. With that settled once and for all, we can then begin to concentrate on friendly Jewish–Christian relations and on the teaching of Jesus as the flower of Jewish spirituality.

Notes

[1] See "On the Embassy to Gaius," in *The Works of Philo: Complete and Unabridged*, translated by C.D. Yonge (Peabody, MA: Hendrickson Publishers, 1993), 784, #301–302.

[2] Loc. Cit.

[3] Josephus, *The Antiquities of the Jews* 18,4,2; *The Wars of the Jews* 2,9,4.

[4] David Flusser, a leading Jewish New Testament scholar, calls attention to expressions of sympathy, especially in Luke's Gospel, on the part of various segments of the Jewish population while Jesus hung on the cross. While the rulers and some of the soldiers may have mocked Jesus, Luke says that "a great number of people followed [Jesus] and among them were women who were beating their breasts and wailing for him." Far from scoffing, many Jews stood by the cross watching in silence, including Jesus' acquaintances and the women who had followed him from Galilee. One Jewish criminal crucified with Jesus declared him innocent, as did the Roman centurion. When Jesus breathed his last, "all the crowds who had gathered there for this specta-

cle saw what had taken place, and returned home beating their breasts" (Lk 23:27, 41, 47–49). See David Flusser, *Jesus, in collaboration with R. Steven Notley* (Jerusalem: Magnes Press; 2nd edition, Corrected and augmented, 1998), 224. Luke in Acts continues to insist on Pilate's desire to free Jesus (Acts 3:13).

[5] Two books, one by a Roman Catholic priest and the other by a former Anglican priest, document the history of Christian anti-Semitism: *The Anguish of the Jews: Twenty-three Centuries of Antisemitism* by the late Edward H. Flannery (Mahwah, NJ: The Paulist Press, 1985), and *Christian Antisemitism: A History of Hate* by William Nicholls (Northvale, NJ: Jason Aronson, 1986). While Nazism was a pagan movement, inimical to all religion, the long tradition of Christian anti-Semitism was largely responsible for the atmosphere that made the Holocaust possible. Exclusive of the several million Poles, Gypsies, and physically and mentally defective men and women, six million Jews died in Nazi concentration camps and gas chambers.

To get an idea of what six million human beings looks like in the concrete, picture a column of six million people marching three abreast with a yard between them. Their marching bodies take up another yard for a total of two yards. The moving column of threes would reach from New York to Utah, or from New Orleans to Idaho, just short of 2,272 miles. Driving 400 miles a day, it would take nearly six days to travel the length of the column. Add three million non-Jews and you are on your way from New Orleans to Alaska.

[6] The Dead Scrolls Community at Kirbet Qumran withdrew from the cities and the Temple in protest. They believed in the coming of two Messiahs, one a priest and the others a king–warrior. They set up their "Temple–in–Exile" at the northwest end of the Dead Sea. They were not alone in regarding the Temple high priests as usurpers. Most of the people, however, accepted them because the Temple service was important and no other substitute was available.

[7] Josephus, *The Wars of the Jews* 7,5,3.

[8] Although "The perfidious Jews" was retained in the Roman Catholic liturgy for Good Friday until Pope John XXIII eliminated it in the middle of the twentieth century, it is not quite as bad as it sounds. "Perfidious" in this case does not mean treacherous or deceitful, but "unbelieving," for example, in the divinity of Christ. The same word could be applied to Moslems. The word occurs in a prayer for Jews: Oremus *et pro perfidis Judaeis*. In a somewhat twisted way one is praying for one's adversaries.

Chapter Twenty-five

BARABBAS

Would Pilate Have Released an Insurrectionist Murderer?

Many scripture scholars hold that the name "Barabbas" is an invention of the evangelists.[1] As for the custom of releasing a prisoner of the people's choice at festival time, it cannot be verified outside the Gospels. However, the idea of commuting the sentence of a prisoner was not unusual. The Gospels say, however, that Barabbas was no ordinary prisoner. Mark and Luke say that he was involved in sedition and had committed murder (Mk 15:7; Lk 23:19). Matthew is content with saying that he was a "notorious" prisoner (Mt 27:16) without mentioning any particular crime. The Fourth Gospel, likewise, does not mention the crime of Barabbas, and it gives no indication that he was ever actually released (Jn 18: 39–40). It is possible that Pilate released neither Jesus nor Barabbas, but sent both of them to the cross. From this it would follow that Barabbas would have been one of the men crucified with Jesus. Certainly, if Barabbas had been guilty of sedition and was one of those mentioned in Mark's Gospel who was involved in "the insurrection" (Mk 15:7), we can be sure that Pilate would not have released him.

Just because we have no other records outside of the Gospels to back up the custom of releasing a prisoner at festival time does not mean that some such custom did not exist. There must have been hundreds of petty customs that were in place two thousand years ago in distant Palestine about which we have no knowledge. To win favor with people under Roman rule, it would not be untypical of the Roman legal system to call for the release of a prisoner, for example, from debtor's prison, at festival time. After all, the Jews were commanded to forgive all debts at the start of the Sabbatical year. Releasing a prisoner during Passover for a minor infraction of the law or because of a debt is not as farfetched as some might think. However, we are certainly right in holding that Pilate would never have released anyone who had been engaged in anti-Roman activity, including violence and murder.

So, that leaves us with the suspicion that Mark, followed and copied by Matthew and Luke, heard about the idea of an amnesty for certain prisoners at festival time and during the Sabbatical year. They then introduce the idea that the innocent Jesus was sent to the cross in place of Barabbas. The murderer and great sinner was set free, and Jesus went to the cross in his stead. This theme will be developed further in the Excursus on Substitutionism.

Meanwhile, who was Barabbas? One charge against the actual existence of such a man is the fact that we seem to be dealing with a made-up name. Barabbas simply means "son of the father," which could apply to any man in existence. So there is a fair chance that the name is fictional. However, Robert W. Funk calls attention to the existence of ossuaries (bone boxes) from the first century with the name "Barabbas" clearly carved on the stone receptacle. So at least one argument against the man's existence has to be scrapped.[2]

Perhaps the evangelists did not know what the man's name really was and simply used a name that was in circulation. So I am not convinced that Barabbas is fictional and that no such person was involved in the trial of Jesus.

The *Nestle-Aland Novum Testamentum Graece et Latine* preserves a curious manuscript tradition. It holds that the full name of the man who was paired against Jesus also bore the name Jesus.[3] *The New Oxford Annotated Bible* also supports the inclusion of Jesus as the given name of Barabbas.[4] Pilate asks, "Whom do you want me to release, Jesus Barabbas or Jesus who is called Messiah?" Since the Fourth Gospel says nothing about the release of Barabbas, I contend that he was not released; or, if you prefer, he was released from prison and sent to the cross with Jesus. He may have been a freedom fighter and would be regarded as a martyr by the masses, but from Pilate's point of view he was an enemy of everything that symbolized Rome. For the moment Pilate was simply amusing himself when he asked the people, "Which Jesus do you want released?" He had not the slightest intention of releasing either of them.

Excursus on Substitutionism

Mark, Matthew, and Luke saw in the figure of Barabbas a lesson to be learned, something homilists have made use of for centuries. Like Barabbas, we are sinners. We are the ones who should have been sent to the cross, but Jesus went in our place. This is the essence of the theory of salvation known as Substitutionism: Jesus took upon himself the punishment that was our due; by substituting for us, he paid the price required by an all-just Creator for the remission of sin. Mark and Matthew develop this theme when they have Jesus say, "The Son of Man came not to be served but to serve, and give his life a ransom for many" (Mk 10:45; Mt 20:28). Jesus' death thus became a ransom payment, an act of expiation for the sins of men.[5]

For Origen and Gregory the Great, Satan had kept men in dire bondage until the time of Christ. He was finally defeated by the death of Jesus who, being innocent, invalidated Satan's hold on humanity. St. Anselm (1033–1109) rejected this theory, saying that the ransom had to be paid to God the Father, the one who had been offended by the sins of men. A legalistic form of the Ransom motif holds that the divine books had to be balanced. God must, in justice to himself, require satisfaction for the outrage to His Divine Majesty resulting from Adam's sin and ours. The only one equal to the task of giving due satisfaction was God's only Son. He was sent to suffer and die in order that through the death of one just man the Father would receive the kind of satisfaction that his mercy and justice required.

Thoughtful people today are uncomfortable with this kind of accounting system. Among the factors that led to the death of Jesus was his program of support for the poor, outcast members of his society. His cry, "Woe to you who are rich" (Lk 6:24) threatened the privileged classes, both Jewish and Roman. His talk of a "kingdom to come" sounded far too much like a regime that would replace the princedom of Herod Antipas and subvert Roman rule. It convinced very few of those who exercised power to be assured that Jesus' kingdom was "not of this world" (Jn 18:36), when it was obvious that Jesus envisioned a new social order in this world. Although he might sternly order his adherents not to go about declaring that he was the Messiah–King (Mk 8:30), his admonitions were ignored by the more zealous patriots.

John the Baptist, Jesus' original mentor, had vigorously attacked the Temple Sadducean High Priests (Mt 3:7) and Herod Antipas (Mk 6:18). As heir to John's messianic movement, Jesus was under suspicion from the start by both the nation's secular and religious rulers. His modest but very public "triumphal entry" into Jerusalem seated on a donkey, following the prophetic model described in Zechariah (Zech 9:9), where a victorious warrior king enters the city in humble guise, only confirmed the suspicion of those who heard the shouts of the people who hailed Jesus as David's heir and rightful King of the Jews.

Not to be overlooked is the wording of the notice posted over the cross of Jesus in three languages. It declared that the crucified man was condemned to death on a charge of sedition, of pretending to be King of the Jews. Whether or not Jesus ever claimed to be king, those who died with him were insurrectionists. The dragnet that brought them to prison also caught Jesus.

The last thing Pilate needed to put an end to his career was to have been proven dilatory in arresting and condemning the apparent ringleader of a potential rebellion. So he did not have to think twice about what to do to halt Jesus' "Kingdom" movement. The ambush that netted Jesus one moonlit night was one of several forays into the hills that trapped a number of those who would have been glad to co-opt Jesus and his movement and make them the focus and rallying point for heralding the coming of a kingdom free from Roman rule and foreign domination.

Pilate may have asked teasingly, "Which Jesus do you prefer?" and this gave Mark the inspiration to pit Jesus against Barabbas. We are Barabbas, sinful children of Adam, saved from our just punishment by the death of the innocent Jesus who substituted for us and became a whipping boy for our sake. This was already a well-developed thesis in the mind of St. Paul when he wrote that Jesus "was handed over to death for our trespasses" (Rom 4:25). There is a prophetic model for this, as we read in Isaiah: "He was wounded for our transgressions; . . . upon him was the punishment that made us whole; . . . and the Lord laid on him the iniquity of us all" (Isa 53:4–6). Paul dramatizes this when he declares that on the cross Jesus "became a curse for us" (Gal 3:13), and that "for our sake [God] made him to be sin who knew no sin" (2 Cor 5:21). Less rhetorically, Paul finally speaks from the heart when he says that he lives "by faith in the Son of God who loved me and gave himself for me" (Gal 2:20). This is the essence of Jesus' teaching: to give of oneself for love of others. That is what he did, and the true disciple should do nothing less.

Luke tells us that two men are crucified with Jesus, one on either side of him. One of the condemned men derides Jesus, saying, "'Are you the Messiah? Save yourself and us.' But the other rebuked him, saying, 'Do you not fear God, since you are under the same sentence of condemnation? And we indeed have been condemned justly, for we are getting what we deserve for our deeds, but this man has done nothing wrong'" (Lk 23:40–41). I suggest that "the good thief" was none other than Barabbas.

Notes

[1] The scholars who belong to The Jesus Seminar reject the historicity of the Barabbas incident out of hand. The account in the four gospels is printed in black, meaning that "This information is improbable; it does not fit verifiable evidence; it is largely or entirely fictive." *The Acts of Jesus: The Search for the Authentic Deeds of Jesus*, by Robert W. Funk (HarperSanFrancisco, 1998), 36–37, 153. "The Barabbas segment is wholly fictitious, in spite of the fact that the name Barabbas is actually attested on ossuaries (small stone coffins) from the period."

Raymond E. Brown, in his massive two-volume work, *The Death of the Messiah* (New York: Doubleday/Anchor, 1994) is hesitant. In the long section 34 in volume 1 on Barabbas, pp.787–820, he does not definitely discount some aspects of the Barabbas story. On page 820, he concludes rather weakly, saying that evil was chosen over the innocent Jesus, so that, "The story of Barabbas with a basis in fact was dramatized to convey that truth."

[2] Robert W. Funk seems to contradict himself when he holds that the name Barabbas is fictional, yet allows that it exists on ossuary boxes. See note 1 above.

[3] In the Greek text, Pilate asks the people which of the two men named Jesus they wanted released, "Jesoun ton Barabban e Jesoun ton legomenon Christon?" *Novum Testamentum: Graece et Latine* (Stuttgart: Deutsche Bibelgesellschaft, 1989, 1984), 81.

[4] See note "y" in the New Annotated Revised Standard Version for Matthew 27:17.

[5] For a condensed history of the theories on expiation and satisfaction, see Gerard S. Sloyan, *The Crucifixion of Jesus: History, Myth, Faith* (Minneapolis: Fortress, 1995), chapter 4.

Chapter Twenty-six

SIMON OF CYRENE

A Surprising Day for a Common Man

Simon, a man from Cyrene, present-day Shahat, in the province of Cyrenaica (Libya), happens to be on the road leading to the center of Jerusalem when he meets a party of soldiers who are leading Jesus out to be crucified. They are heading for the place of execution called Golgotha. This is an Aramaic word that means "skull," or "Place of the skull" (Mk 15:22). It may refer to the shape of a knobby rise in the midst of an old quarry or to the fact that a skull is a symbol of death. The Latin word, "Calvary," to designate the same place, is also related to the skull. In Latin *calva* means a bald head and suggests the skull beneath the scalp.

When Simon meets Jesus on his way to be executed, he is coming in from the country (*ap' agrou*). Because this is Passover season, he is probably staying with friends in the suburbs away from the overcrowded city or simply camping out. We have no reason to believe that he knew Jesus or even knew who he was, since he was but a visitor from another part of the Empire. The last thing he could have anticipated upon awakening that morning was that shortly before 9:00 A.M. he would be carrying another man's crossbeam to a place of execution. When Jesus could no longer carry his burden, Simon was compelled to carry it. He had no choice. A Roman soldier had the right to commandeer anyone he needed to carry out an unpleasant task.

When we see pictures portraying Jesus carrying his "cross" to Calvary, artists often represent him as bearing the whole instrument of execution over one shoulder. We see it as composed of a vertical beam that will be sunk in the ground supporting a horizontal crossbeam. It is unlikely that the Romans supplied each of the many victims they sent to the cross with the luxury of a complete instrument of torture. Nevertheless, what we often see on television are devout men in Jerusalem carrying imitation crosses during Holy Week. What a condemned man had to carry was only the crossbeam. It was laid on his shoulders with this outstretched arms tied to it at the wrists.

A sign or board bearing an inscription indicating the crime of the condemned man was carried before him as he walked to his death, or it might be hung around his neck. The sign placed over the cross of Jesus read, "Jesus of Nazareth, the King of the Jews." The chief priests complained about the wording, saying, "Do not write, 'The king of the Jews,' but this man said, 'I am the King of the Jews.'" Pilate answered, "What I have written I have written" (Jn 19:19–21). Pilate's wording was meant to be mockery. The evangelists took it to be a title Jesus richly deserved.

If Jesus was tied to the crossbeam, it must have weighed heavily on his wounded shoulders, neck, and arms. They had been flayed by leaded, leather thongs. Weakness would have caused Jesus to stumble and fall. The Stations of the Cross memorialize three such falls. When it was clear after several falls that Jesus could no longer carry the weight of the crossbeam, the soldiers guarding him looked around for a strong, healthy-looking young man. They spotted Simon and pressed him into service, because no Roman soldier would help.

So Jesus was probably untied from the crossbeam. Simon was then engaged to carry it in some fashion until they all reached the place of execution. There, the uprights were already in place, awaiting the hanging of the unfortunate men who were to die that day. It harrows the human spirit to dwell on the calculated cruelty of the Romans. The purpose of the scourging before crucifixion, for those who were not simply being punished and then released, was to cause the victim as much pain as possible while he was still alive and capable of suffering before being nailed to a cross. Even though Simon must have been familiar with crucifixions, actually carrying the instrument of death on his shoulders must have made a deep impression on him.

Isaac, carrying on his shoulders the wood that was to be used in a sacrifice in which he was to be the victim (Gen 22:6), has been traditionally seen as a prophetic model anticipating Jesus, who would carry the wood of the cross on which he would be sacrificed. "Carrying one's cross" became a symbol for the authentic disciple of Jesus. "He called the crowd with his disciples, and said to them, 'If any want to become my followers, let them deny themselves and take up their cross and follow me'" (Mt 16:24). The Fifth Station of the Way of the Cross represents Simon of Cyrene carrying the cross of Jesus. Not figuratively but literally, he took up and carried the *patibulum*, (transverse beam) to which Jesus would be nailed.

If Simon waited around with the ever-curious crowd that seems to be attracted by public executions, he must have come to realize that Jesus was no ordinary criminal. He prayed for his executioners and actually forgave them for what they were doing (Lk 23:34).

Simon, After His Experience on Calvary

It is all but certain that Simon and his two sons were converts to the Way, as the teaching of Jesus came to be called. Mark in his Gospel gives us the names of his two sons, Alexander and Rufus. So the three of them, the father and his two sons, were known to the community for which Mark's Gospel was intended (Mk 15:21). Not everyone gets the chance to carry the cross of Jesus. It must have been considered a great privilege for Mark's community to have in its midst, if not Simon himself, at least two of his sons. It is generally assumed that the Gospel according to Mark was composed in Rome and disseminated from there, which must have been where Alexander and Rufus lived. In fact, Paul concludes his Letter to the Romans asking to be remembered to Rufus whom he esteems as a chosen soul, and to his mother, "a mother to me also" (Rom 16:13).

The Rufus here may not be Simon's son and Alexander's brother. But the early Christian community in Rome could not have been very large. In fact, when Paul greets twenty-four of them in his Letter, this may very well exhaust the list of those who stood out, with Rufus, "chosen in the Lord," among them. What happened to their father? It is possible that he may have stayed in Cyrene or died before Paul wrote his letter to the Romans, around 56 CE, about a quarter of a century after the death of Jesus.

However, Simon may have kept his headquarters in Cyrene and become a missionary of sorts. Cyrene, like Alexandria, was a busy Mediterranean port with a large Jewish population. For them, Jerusalem was the center of the earth, and the sea passage from Cyrene to the Palestinian ports of Joppa and Gaza was not overly difficult. So we find Simon in Judea for Passover. Luke tells us that among those present at Pentecost were pilgrims from "the parts of Libya belonging to Cyrene" (Acts 1:10).

From Acts we also learn that in Paul's day among those who came to Antioch to preach the Word were some Cyrenaians, who proved to be very effective missionaries (Acts 11:20). Simon may have been among them. Indeed, it may have been he who brought the faith to

Cyrene and later spearheaded the preaching mission to Antioch. This is not as improbable as it might seem. Although separated by miles, these early Christian communities managed to keep in touch with one another. Long before Paul visited Rome, albeit under house arrest, there was a small but well-established Jewish Christian community there. It may have been the butt of an attack by Orthodox Jews, because Claudius (41–54 CE) expelled the Jews from Rome, making no distinction between Christians and Jews. Then in 62 Nero blamed the Christians, now distinct from the Jews, for setting fire to a large section of the city, a fire that Nero is said to have ordered to make room for his grandiose building plans. As a result, many Christians were exposed to the beasts in the Colosseum.

It was shortly after this that Mark wrote his Gospel, presumably in Rome with the mention of Alexander and Rufus. The fact that Paul does not mention Simon in his greetings to the Romans could be explained if Simon was among those Cyrenaians who went to Antioch to preach the Gospel. Luke (Acts 13:1) says that among the leading missionaries in Antioch was a certain Lucius of Cyrene and a coworker called Simon the Black (*Symeōn ho kaloumenos niger*). Presumably the man called Simon (Symeon) was dubbed "the black" because of the color of his skin, not because of the color of his hair, because most North Africans have black hair. Artists have portrayed Simon of Cyrene as white. But the Jews of the Diaspora lived in many different nations and climates. Today there are black Jews in Ethiopia, some of whom have emigrated from their own country to Israel. They are a standing refutation that Judaism is a religion based strictly on race. There are blond Jews, fair-skinned Irish Jews, and brown-skinned Jews in India. It would be interesting if Simon the Black and Simon of Cyrene were one and the same person. Short of that, we are told that the man who carried the cross of Jesus was an African.

Chapter Twenty-seven

LONGINUS

The Spearman: "A Gentile Has the Last Word"

W e do not know the name of the centurion who stood by the cross when Jesus died and declared, "Truly this man was God's Son!" (Mt 27:54). Tradition has dubbed him Longinus, the man with the spear, *Longchē* ($\lambda o\gamma\chi\eta$).[1]

Centurions were men of stature. Some, if they had been outstanding for services to the army and the Empire, would have been granted Roman citizenship.[2] They were in a class apart from the rough soldiers who served under them. The centurion in charge of the execution of Jesus would not have been engaged in the actual nailing of Jesus to the cross. That was a task for the soldiers. They were a crude lot, not above engaging in tomfoolery at the expense of a prisoner about to be executed. The centurion's role was to direct the procedure. He was less likely than the common soldiers to make sport of Jesus and plait for him a crown of thorns (Mk 15:17; Mt 27:29).

Although a centurion could be in charge of as many as a hundred men, he would not have employed a great number of soldiers to escort Jesus and the other two men to be crucified with him from Pilate's headquarters to Calvary. Bound to their transverse beams, the three prisoners were in no condition to attempt to run away. But even an escort of a few armed soldiers, making its way along the narrow streets of Jerusalem and shepherding their victims to the place of execution, would have created quite a stir.

One of the tasks of the soldiers was to clear the way so that the condemned men could move along. We are told that pious women stood along the street, lamenting the sight of Jesus carrying his crossbeam. According to Luke, Jesus tells them not to weep for him but for themselves and for their children: "For if they do these things when the wood is green, what will happen when it is dry?" (Lk 23:31). Luke here has Jesus refer to the future destruction of Jerusalem that would take place forty years later. "For the days are coming when they will say, 'Blessed are the barren, and the wombs that never bore, and the breasts that never nursed'" (Lk 23;29).

Luke disagrees with Mark and Matthew regarding what the centurion said at the time of Jesus' death. Matthew says that there was an earthquake and that the frightened centurion, taking this as an omen, declared that Jesus was God's Son. In Luke there is no earthquake but Jesus cries out with a loud voice just before he dies. Whereupon the centurion says to himself or to somebody nearby, "Certainly this man was *dikaios*," that is, just or innocent of the charges against him (Lk 23:47).

The evangelists have different reasons for the words they select. In Matthew's Gospel Jesus is mocked for having claimed to be "the Son of God" (Mt 27:40, 43). The centurion professes faith in his divinity to rebut the taunts hurled at Jesus as he hung on the cross. In Mark and Luke the taunts center on the alleged claim of Jesus that he was "King of the Jews." Luke's centurion responds, saying that Jesus was innocent, not an imposter. This was also the judgment of the "good thief," or brigand, who was crucified with Jesus. For reasons indicated in chapter 25, I have maintained that the outlaw who declared that Jesus had done no wrong was Barabbas (Lk 23:41).

Background Considerations

Who were these "bandits" who were crucified with Jesus? They were not ordinary thieves, as the King James and Douay Versions would claim. Ordinary robbers were not likely to be crucified. Crucifixion was reserved for insurrectionists, runaway slaves, and even Roman citizens who had become traitors to the Empire. These two men were freedom fighters, to use a contemporary word. Richard A. Horsley would classify such men as bandits, meaning that they belonged to marauding bands of patriots who sought to right wrongs and fight for justice.[3] It was a form of social banditry, very often aimed at Jews who collaborated with the Romans or the wealthy who oppressed the poor. The two men would not have regarded themselves as criminals, but as fighters for justice and freedom, for the redemption of Israel. That any of these men who had been caught and crucified would have felt that, "we indeed have been condemned justly," seems unlikely, although one of the bandits might have said that Jesus was innocent, because he had not been involved in killing people.

Still, this brings up the question of who was present to hear what the "good thief " had said, or what the centurion had said, and to whom. The apologetic tone of these utterances is part of the type of reconstruction that the evangelists engaged in for the edification of their Christian readers and hearers.

The centurion played a significant role in certifying the death of Jesus. When Joseph of Arimathea went to Pilate to beg for the body of Jesus so that he might bury it in his own family tomb, the prefect would not release the body until he had learned from the centurion that Jesus was really dead. He was frankly astonished that Jesus had died so soon (Mk 15:44). After all, the two men crucified with him were still alive. Why did Jesus die so soon, given the fact that crucified slaves could live several days after being crucified? Was it because Jesus' ordeal was so much more debilitating than the experience of the two bandits? He was buffeted during his trial, both before Caiaphas and Annas (Mk 14:65; Jn 18:22). In addition, he was scourged later by the Roman soldiers with no limit to the number of lashes that could be inflicted, and he had a plaited crown of thorns pressed down on his head. Those who died with Jesus seem to have escaped some of this violent treatment and obscene mockery.

Such abuses must be taken into consideration, if we are to account for the death of Jesus after only six hours. There may be an indication in the Gospels of both Luke and John that Jesus willed to expire when he actually did so. Indeed, rather than dying in a weakened condition, Luke says that Jesus cried out with a loud voice, indicating that he was still in command of his breathing (Lk 23: 46). According to John, his death was more deliberate but he was still in control: "Then he lowered his head and gave up his spirit" (Jn 19:30). Hindu yogis, such as Swami Vivekananda, were able to cease breathing and expire when they chose, though they appeared to be in good health only hours before.[4]

Whether or not Jesus deliberately willed to expire when he did would not be an immediate concern of the soldiers or the centurion in charge of them: "One of the soldiers pierced his side with a spear, and at once blood and water came out" (Jn 19:34). The separation of the fluids would indicate that death had already taken place. So they did not bother to break the legs of Jesus, a gesture that would hasten death by asphyxiation. The text does not say whether or not it was the centurion who bore the spear that opened the side of Jesus, tradition holds that it was he. In any case, he was there to witness what had happened, so he was able to assure Pilate that the prisoner was dead. The separation of the blood and serum also served as a refutation for those who, recently and in ancient times, have maintained that Jesus did not really die on the cross but actually survived his crucifixion.

John calls to mind two prophetic models to assure readers that the circumstances of Jesus' death had been foreseen in prophecy. The bones of the paschal lamb are not to be broken (Ex 12:46), and we read in Zechariah, "when they look on the one whom they have pierced, they shall mourn for him, as one mourns for an only child" (Zech 12:10). Both of these anticipations were fulfilled in the death of Jesus. His bones were not broken and after his side was pierced the soldiers who had been keeping watch looked on the one whom they had pierced.[5]

The editors of the Fourth Gospel insist that the source of their information about the events of Jesus' public life was an eyewitness. Even if their Gospel had not introduced the spear thrust into Jesus' side, one could be certain that the centurion, if he found Jesus apparently dead, would have taken no chances. He would have caused the side of Jesus to be opened with a lance to make sure that his mission, which was to execute three men, had been successfully accomplished.

One last item needs attention in this chapter on the death of Jesus. All four evangelists say that the soldiers cast lots for his garment, and that this, too, was done in fulfillment of the prophecy found in the twenty-second Psalm: "They divide my clothes among them, and for my raiment they cast lots" (Ps 22:18). Did this event actually happen; or was this prophecy historicized? John's Gospel, which tends to be much more precise on details than the other Gospels, adds an interesting observation. The soldiers did not cast lots for Jesus' garments but only for his tunic which, being woven in one piece from top to bottom, could not be divided. As for his other garments, they were divided in four parts, "one [part] for each soldier" (Jn 19:23). This seems to indicate that there were only four soldiers who took part in the crucifixion episode, not counting the centurion, who might not have been interested in the blood-soaked garments of a man who had been scourged. In any case, there seems to be no compelling reason against the idea that the dividing of Jesus' clothing may be historical. Who received the clothing? Even ordinary clothing was expensive in the first century, and a seamless robe would be especially coveted by poor soldiers. The soldiers loved to gamble, and the idea of drawing lots for the robe makes sense. So, even if the evangelists were only guessing about dividing the garments of Jesus, it was the kind of thing that, independent of the twenty-second Psalm, very likely happened. If there were any doubt about dividing the garments, one could always have recourse to the prophetic model in the Psalm.

Could the Evangelists Have Guessed Right?

Anyone familiar with the procedure in routine crucifixions could have guessed what might have happened when Jesus was executed. He would have been flogged, which was standard practice. He would have carried his *patibulum* to the place of execution. Falling along the way after a thorough scourging is not out of the question. Requiring a strong and healthy bystander to help the condemned man carry his crossbeam would not be unusual. Offering the crucified man a drink of crude wine (Mt 27:48), or a narcotic, "wine mixed with gall" (Mt 27:34), was permitted as an act of mercy. Dividing the condemned man's garments may well have been customary in such circumstances, because criminals were stripped naked before being crucified. The Romans would not usually crucify a single man but several men at the same time. Because the bodies had to be removed from their crosses before sundown, had one of the three men been found already dead, the thrust of the spear would be used to make sure that the victim was not simply in a coma. Finally, all this would have been under the supervision of a centurion.

What may not have been historical was the confession of the centurion to the effect that Jesus was God's Son.[5] Did he say this out loud or to the crowd or to other soldiers? If he made some kind of declaration about the divine sonship of Jesus, it is strange that it does not appear in the Fourth Gospel, the one so insistent about the divinity of Jesus, the one that has the best chance of being based on an eyewitness's account. One of the polemical reasons for introducing the testimony of the centurion was to emphasize the contrast between his faith and the behavior of the Jewish bystanders. Some, we are told, were mocking Jesus, while the Gentile was praising him. This should have encouraged other Gentiles to embrace the faith, even though Jesus was put to death as an enemy of the Empire.

Independent of the eyewitness whose recollections play so prominent a role in the Fourth Gospel, a good number of the events described in the Synoptic Gospels could have been guessed correctly by writers who, although not witnesses to the crucifixion of Jesus, were familiar with Roman procedures in such matters. Beyond that, the evangelists would have filled in the gaps by combing through the Hebrew Scriptures. The twenty-second Psalm, for example, includes a story about a suffering man who feels forsaken by God, whose "hands and feet" have been pierced (according to the Greek Septuagint Version of the Hebrew Bible), whose bones are out of joint as he suffers from thirst and is mocked by his captors.[6] This was an almost perfect fit for a crucified man. Putting together the Psalm and the list of probabilities mentioned above, the evangelists could have created the kind of account found in the four Gospels, even without the alleged recourse to the recollections of an eyewitness or to the oral tradition.

Was this history remembered or prophecy historicized? Probably a little bit of each, along with a certain amount of guessing. But I would add to this the fact that very shortly after the death of Jesus his followers and disciples could already be found in such cities as Antioch, Edessa, Damascus, and Ephesus. Among them there must have been a few older men and women who had been in Jerusalem for the festival at the time of Jesus' crucifixion, people who could report on it thirty or forty years later, or pass on what they had witnessed to a younger generation. In other words, the evangelists did not have to depend entirely on guesswork and historicizing the prophecies, although the latter played a role in the Gospel accounts.

Excursus: When Was Passover?

All four Gospels agree that Jesus died on Friday, the day before the Sabbath. Mark and the other Synoptic evangelists hold that the Last Supper as well as the arrest, trial, and death of Jesus took place on the same "day", that is, on a day beginning at sundown Thursday and ending at sundown Friday. The Last Supper was *prepared* on "the first day of the Unleavened Bread, when the Passover lamb is sacrificed" (Mk 14:12). That is 14 Nisan, or Holy Thursday according to our way of marking the days of the week. The farewell meal then took place on that night after sundown, that is, on 15 Nisan.

According to the Fourth Gospel, however, the high priests refused to enter Pilate's headquarters on the day Jesus was condemned and executed to avoid defilement *before eating the Passover* (Jn 18:28). This would clearly indicate that the Passover meal had not already taken place but was to be eaten at some future time, for example, that night when the Sabbath began after sundown. This could mean that in that particular year Passover fell on Saturday, the Sabbath. John called that Passover a day of Great Solemnity, *megalē hēmera* (Jn 19:31). Was it a Great Solemnity because Passover fell on the Sabbath? In that case, as Hillel points out, Passover and its activity take precedence over Saturday and the Sabbath rest.[7]

If the "Great Sabbath" is what we now refer to as *Shabbas* or *Shabbat Hagodol*, it falls on the Sabbath before Passover.[8] So, if Saturday was the Great Sabbath, then Passover must have been celebrated on some day after the Great Sabbath, which could mean Sunday or any day during the following week. It is more probable, then, that when the Fourth Gospel mentions *hē megalē hēmera,* the reference is *not* to *Shabbat Hagodol.* John was simply calling attention to the fact that in that year Passover, 15 Nisan, fell on the Sabbath.

According to John, because Jesus' Last Supper, arrest, crucifixion, death, and burial all took place on the same day, 14 Nisan, the last Supper could not have been, strictly speaking, a Passover meal. Could Jesus have anticipated Passover and taken his Passover a day earlier? He likely did not, because, again according to the Fourth Gospel, the Last Supper took place before the Pascal lambs eaten at Passover were slain.

Time Warps in the Fourth

In the Fourth Gospel, events occur when it pleases the author, when it seems appropriate, and not necessarily in the correct historical sequence. He has Jesus standing before Pilate at the sixth hour, that is, at noon. But Mark says that Jesus was crucified at nine in the morning (Mk 15:25). Matthew and Luke omit the exact time of the crucifixion but they say that darkness covered the whole land from noon until three (Mt 27:45). However, Jesus had been on the cross for some time before the darkness occurred, because he had been mocked by the Chief Priests, those who passed by, and by at least one of the men crucified with him. So, Mark's 9:00 AM to 3:00 PM period seems to be approximately correct. But this cannot account for John, who has Jesus still standing before Pilate at noon when he was supposed to have been hanging on the cross for three hours.

John evidently wanted to represent Jesus as a sacrificial victim condemned at noon because that is the hour when the priests began to slaughter the Pascal lambs. In the Fourth Gospel, John the Baptist calls Jesus "the Lamb of God" (Jn 1:29). So it looks as though John chose to have Jesus condemned at noon by Pilate to suit his purpose, which was to remind readers that Jesus was the true Passover Lamb, slain for the atonement of the sins of the world. The Book of Common Prayer echoes the words of John's Gospel when the celebrant says, after the breaking of the bread, "Christ our Passover is sacrificed for us."

The displacement idea is supported by the fact that John situates the cleansing of the Temple at the beginning of Jesus' public ministry (Jn 2:13–22), instead of just a few days before his death. He omits the institution of the Eucharist from the Last Supper account, and has Jesus speak of it in chapter 6. Instead of describing Jesus' agony in the Garden of Olives, John has him groan in spirit while standing in the midst of a crowd, saying, "Now is my soul troubled. And what shall I say—Father, save me from this hour'? No, it is for this reason that I have come to this hour" (Jn 12:27). These words echo what Jesus said in the Synoptic Gospels during his agony in the Garden. Finally, the miraculous catch of fish, which is described in the fifth chapter of Luke's Gospel as occurring in Galilee before Jesus' resurrection, is placed after his resurrection in John's Gospel. So, having portrayed Jesus as standing before Pilate at noon on the day of Preparation when the lambs were sacrificed may be one more example of a symbolic displacement of an historic event, a *theologoumenon*, that is, a theological insight narrated as an historic event. This belongs to the class of those instances when the evangelists turn something Jesus said into something he did.

Such tampering with time and event helps confirm the belief that John changed the day on which Jesus, the Lamb of God, was judged, in order to make it coincide with the Day of Preparation. The alternative is to go back to Synoptic Gospel accounts. This poses another kind of problem. If Jesus' Jewish trial and execution took place on the day of Passover itself, if he was judged and condemned at night by a hand-picked rump session of the Sanhedrin, if he was executed on the same day, as the Jews count days, that is, from sundown Thursday to sundown Friday, the entire proceeding was illicit, illegal, and immoral by every canon of Jewish practice. Incidentally, according to the Synoptic Gospels the high priests went against their own better judgment. They had agreed not to arrest and condemn Jesus "during the festival, or there may be a riot among the people" (Mt 26:5). Having taken this decision, they then went ahead and arranged to have Jesus arrested and crucified on Passover.

Regarding the day on which Jesus is supposed to have died, a last desperate option is to hold that Jesus did not die on either of the two days proposed by the evangelists, although his death may have taken place some time during the Paschal season. Both the Synoptic writers and John would have chosen the day on which Jesus died to make it coincide with the Day of Preparation (in John) or Passover itself (in the Synoptics) because of the symbolism of the day. In either case, Passover commemorates the day on which the people of Israel were saved from bondage and the pursuing army of Pharaoh by daubing the "blood of the lamb" on the lintels of their houses, even as Jesus' blood stained the wood of the cross. (Ex 12:21–22).

Notes

[1] Joseph A. Fitzmyer, *The Gospel according to Luke* (Garden City, NY: Doubleday/Anchor, 1893), 1, 1519. "Longinus" first turns up in the apocryphal Acts of Pilate, fourth to sixth century.

[2] Denis Bain Saddington, *The Oxford Commentary on the Bible* (New York: Oxford University Press, 1992), 105.

[3] Richard A, Horsley, *Bandits, Prophets & Messiahs: Popular Movements in the Time of Jesus* (Harrisburg, PA: Trinity Press International, 1983, 1999), 48, 67, 256.

[4] Christopher Isherwood, *Biographical Introduction to What Is Religion? In the Words of Swami Vivekananda* (New York: Julian Press, 1952): "His health was better. He ate his midday meal with relish, talked philosophy and went for a two-mile waLk In the evening he passed into deep meditation, and the heart stopped beating. For hours they tried to arouse him" (xx).

[5] Few scholars regard as literally and historically true the signs that are said to have marked the moment when Jesus died, signs that were introduced to mark the magnitude of the event: "The earth shook, and the rocks were split. The tombs were opened and the bodies of the saints who had fallen asleep were raised" (Mt 27:51–52). None of these "signs" appear in the eyewitness's account in John's Gospel. It is not to be supposed that the tombs of those who "were raised" would have been found empty the next day. The rending of the veil of the Temple from top to bottom (Mk 15:38; Mt 27:51) was also symbolic. It meant that those who believed in Jesus had now been given access to the Holy of Holies, that is, God's dwelling place; or that Judaism had been "superseded" by a New Covenant.

[6] As indicated earlier, the translation of the Hebrew text on which the Septuagint is based mentions "hands and feet," with the idea that they were "shriveled" (Revised Standard Version), or, according to the A. Cohen translation, "gnawed" as if by lions. See *The Psalms* (London: Concino Press, 1965), 64.

[7] On Hillel's belief that Passover should override the Sabbath, see Yitzhak Buxbaum, *The Teachings of Hillel* (Northvale, NJ: Jason Aronson, 1994), 23.

[8] *The Jewish Holy Days and Their Spiritual Significance* (Northvale, NJ: Jason Aronson, 1996), 307. Mosche A. Braun, the author, adds: "Why was Shabbat [Hagodol] so special? It was because the Israelites had to take a sheep on that day,

inspect it, and keep it until the fourteenth day of Nisan for the Passover Sacrifice" (308). If the Great Sabbath was on the Saturday before Holy Week, this might lend credibility to the Synoptic accounts. For 14 Nisan would then have coincided with Wednesday–Thursday, according to the Hebrew way of defining a day. It was on that day that the apostles arranged for the Passover meal. And 15 Nisan, which began on Thursday at sundown, would include the Last Supper, the agony in the Garden, the arrest, trial, death, and burial of Jesus, as the Synoptics have maintained. But there is no mention of a Great Sabbath in the first three gospels. Since the Fourth Gospel situates it on the day after Jesus' crucifixion and death, this means that 14 and 15 Nisan would have occurred some time during the following octave, if Shabbat Hagodol and The Great Sabbath are one and the same. But John has Jesus judged and crucified on 14 Nisan, a day before the Great Sabbath. We cannot have it both ways. Conclusion: we do not know when Jesus was crucified. John's timetable ends in confusion, and the Synoptics have Jesus judged and crucified on Passover, a highly unlikely day. So, while the evangelists arrange their timetable in order to have Jesus die on a day that is theologically appropriate, one has to conclude that they truly did not know when Jesus died.

PART SEVEN:

Resurrection

Chapter Twenty-eight

JOSEPH OF ARIMATHEA

You Get What You Pay For

Joseph of Arimathea, the man who is reported as having participated in the burial of Jesus, was said to have been one of his disciples according to Matthew and John. John adds that he, like Nicodemus, was a secret disciple "because of his fear of the Jews" (Jn 19:38). Mark calls him a respected member of the Council, presumably that over which Caiaphas the High Priest presided (Mk 15:43), while Luke adds that he "had not agreed to [the Council's] plan and action" (Lk 23:51), meaning that he disagreed with the plan to arrest and condemn Jesus. Mark and Luke say that he was among those who were awaiting the coming of the kingdom of God.

If Joseph were a member of the Supreme Council (Sanhedrin), he would have to be readily available for Council meetings. So, although he was identified with the town he came from, he also would have had a residence in Jerusalem. Arimathea has been tentatively identified with present-day Rathamin, a village that lies about twenty-five miles from Jerusalem, too far away for a man who had to be available for emergency Council meetings, such as the one to condemn Jesus. Joseph not only lived in Jerusalem, but like all Jews he also considered it a blessing to be buried near the city. For that reason he had a tomb prepared for his own death and burial and for the members of his family. It was a new tomb located just outside the city walls, because tombs were not permitted inside the city.[1] Although a few scripture scholars call into question the existence of Joseph of Arimathea, the descriptions of him in the accounts of the four evangelists tell us quite a bit about him. His existence has double attestation in the three Synoptic Gospels and in the Fourth Gospel. His name and place of origin are known. He is described as wealthy and influential enough to have enjoyed ready access to Pilate. He was a secret disciple of Jesus, was involved in the Council's deliberations about the fate of Jesus, had a tomb of his own, bought the shroud in which Jesus was buried, and cooperated with Nicodemus in the actual burial of Jesus. According to the skeptics, all of these details are a pure invention of the evangelists.[2] Because the four Gospels agree on the existence and basic description of Joseph, those who hold for his nonexistence are guided by fixed presumptions rather than on positive evidence that he is a pure fiction.

Joseph's tomb was no ordinary one.[3] Matthew calls it a *mnēmeion*, a sepulcher, in the form of a cave hollowed out of solid rock. Luke maintains that it had never been used before to assure readers that it had not been contaminated by an earlier corpse that rotted away. These Jewish cave tombs were not permanent burial places. After the flesh had decomposed, the bones were collected and placed in an ossuary, or bone box. This might be buried again in the tomb, buried in the ground, or shelved in a memorial vault. The tomb would then be reused for later temporary burials.[4] Had Jesus, body and soul, risen from the dead, there would have been no bones left behind, and no ossuary, only an empty tomb.

The fact that Joseph had his own tomb hewn out of rock indicates he that he was a man of substance, a fact confirmed by Matthew (Mt 27:60). The Fourth Gospel adds that Joseph's tomb was in a garden, because Mary Magdalene mistook the risen Jesus for "the gardener."[5] In any case, because the sin of Adam was committed in a garden and because death followed from his sin, it may have seemed appropriate to the author of the Fourth Gospel to have the risen and sinless Jesus appear to Mary in a garden (Jn 20:15).

Why Would Pilate Release the Body of Jesus to Joseph?

Mark says that Joseph "went boldly to Pilate and asked for the body of Jesus" (Mk 15:43). I doubt that Pilate granted favors for the asking. Everything had a price. You get only what you pay for. Today in the United States we call it graft. In other parts of the world it is a way of life. Joseph was a rich man. Had it not been so, he probably could not have secured an interview with Pilate the governor, and Pilate probably would not have released the body of Jesus. So Joseph had to lay his purse on a table and let Pilate take what he thought his favor was worth. But before Joseph could have the body, Pilate had to make sure that Jesus was dead. When the centurion in charge of the execution assured Pilate that all three men whose crucifixion he had overseen were truly dead, Pilate informed the soldier that Joseph could have the body.

Given permission to possess the body of Jesus, Joseph was ill equipped to remove it from the cross. How would he manage to pull out the nails from the solid wood of the cross without inflicting further injury on the body? Perhaps some Roman soldiers who had the proper tools could be paid to help. Events get cloudy when we try to plot the details. If the soldiers buried Jesus in a common grave, Joseph would not be needed. If the body were to be turned over to Joseph, he would need help in removing it from the cross and carrying it to the awaiting tomb. According to the Fourth Gospel, he had the help of Nicodemus, the Pharisee who had secretly visited Jesus by night (Jn 3:1; 19:39), and probably some of his own servants and slaves.

After his interview with Pilate, Mark says that Joseph went out and bought the linen shroud used to bury Jesus (Mk 15:46). Gaining access to Pilate, waiting for the centurion to certify that Jesus was dead, along with the task of purchasing a shroud and engaging in the delicate task of removing the body of Jesus from the cross, all took time. As a result, the usual burial amenities could not be completed before sundown, before the Sabbath rest began.

The Turin Shroud

Some believe that the Holy Shroud of Turin is the very burial cloth that Joseph provided.[6] Even those who reject the authenticity of the Shroud cannot explain how the faint straw-colored image of what purports to be the front and back of a crucified man was created. There are stains seemingly left by the flow of blood from the wounds in the figure's wrists, feet, side, and head, along with the wounds resulting from a severe scourging. The astonishing thing is that when the Shroud is photographed, the negative, when developed, turns out to be a positive. If the image were somehow imposed on the cloth in the fourteenth century, as the carbon dating would seem to indicate, who was the genius who, without paint or scorch, managed to create a work of art whose anatomical accuracy surpasses any known fourteenth century painting? And did the presumed "artist" know how to create an image with the lights and shadows reversed so that, when photography would later be invented, the resulting image would be a figure of haunting majesty? Those scientists who have worked closely on the Shroud have been interested not so much in whether the Turin cloth is the burial shroud of Jesus but in the mystery of how the image was created. The very best efforts to duplicate the process, apparently known to a fourteenth-century craftsman, have resulted only in grotesque imitations.

Wisely, the Church has never claimed that the Shroud of Turin is the shroud of Jesus. But the mystery remains. John says that when the two disciples visited the empty tomb of the risen Jesus, they found a collapsed shroud with no body wrapped in it "and the cloth that had been on Jesus' head, not lying with the linen wrapping but rolled up in a place by itself" (Jn 20:7). The face cloth that had covered the head of Jesus had been taken off and tossed aside. Had it been covering the face of Jesus as he lay in the tomb, the image of his majestic face would not have been imprinted on the shroud.

These are some of the things that must be taken into consideration before the Shroud of Turin is definitely dismissed as a deliberate hoax. If Peter and the Beloved Disciple (or Peter alone according to Luke's Gospel) had discerned the strange markings on the shroud of Jesus, they might have decided to preserve it and show it to others as proof that not only the tomb but also the shroud was empty. The telltale markings would indicate that something out of the ordinary had taken place. Whether authentic or not, the Turin Shroud is a striking reminder of what Jesus endured when he was scourged and crucified. There were not simply "five wounds," but hundreds, if one counts the head wounds resulting from the crown of many thorns and the forty or more lashes on the front and back.

None of the Synoptic Gospels mentions treating the body of Jesus with myrrh and aloes at the time of his burial. This omission is rectified by the author of the Fourth Gospel. He introduces Nicodemus who supplies the spice and healing aloes for the purpose of preserving and perfuming the body (Jn 19:39). The Synoptic Gospels speak of some women coming to anoint the body of Jesus, but they are preparing to perform this service only on Easter Sunday morning. We owe to John's Gospel the account of the anointing at the time of burial. Few who are acquainted with the New Testament or hear the Gospels read in church realize that three of the four accounts of the burial of Jesus make no mention of his being anointed on Friday. Thus, one Gospel complements another. Similarly, if we had only Matthew's Gospel, we would hear nothing about the birth of Jesus in a stable, about a choir of angels heralding his birth, or about shepherds coming to the stable. All of these latter details appear only in Luke's Gospel, which is why writers from the earliest days tried to create a Gospel harmony that would weave together into a single story the different accounts of the same event.

Matthew introduces what seems at first like an odd detail. He maintains that Joseph of Arimathea wrapped the body of Jesus in a clean (*kathara*) cloth. He would hardly have supplied a soiled or used one, so by a "clean" cloth, Matthew may mean one that was ritually pure, made out of pure linen with no admixture of wool. In Leviticus, Moses warns the congregation, "[You shall] not put on a garment made of two different materials" (Lev 19:19). For example, a cloth woven of wool and linen would be made of the product of an animal and a plant. So, for Matthew, the evangelist who seems to know the most about Jewish customs, a clean cloth must be one that is kosher, made of pure linen. In fact, the Shroud of Turin is woven of pure linen.

The History of the Tomb

Was it wise for Pilate to have granted Joseph permission to bury Jesus honorably in an impressive tomb? Such a burial could easily have become a shrine to keep alive the memory of Jesus and his movement. Fearing that Hitler's mountain hideout in the Bavarian Alps could become a place of pilgrimage by unregenerate Nazis, or a curiosity for tourists, the Germans, on American instruction, dynamited and bulldozed the rambling three-story Berghof.[7]

But did the tomb of Jesus become a place of pilgrimage? The fact is that until the fourth century we have precious little evidence that the tomb of Jesus was turned into a shrine for the early disciples of Jesus and their converts. It is mentioned once in the Acts of the Apostles. The reference to the tomb occurs when Paul, speaking in the synagogue of Pisidia, confirms the contention that Jesus was properly buried in a tomb (*ethēkan eis mnēmeion*) (Acts 13:29).[8]

This passing reference to a tomb on the part of Paul does not impress John Dominic Crossan. He holds that there never was a tomb and that Jesus, as mentioned earlier, was probably buried by Roman soldiers in a quickly dug shallow grave. Yet, the fact remains that the Gospels provide us with the names of the women who came to the tomb on Easter Sunday as well as the names of the men who buried Jesus. Even so, it is only fair to note that Paul in his several trips to Jerusalem makes no mention of the tomb of Jesus that he might have visited. Paul's defense would probably be in line with the question the angels ask the women who come to the tomb, "Why do you seek the living among the dead?" (Lk 24:5). We honor the tombs of the dead, not of those who are still alive.

Still we must recognize how avid people are for keepsakes and relics of famous people. A dress once worn by a movie star may fetch thousands of dollars when sold at auction. Recognizing how much Jesus meant to many people, it is strange that his tomb all but dropped out of history for the first three centuries. Before St. Helena, mother of the Emperor Constantine, "rediscovered" Jesus tomb, pilgrims like Origen, who visited Jerusalem talked of seeing the sights, visiting Bethlehem, and so on, but made no mention of the tomb.[9] Indeed, when Helena and her party came to raise a basilica at the sight of the tomb, they got no help from the local people and could only guess where the original tomb was. Associated with the alleged discovery of the actual tomb of Jesus, we are told by St. Ambrose that Helena and her party found three crosses, the one Jesus died on, and the two others belonging to the two "thieves" crucified with him. They also found the title board placed at the head of Jesus' cross stating that he was "The King of the Jews."[10] Needless to add that somewhere nails were also found, the very nails used to pinion Jesus to the cross. The most we can say, faced with such fantastic and improbable tales, is that, if the present site of the tomb inside the Church of the Holy Sepulcher is not the correct one, the correct one—if it exists—cannot be far away.

Guarding the Tomb

Along with an existing tomb perpetuating Jesus' memory, Pilate and the high priests had to deal with the preaching of the zealous apostles of Jesus who, declaring that Jesus had been raised from the dead, were making numerous converts, even among the lower clergy. Matthew tells of the high priests going to Pilate and securing permission to set a guard before the tomb, lest the disciples of Jesus come during the night, steal the body, and then claim that he had risen from the dead (Mt 27:64). This unlikely theory assumes that well before he died Jesus had been going around publicly declaring that, if executed, he would rise from the dead. Otherwise, how could the high priests have learned that Jesus had made such a prediction?

Where did Matthew, acting as God's spin-doctor, get the idea of introducing a military detachment to guard the tomb? It was to refute a contemporary charge that the resurrection was a hoax. If soldiers were posted to guard the tomb, no one could have stolen the body. But even Augustine saw through the weakness of the Gospel story, while failing to draw the obvious conclusion. He asked how the soldiers, if they were all asleep, could testify that the body was stolen and know who the thieves were? One would, in addition, have to assume that all of the soldiers slept while on duty and that the commotion caused by rolling back the stone from the tomb and spiriting away the dead body of Jesus did not awaken a single guard.[11]

In any case, Pilate did not have to worry about the body being stolen. As far as he was concerned the execution of Jesus wrote finis to the story of the Galilean preacher. Little did he know that he would be remembered in history primarily as the man who condemned Jesus to death, allowed him to be properly buried, and thus set the stage for a glorious resurrection.

Joseph of Arimathea in Legend and Story

We know very little about the subsequent history of Joseph of Arimathea. The apocryphal Gospel of Nicodemus (also known as the Acts of Pilate) holds that he was arrested and imprisoned for burying the body of Jesus. Later legends have him travel to Britain, bringing with him the Holy Grail containing the precious blood of Christ. Frank C. Tribbe, known for his early and well-documented book on the Shroud of Turin (*Portrait of Jesus*, 1983), has recently published an historical novel, entitled, *I, Joseph of Arimathea*.[12] Making use of bits and pieces drawn from the legends and apochrypha, plus a lively creative imagination, he portrays Joseph of Arimathea as the rich uncle of Jesus. He was engaged in importing tin from Britain and took Jesus with him to Britain on one of his business trips when Jesus was a youth. Years later, after escaping from prison, Joseph retired for safety to the Britain he knew so well and learned to love as a trader. There he got to know and convert to the Christian Way members of the leading Druidic families. Some of them were sent to Rome as honorable hostages, and they brought Christianity with them to the capital of the Empire in the forties, before the arrival of Peter and Paul. Today, Joseph is honored as the patron of Glastonbury, the Avalon of the Arthurian legends, and for having introduced Christianity to Britain before the middle of the first century.

Apologists for the antiquity of the Church in England have used this rumor of an early flowering of Christianity there as proof of its origin in apostolic times. Although the Church of England also bases the validity of its ministry on the concept of apostolic succession, dating back to the time of Augustine, Archbishop of Canterbury, and through him to first and second century bishops, the Celtic Church with its native clergy already existed in Britain centuries before the arrival of Augustine. The compromise settlement at Whitby (664) introduced the customs of the Roman Church into Britain, and they eventually prevailed. The original Celtic Church, however, traces its origin back to apostolic times. If the stories and legends about Joseph of Arimathea coming to Britain can be credited, it is possibile that he may have helped introduce an early version of Christian beliefs to what would later be known as England.

Notes

1 Even prominent Jews were buried outside the city walls. The ossuaries discovered in 1990 two kilometers south of the Temple Mount turned out to be those of the Caiaphas family. As pointed out in chapter 22, note 2, one of them turned out to be that of Joseph Caiaphas, the high priest who cross-examined Jesus according to the Synoptic Gospels. Even King Herod's tomb was beyond the ridge of the Valley of Hinnom, that is, outside the old city wall. See John J. Rousseau and Rami Arav, *Jesus & His World: Archeological and Cultural Dictionary* (Minneapolis: Fortress Press, 1995). Pages 164–165 deal with Jerusalem tombs. For the tomb of Caiaphas, see 139–140.

2 Robert W. Funk, *Honest to Jesus* (San Francisco: HarperSanFrancisco, 1996) is among those who hold that "Joseph of Arimathea is probably a Markan creation." "At the hands of Matthew, Joseph becomes rich and a disciple of Jesus." Nicodemus is "a fictive burial assistant." "Barabbas is certainly a fiction." "Judas Iscariot the betrayer is in all probability a gospel fiction." His name is probably symbolic because "Jesus was betrayed by descendants of Judah." Other fictional characters are Simon of Cyrene, Pilate's wife who warned him of a dream she had about Jesus, and, finally the soldiers posted to guard the tomb of Jesus lest his disciples come and steal the body. See 234–236. While the story about the soldiers set to guard the tomb and the warning by Pilate's wife may be fictitious, the other persons mentioned do not fall so easily into the class of creations of the evangelists. This is especially true of Simon of Cyrene and his sons, Rufus and Alexander. The two sons were known by members of the community for which Mark's Gospel was composed. Funk argues that Joseph of Arimathea must be a fiction because "Jesus lacked friends in high places." The argument assumes what has to be proved, namely, that under no circumstances could Jesus have had any well-placed friends. Why not? According to the Fourth Gospel, Jesus had been to Jerusalem many times over a period of several years. He had friends there, including the Bethany family. And, given his charismatic personality and powerful message, there is little reason to claim that he had no disciples and admirers who were

educated or well placed. Luke points out that Joanna, the wife of the steward of Herod Antipas, was a follower of Jesus.

[3] St. Paul says that Jesus was buried in a proper tomb. Those who hold that he was not buried honorably will have to explain why Paul, who knew Peter, John, and James the brother of Jesus, thought there was a tomb. The Greek words used in the body of this chapter refer to what is known the world over as a tomb. They are the words used by Paul in his talk in the Synagogue at Pisidia (Acts 13:29), and also in his own writings (1 Cor 15:4). Are we to suppose that when Paul met the three "Pillars" of the Church, they deceived him or, perhaps, did not tell him that actually Jesus' body was thrown into a common pit or buried in a shallow grave? I do not think there can be any serious doubt about Paul's belief that there was a tomb.

[4] In 1968, in the course of the discovery of three family burial caves northeast of Jerusalem on the Nablus Road, at the site of the Giv'at ha-Mivtar excavations, an ossuary dating from the first century was found. It contained the heel bone of a man in his twenties. He had been crucified and a 4.5-inch nail was found piercing his heel. It indicated that a crucified man could be buried in a family tomb, with the bones later transferred to an ossuary. This was more likely to happen when only two or three men were crucified, as in the case of Jesus. In mass crucifixions, if corpses were buried at all, they would have been dumped into a mass grave, or left to rot on their crosses.

[5] In 1867, a tomb at the foot of a hill was discovered west of the Nablus Road. The property was sold in 1870 and General Gordon of Khartoum fame visited the site. He was convinced that it was the tomb of Jesus. This garden setting is more pleasing than the bustling Church of the Holy Sepulcher. On the Garden Tomb, See Rousseau and Arav, *Jesus and His World*, 104–109.

[6] Books on the Shroud abound. To mention a few: *Report on the Shroud* by John H. Heller (Boston: Houghton Mifflin, 1983). *Portrait of Jesus* by Frank C. Tribbe (New York: Stein & Day, 1983). *The Blood and the Shroud* by Ian Wilson (New York: The Free Press, 1998). *The Jesus Conspiracy: The Turin Shroud and the Truth about the Resurrection* by Holger Kersten and Elmar H. Gruber (Rockport, MA: Element, 1994). The coauthors think that Jesus survived his crucifixion.

[7] For the destruction of Hitler's Berghof, see Timothy W. Ryback, "Hitler's Lost Family," *The New Yorker*, July 17, 2000.

[8] John Dominic Crossan writes, regarding the burial of Jesus, "The soldiers who crucified Jesus would probably have done it [taken him down from the cross] and buried him speedily and indifferently, in a necessarily shallow and mounded grave rather than a rock-hewn tomb. That would mean lime, at best, and the dogs again, at worse," in *Who Killed Jesus?* (HarperSanFrancisco), 188.

[9] Jerome in *De viribus illustribus* 3,34, cited in Rousseau and Arav (112), speaks of Origen's pilgrimage to the Holy Land. During and after the Jewish War (66–70), many Christians left Judea. After the Bar Kokhba War (132–135), Hadrian destroyed what was left of Jerusalem and built there a new Roman city, Aelia Capitolana. What remained of what had been the tomb of Jesus and memory of exactly where it was probably lay buried beneath the rubble.

[10] Rousseau and Arav, 113.

[11] The Second Nocturn in the Divine Office for Holy Saturday, Lesson IV, ridicules the instruction given to the soldiers who were supposed to be guarding the tomb: "Say that when you were sleeping 'His disciples came and made off with him.' You sum-

mon sleeping men as witnesses! Really, shrewdness itself has fallen asleep when its search can come up with no better plot than this!"

[12] See Franck C. Tribbe, *I, Joseph of Arimathea, A Story of Jesus, His Resurrection, and the Aftermath. A Documented Historical Novel.* (Nevada City, CA: Blue Dolphin Publishing Co, 2000).

Chapter Twenty-nine

CLOPAS/CLEOPAS

The Jesus Dynasty

C leopas is one of the two travelers mentioned by Luke. The second is unnamed. They are making their way from Jerusalem to the town of Emmaus, some seven miles away on the day of Jesus' resurrection. They know that some women have found the tomb of Jesus empty and have reported this information to the apostles. The women say that they have seen Jesus alive, but the men do not believe them. When the men go to the tomb, they find it empty with no sign of Jesus (Lk 24:22; Jn 20:3). Meanwhile, Cleopas and his companion are discussing the tragic way Jesus has died. This is now the "third day," as the Jews count days, since these things had happened, and the disciples of Jesus were despondent.[1]

The two travelers tell all of this to a stranger who joins them. It is the risen Jesus, of course, but in their downcast state they fail to recognize him. He wonders why they are so sad. They express astonishment that their companion does not know how the high priests condemned Jesus and crucified him.[2] Then Jesus begins to show them how everything that happened was foreknown and foreshadowed in the scriptures: "Was it not necessary[3] that the Messiah should suffer these things and then enter into his glory? Then beginning with Moses and all the prophets, he interpreted to them the things about himself in all the scriptures" (Lk 24:26–27).

This is, above all, a teaching story. It is meant to assure believers and potential converts that Jesus was the Messiah and that his death was part of a divine plan, leading to his glorification. Did the encounter ever take place, or did the evangelist invent the story? Not necessarily. It is possible that two of Jesus' despondent disciples on the road to Emmaus were met by a stranger who showed them how the death of Jesus took place in fulfillment of the scriptures. Was the stranger Jesus? Luke intends this to be the case, because the episode ends when the stranger, asked to dine with the two disciples, "took bread, blessed and broke it, and gave it to them," and then disappeared (Lk 24:31).

The Eucharist

The Eucharistic formula is present in the words" took . . . blessed . . . broke . . . gave."[4] In Acts, Luke tells how the followers of Jesus, "devoted themselves to the apostles' teaching and fellowship, to the breaking of bread and the prayers. . . . Day by day, as they spent much time together in the temple, they broke bread at home [or from house to house]" (Acts 2:42 and 46). Breaking bread together is, at the very least, a sign of fellowship. But in the early Church it stood for something more. It invoked the presence of Jesus, not just in memory but in fact. It symbolized the continued real presence of Jesus among those who came together in his name. "For where two or three are gathered in my name, I am there among them" (Mt 18:20).

The notion of a sacramental Real Presence took on a more literal meaning in the decades that followed the writing of the Gospels. Christ was said to be substantially present in or under the figures of bread and wine, which is the Catholic position. The reformers disagreed among themselves on the meaning of the Real Presence, some leaning to the Catholic position, such as Luther. Others adopted the idea of the co-presence of Jesus according to the faith of the community or the individuals gathered in his name. Finally, some felt the Eucharist was simply a memorial or commemorative rite.

The Continuing Presence of Jesus

According to the Fourth Gospel, Jesus promised his apostles to send the Holy Spirit to guide them (Jn 16:7–8). This represents a different kind of presence when compared with the Eucharistic presence. There is a kind of presence, the kind experienced by St. Paul when he learned that, in persecuting the followers of Jesus, he was in fact attacking Jesus: "Saul, Saul, why do you persecute me?" (Acts 9:4).

In John's Gospel, ten of the apostles experienced this presence. Although the doors are closed, Jesus suddenly stands in their midst and says, "Peace be with you" (Jn 20:42). Then he shows them the wounds in his hands and side. Luke writes of a similar, even more vivid, appearance, when Jesus eats broiled fish in their presence (Lk 24:42). The most realistic appearance of all occurs in the Appendix to John's Gospel. There, Jesus has returned to Galilee. He stands on the shore of the lake and has prepared breakfast for seven of his disciples (Jn 21:9–12).

What the evangelists are saying by using all of these concrete episodes is that the Jesus who died on the cross on Friday is alive. His presence has been experienced by his chosen witnesses. These experiences are called "appearances."[5] Scripture scholars debate whether they were simply visions or real-life, three-dimensional, warm-body visitations. One thing is sure: the apostles and the evangelists were convinced that Jesus rose from or was raised from the dead. They staked their lives on it. It is the very cornerstone of the Christian faith; without it there would have been no Church.

Who Was Cleopas?

According the evangelists, several women were present when Jesus died. John identifies them as Mary the mother of Jesus, "his mother's sister, Mary the wife of Clopas, and Mary Magdalene" (Jn 19:25; Mt 27:61; Lk 23:49). How many women does that add up to? If "his mother's sister" is "Mary the wife of Clopas," then there were only three women present. If Mary the wife of Clopas is not the sister of the mother of Jesus, then there were four women present. I have opted for three, thus identifying Mary's "sister" with the wife of Clopas. Because the mother of Jesus could hardly have a blood sister also named Mary, this other Mary must have been a sister-in-law. Is she the sister of her husband Joseph (Mary's sister-in-law) or is Clopas a brother of Joseph (Mary's brother-in-law)? The Church historian Eusebius settles the matter by maintaining that Clopas was Jesus' uncle, either his mother's or his father's brother. In that case, the other Mary would be his aunt or aunt-in-law.[6]

Can we assume that Clopas, who was Jesus' uncle, is the same as the man named "Cleopas" in Luke's Gospel? Fitzmyer holds that Clopas is a Hebrew or Aramaic name, whereas Cleopas, or Kleopas, is of Egyptian derivation, like the name "Cleopatra."[7] He could be right. On the other hand, we know of no other disciple of Jesus named Clopas/Cleopas associated with him at the time of his death and resurrection. So there is a good chance that we are dealing with only one man. Very often Jews bore two names, one a Romanized or Grecized name along with a Hebrew one. John Mark combines a Hebrew and a Roman name. Saul became Paul; the Hasmonean Jannaeus was known as Alexander; the two apostles, Philip and Andrew, bore Greek names, but they must also have been given Hebrew names. So I think that Cleopas, an Egyptianized form of Clopas, is the same man as Clopas. Luke would be referring to him under his Egyptianized name, and John under his Hebrew name.[8]

Dynasty

These family ties of Jesus have an interesting history. Jesus was very clear on his attitude toward clannishness: "Who are my mother and my brothers? Whoever does the will of God is my brother and sister and mother" (Mk 3:33–35). Eusebius, now quoting Hegesippus, says that Symeon, the son of Clopas and Mary, and a first cousin of Jesus, became the second Bishop of Jerusalem after the execution of James the brother of Jesus. There seems to have been the beginnings of a dynastic movement in the early Jewish Christian Church. We have no way of knowing, had there been peaceful times, how long the family of Jesus could have kept in its hands the headship—Eusebius calls it "the throne"—of the Jerusalem Church. After the fall of Jerusalem, when many Jewish converts migrated to other parts of the Mediterranean world, the names of the successors of James and Symeon are lost in the dust of history. But at least the first two bishops of Jerusalem were relatives of Jesus. The first bishop, James, was Jesus' brother and the second, Symeon, a first cousin. It may be significant that none of Jesus' chosen twelve apostles were members of his immediate family. In fact, during his lifetime the relations between Jesus and his family were anything but cordial. One strongly suspects that among the reasons for this estrangement was the fact that during his ministry Jesus refused to favor members of his family or comply with their conception of how he ought to conduct his affairs. See, especially, John 7:1–7. But after his passing, family interests seem to have prevailed, at least in the Judean Church.

Hegesippus goes on to say that under the Emperor Domitian a determined effort was made to seek out for execution the relatives of Jesus, "all those who were of David's line," so that among the martyrs for the faith were not only Symeon, who was very old when he was executed, but many others, including Jude, one of Jesus' brothers.

Luke does not give the name of the "other disciple" who traveled with Cleopas on the road to Emmaus. It could have been his wife Mary. The longer ending appended to Mark's Gospel also refers to an appearance of Jesus "to two of them, as they were walking into the country" (Mk 16:12). Was this account an abbreviated form, borrowed from Luke's Gospel, or did the oral tradition include a story about two people to whom Jesus appeared while they were on a journey? The original story may have preceded Luke's development of it. If that is the case, Luke's enhanced version is one of the gems of the four Gospels. Like the Parable of the Prodigal Son, another of Luke's compositions, the story of the travelers is well told and dramatically presented. It compares well with John's account of Jesus' encounter with the Samaritan woman and the way John's blind man outwits the Pharisees who believe that the man must be deep into sin because he was born blind (Jn 9:1–41).

If Cleopas was the father of Symeon, the second Bishop of Jerusalem, Symeon may be the source of the story about how his father and another disciple met a stranger on their way to Emmaus, a man who used the scriptures to convince them that it was "necessary" that Christ die and "then enter into his glory." Only after the encounter was over did they become convinced that the stranger had been Jesus.

Notes

[1] Jesus was supposedly in his tomb for approximately 36 hours, that is, parts of three days and two nights. Anticipating his resurrection, Jesus, according to Matthew, cited the Book of Jonah, where it is stated that "Jonah was in the belly of the fish for three days and three nights" (Mt 12:40; Jon 1:17). This is one night more than the resurrection account calls for.

[2] Luke wants to leave the impression that the Jews, not the Romans, crucified Jesus. He has Cleopas or the other traveler say, "our chief priests and leaders handed him over to be condemned to death and crucified him" (Lk 24:20). The verb, *estaurōsan*, "they crucified" (third person plural, aorist active indicative) refers to the Jewish high priests and leaders, as if the Romans had nothing to do with the execution of Jesus.

[3] In the Preface for the Easter Vigil service, the deacon sings, "O necessary sin of Adam, . . . O happy fault, that merited such a redeemer." The "necessity" here and in Luke's Gospel (24:26) is pronounced in the spirit of joyous hyperbole. But there was a kind of literary necessity in Luke's mind, since Jesus died "that the [Hebrew Scriptures] might be fulfilled."

[4] The words of institution in Luke's Gospel are: "Then he took a loaf of bread, and when he had given thanks, he broke it and gave it to them (Lk 22:19).

[5] The word most often used for an appearance of Jesus is in the verbal form and it is passive. Thus, when Jesus appeared to Peter and James, Paul writes that he "was seen" (*ōphthē/ωφθη*) by them. This is usually translated actively as "appeared to." Paul himself speaks of visions (*optasiai*). But when he gets down to describe the nature of the revelations (*apokalupseis*) he was privileged to enjoy, he speaks of *hearing* words rather then seeing things. He was blinded during his conversion experience and *heard* things that are not to be told" (2 Cor 12:4). So, did Paul really see Jesus or did he not

hear only a voice? In other words, does "appearance" for Paul refer to seeing or only to hearing?

6 Eusebius, *The History of the Church* (New York: Dorset Press, 1984), 124, writes: "The other Mary" the wife of Clopas, would have been the sister-in-law of Jesus' mother. This is consistent with the contention that Clopas was Joseph's brother and an uncle of Jesus.

7 Joseph A. Fitzmyer, *The Gospel according to Luke* (Garden City, NY: Doubleday/ Anchor Bible, 1985), 2: 1563.

8 G.A. Williamson, the translator–editor of Eusebius' *History of the Church*, suggests in a footnote that the Clopas of John's Gospel (Jn 19:25) and the Cleopas of Luke's (Lk 24:18) are the same person. Cf. 123, note 5, and 142.

Epilogue

JESUS AFTER THE RESURRECTION

Luke's Gospel ends with the ascension of Jesus into heaven. It is typical of Luke that he uses concrete images to convey his message: "While [Jesus] was blessing [the apostles], he withdrew from them and was carried up to heaven" (Lk 24:51). The account of the ascension is even more graphic in Luke's Book of Acts. There it is says, "as they were watching, he was lifted up, and a cloud took him out of their sight." Then two men in white, presumed to be angels, say, "This Jesus, who has been taken up from you into heaven, will come in the same way as you saw him go into heaven" (Acts 1:11), that is, on a cloud.

Luke is the only evangelist who stagecrafts the ascension with concrete images. Matthew concludes his Gospel with some farewell remarks of Jesus, but there is no mention of an ascension. The apostles are authorized to make disciples of all nations, baptizing them in the name of the Holy Trinity, and they are assured that Jesus will be with them "always to the end of the age" (Mt 28:19–20). There is no account of an ascension in the main body of Mark's Gospel, although it is mentioned in the added summary (Mk 16:19–20), much of it borrowed from Luke. Finally, there is no actual ascension in the Fourth Gospel, although Jesus does mention it when he says to Mary Magdalene, "I have not yet ascended to the Father" (Jn 20:17).

The ascension is an important piece in the story of Jesus. Some forty days after the resurrection and the post-resurrection appearances, he is seen no more. What happened? Where did he go? Did he go into hiding, flee into Egypt, change his identity? Kersten and Gruber maintain that he survived the crucifixion, was found barely alive in the tomb on the third day, and was taken to recover among the Essenes.[1] What happened to Jesus after that they are unable to say, beyond the fact that he must eventually have died some time somewhere. After his death he was later seen by a few of his disciples in Galilee. What then?

Coming Again

As indicated earlier, Jesus frequently spoke of the Son of Man. Most often he was referring to himself, as when he says, "The Son of

275

Man has nowhere to lay his head," or "The Son of Man will be betrayed" (Mt 8:20, 17:22). At other times, he seems to be referring to someone else, or to himself as a transformed being. Thus, the evangelists will have him say, "Those who are ashamed of me and my words in this adulterous and sinful generation, of them the Son of Man will also be ashamed when he comes in the glory of his Father with the holy angels" (Mk 8:38). Or, again, "Then the sign of the Son of Man will appear in the heavens, and then all the nations of the earth will mourn, and they will see the Son of Man coming in the clouds of heaven with power and great glory" (Mt 24:30). The Son of Man coming in the clouds is based on Daniel 7:13. Luke anticipates it in his ascension account in Acts.

I am convinced that when Jesus speaks of himself as "Son of Man," he uses the term simply to mean "this person" or "this human being" and nothing more. It was a way of avoiding self-promoting language and not making politically dangerous claims. But in view of the apocalyptic atmosphere connected with the night visions of Daniel, Mark, followed by Matthew and Luke, could not resist the temptation to equate Jesus, as Son of Man, with a triumphalist interpretation of Daniel's vision. Hard upon the wartime suffering of "those days" (Mk 13:19), culminating in the fall of Jerusalem and the destruction of the Temple, it was clear to Mark that a new day was dawning and that Jesus would soon return in glory. The fall of Jerusalem was the cue for the coming of the Day of the Lord in fulfillment of the "prophecy" of Daniel.

The earlier tradition in which Paul had been instructed was acquainted with the idea that Jesus would soon come and gather to himself the living as well as those who had died in Christ. "For the Lord himself, with cry of command, with the archangel's call and with the sound of God's trumpet, will descend from heaven and the dead in Christ will rise first. Then we who are alive, who are left, will be caught up in the clouds together with them to meet the Lord in the air; and we will be with the Lord forever" (1 Thess 4:16–17).

This is not the "Son of Man" version of a second coming. Paul never refers to the night visions of Daniel, and the words, "the Son of Man" are not in his vocabulary. Interestingly, he seems not to have known about what would later be Mark's interpretation of the Son of Man passage in Daniel because it indicates that Paul was not acquainted with the coming of the Lord on a cloud in the company of his angels. The introduction of Daniel's vision as prophetic of a second coming of Jesus was a later invention of the Gospel writers, prompted by the fall of Jerusalem and the destruction of the Temple, a sure sign according to the calculations of the first three evangelists that the end time was imminent and that Jesus would soon return in power.

The Fourth Gospel portrays Jesus as speaking a dozen times of the Son of Man, thus supporting the view that Jesus used the words. However, except for a single instance when the phrase refers to the preexistence of the Son of Man (Jn 3:13), it always describes the earthbound Jesus in his mortal, pre-resurrection humanity. So we have three conflicting versions of what the coming of one like a Son of Man might mean. For John, the Son of Man means the historical Jesus. For the Synoptic evangelists, it refers to the Jesus of history and to the same as a celestial figure coming with the clouds and seated at the right hand of God. Paul, for his part, thinks that a rapture will soon take place when the dead will rise and the faithful followers of Jesus will be taken up to live with the Lord forever.

Although Paul thinks that Jesus will come and take to himself a select few, that is, those who have lived and died in Christ, the Synoptic evangelists dream of a public manifestation. During his post-resurrection phase, the risen Jesus appeared to only a few chosen disciples, but when he comes again in glory everyone will see him, even Caiaphas the High Priest and the members of his council. "But I tell you, From now on you [Caiaphas etc.] will see the Son of Man seated at the right hand of power and coming on the clouds of heaven" (Mt 26:64). Some thought he would appear only in Jerusalem; others thought that his coming would be a worldwide public appearance. It would take place everywhere simultaneously: "If they say to you, 'Look! He is in the inner room,' do not believe it. For as the lightning comes from the east and flashes as far as the west, so will be the coming of the Son of Man" (Mt 24:26–27). It is hard to determine just what Mark and the other evangelists had in mind if they were envisioning a worldwide second coming of Jesus as the Son of Man. For a modern televangelist, it might consist in a simultaneous, global appearance on television. Those who were not tuned in would have missed it and, possibly, be left behind.

Seriously, when Jesus speaks about coming again in John's Gospel, he seems to be referring to two, three, or even four kinds of coming, none of them involving public, celestial phenomena. The first has to do with the post-resurrection appearances. "So you have pain now," says Jesus at the Last Supper, "but *I will see you again*, and your hearts will rejoice" (Jn 16:22). And, indeed, when Jesus appears to his disciples at evening on Easter Sunday, they "rejoiced when they saw the Lord" (Jn 20:20). A second kind of coming in the Fourth Gospel refers to the interior indwelling of Jesus and his heavenly Father in the hearts of those who believe in them: "Those who love me will keep my word and my Father will love them, and *we will come to them* and make our home with them" (Jn 14:23).

The Fourth Gospel seems to go out of its way to avoid any reference to a Son of Man coming in, on, or with the clouds in a public display. Yes, Jesus, with the Father, and presumably the Holy Spirit, *will come* to those who love him and keep his commandments. But "the world" will have no share in it.

There is also a third kind of coming, which refers to the coming of the Holy Spirit at Pentecost. "When the Advocate *comes*, . . . he will testify on my behalf" (Jn 15:26, 16:7–8). Jesus says that if he goes away, he will send the Holy Spirit, the Spirit of Truth, who will teach them everything they need to know and bring back to memory all of the things he had taught them (Jn 14:26). Although the effects are public and visible, the Spirit of its very nature is invisible.

Finally, there is *the coming* of Jesus to greet his disciple at the moment of death. This could be the implication in the last chapter of the Fourth Gospel when Jesus, referring to the Beloved Disciple, speaks of the disciple's not dying "until I come." Because the Beloved Disciple was already dead when the Fourth Gospel was written, the implication is that Jesus had already *come* to him, a coming clearly distinct from any other kinds of coming (Jn 21:22–23).[2]

About Daniel's Vision

A careful reading of the passage in the Book of Daniel that concerns the coming of the Son of Man ("One Like a Human Being, or Son of Man") has persuaded some commentators that the early Christians, including the first three evangelists, misread the meaning of the text. N.T. Wright, speaking of the vision of one like a Son of Man coming with the clouds, has pointed out that "the coming" had nothing to do with a coming to the earth plane. Rather, it referred to the figure of one like a human being coming before God. "And *he came* [*ephthase*] to the Ancient One and was presented before him (Dan 7:13)."[3] So, all the fuss and fury about Jesus, as the Son of Man, returning to earth with the clouds of heaven in glory and power in a celestial second coming, appear to be based on a misreading of Daniel. There, the Son of Man was seen as coming not to earth but to the throne of the Ancient One. It would have made more sense to conceive of Jesus, if he was to be identified with the preexisting Son of Man, as coming back from earth to appear in a cloud of glory before the Ancient of Days. He would then sit at his right hand after his earthly work was done.

Who or What Is the Son of Man?

What kind of being is it that has the appearance of a Son of Man, that is, of a human being? In chapters eight, nine, and ten of the Book of Daniel, the apparitions in human form turn out to be angels, sometimes Gabriel and at other times Michael (cf. Dan 8:15–16, 9:21, 10:13, 21). I would agree with Alan F. Segal when he holds that one that looks like a human being (*kbar 'enash*) is exactly *not* a human being but an angel. And not exactly an angel, but an aspect of God, God appearing as an angel in human form and shaped like a man (*kdemuth bnei adam*).[4] God, manifesting as angel in human form, is a divine theophany, like the "men" who visited Abraham in the eighteenth chapter of Genesis. Those men were not simply angels in human form but God manifesting in anthropomorphic dress. In the Hebrew Scriptures the distinction between God and an angel, as an aspect of God, is often blurred.

Philo tackled this problem of the heavenly Son of Man by going back to the Wisdom Figure of Proverbs (8:22–23, 30). He introduces a kind of Demiurge, a second divine being (*deuteros theos*), who is God's Logos (*Questions and Answers on Genesis II, 62*).[5] This is not yet the Logos of John's Gospel, one later defined as equal to and consubstantial with the Father. Philo's Wisdom Figure is subordinate to the Supreme Being but partakes of some of his qualities, such as the divine *kavod*, or glory. The rabbis in the Merkabah tradition called the one like a human being *Metatron*, the highest angel, the one who stands behind, or perhaps even at the right hand, of the one who sits on the throne.

Man is made after the image and likeness of this *deuteros theos*, because the ultimate God, YHWH, cannot be adequately imaged by any creature, not even an angel.[6] This being that shares in the likeness of God and the likeness of Man, is a subordinate intermediary between God and humanity, God's vicegerent and principal agent in relation to creatures. For Philo, in any case, the "One Like a Son of Man" includes the perfection of Man as it existed in the mind of Divine Wisdom before creation and the fall. It is against this Proto-Man that all humankind will be measured and judged. When that day comes, the ideal Son of Man, very much like a living Platonic *Eidos,* or Form, will become the touchstone for determining the spiritual and moral worth of souls. Lower than the Godhead, and higher than individual human beings, Proverb's archetypal Wisdom shares divine and human characteristics

The Fourth Gospel sees Jesus as the embodiment of this preexisting *Eidos,* who was in the beginning, became incarnate, and now sits at the right hand of God in the likeness of a human being (Son of Man). John has Jesus speak of himself as "the one who descended from heaven" (Jn 3:13). It is he alone who ascends to heaven, and, according to some manuscripts is always in heaven. But this descent of a preexisting being refers not to a future coming to earth, but to the past, to an event that has already taken place. That same embodied entity returned to its Source and, like Metatron, occupies his post at the right hand of God.

The Author of the Letter to the Hebrews, however, rails against the idea that God's Son—"through whom he created all the worlds" and who "is the reflection of God's glory and the exact imprint of his very being"—could be merely an angel" (Heb 1:2–5). Would he adopt Philo's "*deuteros theos,*" with its implied subordinationism? That is not too clear in Hebrews. The Fourth Gospel, however, goes beyond Philo, subordination, and any form of angelism. This does not quite reflect the view of Mark, Matthew, and Luke who identify Jesus with the *future* coming of a heavenly "One Like a Human Being [Son of Man]." He will come at the end of the age to judge the world. But there is no talk of his preexistence, whether as Metatron or as a "Second God." Jesus' glory accrues to him *after* his earthly travails are complete, whereupon God "raised him up" and "made him both Lord and Messiah," so that he now sits at God's right hand (Acts 2:24, 36).

What has confused generations of New Testament readers and even the evangelists is that the historic Jesus chose to refer to himself not as Messiah or Son of David or King of the Jews, but simply as this human being, this Son of Man, a neutral word that was not supposed to be loaded with political overtones. In Ezekiel, "Son of Man" means an ordinary mortal being, born of woman. The evangelists were not satisfied with so humble a self-identification. So, having searched the

scriptures and intertestamental literature, they thought they had discovered how, by way of conflation, they could identify the human
Jesus, who as the Son of Man suffered and died, with a triumphant Son
of Man coming with the clouds of heaven. The Jesus who died in
apparent disgrace was raised to the right hand of God and would very
soon return in glory.

One can understand why the evangelists chose to identify Jesus
with the Cloud Man. But their identification of the two has led to the
kind of confusion that has given rise to the promise of a victorious and
awesome coming of Jesus in the clouds, and the whole doomsday scenario—something that the framers of the Fourth Gospel were careful
to avoid.

Where Is Jesus Now?

Jesus certainly is not in the Absolute Elsewhere. The divinity that
was in Jesus has not gone off to another distant world but still abides
as a real presence in the lives of those who seek the truth under one
particular religious banner or another or under none at all. Before he
died, Jesus promised that he would come again and that his disciples
would actually see him again. This visible presence ended some five
and a half weeks after the resurrection in the event called "The
Ascension." That disappearance was important for his followers, for
he had said, "It is to your advantage that I go away, for if I do not go
away, the Advocate [the Holy Spirit] will not come to you" (Jn 16:7).
His invisible presence in and through the Spirit would be far more
effective and widespread than Jesus' physical presence could ever be.
The Spirit of Jesus returned "with power" at Pentecost—in what was
the third of the four "comings" mentioned above—when the disciples
of Jesus were filled with the Holy Spirit and overcame the last vestige
of the fear that had immobilized them when he was arrested and crucified.

According to Matthew, Jesus told the high priests that they would
see "the Son of Man seated at the right hand of Power and coming on
the clouds of heaven" (Mt 26:64). Of course, no such event took place,
nor has anything like it happened in the approximately twenty centuries since Jesus' day. Toward the end of the Apostolic Age, when the
return of Jesus was felt to be long overdue, the author of the Second
Letter of Peter consoled those who had grown weary expecting the
return of Jesus in the sky. He wrote, "Do not ignore this one fact,

beloved, that with the Lord one day is like a thousand years, and a thousand years are like one day" (2 Pet 3:8). According to that divine timetable, we are at the beginning of the third day since the time of Christ.

Notes

[1] Holger Kersten and Elmar R. Gruber, *The Jesus Conspiracy: The Turin Shroud and the Truth about the Resurrection* (Rockport, MA: Element, 1994), 281.

[2] The Fourth Gospel was written after the death of the Beloved Disciple. In the final chapter, Jesus is speaking about the future. Members of the Johannine community had fully believed that the Beloved Disciple would still be alive when Jesus returned. However, he had died, and there was no return of the kind expected. But in another sense Jesus had returned to take the Disciple to himself. The words of Jesus at the Last Supper are especially applicable here: "And if I go and prepare a place for you, I will come again and take you to myself, that where I am you may be also" (Jn 14:3).

[3] "Farewell to the Raptures," by N.T. Wright in *Bible Review* (August 2001), 8.

[4] I follow Alan F. Segal here in *Paul the Convert: The Apostolate and Apostasy of Saul the Pharisee* (New Haven: Yale University Press, 1990), 53.

[5] See *The Works of Philo: Complete and Unabridged. New Update Version*, translated by C.D. Yonge (Peabody, MA: Hendrickson Publishers, 1993), 834.

[6] Segal, 45.

BIBLIOGRAPHY

Augustine. 1953. *The City of God.* Translated by Marcus Dods. New York: The Modern Library.

Barclay, William. 1956. *The Gospel of Matthew.* Vol. 1. Philadelphia: The Westminster Press.

Besant, Annie. 1977. *Esoteric Christianity.* Wheaton, IL: The Theosophical Publishing House. Original issue, 1901.

Borg, Marcus J. 1994. *Jesus in Contemporary Scholarship.* Valley Forge: Trinity Press International.

_____.1994. *Meeting Jesus Again for the First Time.* San Francisco: HarperSanFrancisco.

Bornkamm, Gunther. 1960. *Jesus of Nazareth.* New York: Harper & Row.

Braun, Mosche A. 1994. *The Jewish Holy Days and Their Spiritual Significance.* Northvale, NJ: Jason Aronson.

Bouquet, A. C. 1953. *Everyday Life in New Testament Times.* New York: Scribner.

Brown, Raymond E. 1966–1970. *The Gospel According to John.* 2 vols. Garden City, New York: Doubleday.

_____.1979. *The Community of the Beloved Disciple.* Mahwah, NJ: Paulist Press.

_____.1994. *An Introduction to New Testament Christology.* Mahwah, NJ: Paulist Press.

Bruteau, Beatrice. 1995. "The Feast of St. Andrew: A Hundred and Fifty-three Fish," *Living Prayer,* Nov.–Dec: 24–27.

_____, ed. 2001. *Jesus Through Jewish Eyes: Rabbis and Scholars Engage an Ancient Brother in a New Conversation.* Maryknoll, NY: Orbis Books.

Bultmann, Rudolf. 1962. *History of the Synoptic Tradition.* Translated by John Marsh. San Francisco: Harper & Row.

Buxbaum, Yitzhak. 1994. *The Life and Teachings of Hillel.* Northvale, NJ: Jason Aronson.

Campbell, Joseph. 1982. *The Masks of God: Creative Mythology.* New York: Arkana. Original 1968.

Carmichael, Joel. 1984. *The Death of Jesus.* New York: Barnes & Noble. Original, 1962.

Carroll, James. 2001. *Constantine's Sword: The Church and the Jews, A History.* Boston: Houghton Mifflin.

Carter, Warren. 2000. *Matthew and the Margins: A Sociopolitical and Religious Reading.* Maryknoll, NY: Orbis Books.

Charlesworth, James H. 1992. *The Dead Sea Scrolls: A Controversy Resolved.* New York: Doubleday.

Chilton, Bruce, and Jacob Neusner. 1995. *Judaism in the New Testament: Practices and Beliefs.* New York: Routledge.

Chilton, Bruce. 1996. *Pure Knowledge: Jesus' Vision of God.* Grand Rapids: MI: Eerdmans.

Cohen, A. 1965. *The Psalms, with Hebrew Text and English Translation.* London: Soncino Press, Ltd.

Coogan, Michael D. 1993. "Caiaphas." In *the Oxford Companion to the Bible.* New York: Oxford University Press.

Cornfeld, Gaalyah. 1982. *The Historical Jesus: A Scholarly View of the Man and His World.* New York: Macmillan.

Countryman, L. William. 1987. *The Mystical Way in the Fourth Gospel: Crossing Over into God.* Philadelphia: Fortress.

Crossan, John Dominic. 1991. *The Historical Jesus: The Life of a Mediterranean Jewish Peasant.* San Francisco: HarperSanFrancisco.

_____.1995. *Who Killed Jesus: Exposing the Roots of Anti-Semitism in the Gospel Story of the Death of Jesus.* San Francisco: HarperSanFrancisco.

_____.1998. *The Birth of Christianity: Discovering What Happened in the Years Immediately After the Execution of Jesus.* San Francisco: HarperSanFrancisco.

Davies, Stevan L. 1995. *Jesus the Healer.* New York: Crossroad.

Dodd, C. H. 1953. *The Interpretation of the Fourth Gospel.* Cambridge: Cambridge University Press.

Dodds, E. D. 1957. *The Greeks and the Irrational.* Boston: Beacon Press.

Dunn, James D. G. 1997. *Jesus and the Spirit.* Grand Rapids, Michigan: Eerdmans.

Ellsberg, Robert. 1997. *All Saints: Daily Reflections on Saints, Prophets, and Witnesses for Our Times.* New York: Crossroad.

Eusebius. 1984. *The History of the Church from Christ to Constantine.* Translated by G. A. Williamson. New York: Dorest Press.

Feldman, Louis H., and Gohei Hata, eds. 1987. *Josephus, Judaism, and Christianity.* Detroit: Wayne State University.

Fiorenza, Elizabeth Schüssler. 1993. *Discipleship of Equals.* New York: Crossroad.

Fitzmyer, Joseph A. 1981, 1985. *The Gospel according to Luke.* 2 vols. New York: Doubleday.

Flannery, Edward H. 1985. *The Anguish of the Jews.* Mahwah, NJ: Paulist Press.

Flusser, David. 1998. *Jesus, in Collaboration with R. Steven Notley,* 2nd, ed. Jerusalem: The Magnes Press.

_____.1985. *Judaism and the Origins of Christianity.* Jerusalem: The Magnes Press.

Ford, Robert. 1997. *The Parables of Jesus: Rediscovering the Art of Listening.* Minneapolis: Fortress.

Fredriksen, Paula. 2000. *Jesus of Nazareth: King of the Jews: A Jewish Life and the Emergence of Christianity.* New York: Alfred A. Knopf.

Funk, Robert W., and Roy W. Hoover. 1993. *The Five Gospels: The Search for the Authentic Words of Jesus*; *New Translation and Commentary.* New York: Macmillan.

Funk, Robert W. 1996. *Honest to Jesus.* San Francisco: HarperSanFrancisco.

———.1998. *The Acts of Jesus: What Did Jesus Really do? Translation and Commentary.* San Francisco: HarperSanFrancisco.

Grant, Michael. 1977. *An Historian's Review of the Gospels.* New York: Scribner.

Heller, John H. 1982. *Report on the Shroud.* Boston: Houghton Mifflin.

Hervé, J.- H. 1946. *Manuale Theologicae Dogmaticae.* Vol. 2. Westminster, MD: The Newman Bookshop.

Hoehmer, Howard W. 1993. "Herod's Dynasty." In *The Oxford Companion to the Bible.* New York: Oxford University Press.

Horsley, Richard A., with John S. Hanson. 1999. *Bandits, Prophets, and Messiahs.* Harrisburg: Trinity Press International. Original 1985.

Horsley, Richard A. 1993. *Jesus and the Spiral of Violence: Popular Jewish Resistance in Roman Palestine.* Minneapolis: Fortress Press.

Horsley, Richard A., and Neil Asher Silberman. 1997. *The Message and the Kingdom: How Jesus and Paul Ignited a Revolution and Transformed the Ancient World.* New York: Grosset/Putnam.

Ignatius of Antioch. 1985. "Ignatius to the Romans," *Apostolic Fathers.* Vol. 1. Translated by Kersopp Lake. Cambridge: Harvard University Press.

Isherwood, Christopher. 1962. *What is Religion? In the Words of Swami Vivekananda.* New York: Julian Press.

Josephus. 1995. *The Works of Josephus: Complete and Unabridged.* Translated by William Whiston. Peabody, MA: Hendrickson Publishers.

Jones, Jeremiah, and William Wake. 1979. *The Lost Books of the Bible.* Translated by Solomon J. Schepps. New York: Gramercy.

Kapleau, Philip. 1980. *The Three Pillars of Zen.* Garden City, NY: Doubleday.

Keller, Werner. 1981. *The Bible as History.* New York: William Morrow.

Kersten, Holger, and Elmar R. Gruber. 1994. *The Jesus Conspiracy: The Shroud of Turin and the Truth about the Resurrection.* Rockport, MA: Element Books.

Klopenborg, John S. K. 1987. *The Formation of Q.* Philadelphia: Fortress Press.

Klopenborg Verbin, John S. K. 2000. *Excavating Q.* Minneapolis: Fortress.

Lockhart, Douglas. 1997. *Jesus the Heretic: Freedom and Bondage in a Religious World.* Rockport, MA: Element Books.

Lohse, Eduard. 1976. *The New Testament Environments.* Translated by John E. Steely. Nashville: Abingdon.

Maccomby, Hyam. 1987. *The Myth-maker: Paul and the Invention of Christianity.* San Francisco: Harper & Row.

Mack, Burton L. 1993. *The Lost Gospel: The Book of Q and Christian Origins.* San Francisco: HarperSanFrancisco.

Macquarrie, John. 1963. *Twentieth Century Religious Thought: The Frontiers of Philosophy and Theology, 1900-1960.* New York: Harper & Row.

_____.1990. *Jesus Christ in Modern Thought.* Philadelphia: Trinity Press International.

Marion, Jim. 2000. *Putting on the Mind of Christ: The Inner Work of Christian Spirituality.* With a Foreword by Ken Wilbur. Charlottesville, VA: Hampton Roads Publishing.

Meier, John P. 1991-1994. *A Marginal Jew: Rethinking the Historical Jesus.* 2 vols. New York: The Anchor Bible Reference Library.

Mensi, Donald Weldon, and Zwe Padeh. 1999. *The Palace of Adam Kadmon.* Vol. 1 of *The Tree of Life: Chayyim Vital's Introduction to the Kabbalah of Isaac Luria.* Translated with an Introduction by Mansi and Padeh. Northvale, NJ: Jason Aronson.

Meyer, Marvin W., trans. 1984. *The Secret Teachings of Jesus: The Four Gnostic Gospels,* New York: Random House.

_____, trans. 1991. *The Gospel of Thomas: The Hidden Sayings of Jesus.* New York: Harper Collins.

Migliore, Daniel L. 1999. "Mary: A Reformed Perspective," *Theology Today* 56, (3), 346-358.

Moore, George Foot. 1966. *Judaism in the First Centuries of the Christian Era: The Age of the Tannaim.* 2 vols. Cambridge: Harvard University Press.

Oakman, Douglas E. 1986. *Jesus and the Economic Questions of His Day.* Vol. 8 of *Studies in the Bible and Early Christianity.* Lewiston, New York: The Edwin Mellen Press.

Nicholls, William. 1993. *Christian Antisemitism: A History of Hate.* Northvale, NJ: Jason Aronson.

Nolan, Albert. 1992. *Jesus Before Christianity.* Maryknoll, NY: Orbis Books.

Novum Testamentum Graece et Latine. 1994. Stuttgart: Deutsche Bibelgesellschaft.

Otto, Rudolf. 1958. *The Idea of the Holy.* New York: Oxford University Press.

Pelikan, Jaroslav. 1985. *Jesus Through the Centuries.* New Haven: Yale University Press.

Philo. 1993. *The Works of Philo: Complete and Unabridged: New Updated Edition.* Peabody: MA: Hendrickson Publishers.

Pines, Shlomo. 1971. *An Arabic Version of the Testimonium Flavianum.* Jerusalem: The Israel Academy of Sciences and Humanities.

Porter, J. R. 1999. *Jesus Christ: The Jesus of History, the Jesus of Faith.* New York: Oxford University Press.

Reddish, Mitchell G., ed. 1990. *Apocalypic Literature: A Reader.* Nashville: Abingdon Press.

Riley, Gregory J. 1997. *One Jesus, Many Christs: How Jesus Inspired Not One True Christianity But Many.* San Francisco: HarperSanFrancisco.

Robinson, John A. T. 1963. *Honest to God.* Philadelphia: The Westminster Press.

Rousseau, John J., and Rami Arav. 1995. *Jesus and His World: Archeological and Cultural Dictionary.* Minneapolis: Fortress.

Ryback, Timothy, W. 2000. "Hitler's Lost Family." *The New Yorker.* July 17.

Saddington, Denis Bain. 1993. "Centurion." In *The Oxford Companion to the Bible.* New York: Oxford University Press.

Sanders, E. P. 1993. *The Historical Figure of Jesus.* New York: Allen Lane/Penguin.

Schillebeeckx, Edward. 1981. *Jesus: An Experimental Christology.* New York: Crossroad.

Schonfield, High. 1984. *Essene Odyssey: The Mystery of the True Teacher and the Essene Impact on the Shape of Human destiny.* Rockport, MA: Element.

Segal, Alan F. 1986. *Rebecca's Children: Judaism and Christianity in the Roman World.* Cambridge: Harvard University Press.

_____.1990. *Paul the Convert: The Apostolate and the Apostasy of Saul the Pharisee.* New Haven: Yale University Press.

Shanks, Hershel. 1998. *The Mystery and Meaning of the Dead Sea Scrolls.* New York: Random House.

_____, ed. *Christianity and Rabbinic Judaism: A Parallel History of Their Origins and Early Development* .

Shorto, Russell. 1997. *Gospel Truth: The New Image of Jesus Emerging from Science and History, and Why It Matters.* New York: Riverhead Books.

Sloyan, Gerard S. 1995. *The Crucifixion of Jesus: History, Myth, Faith.* Minneapolis: Fortress.

Smith, Morton. 1978. *Jesus the Magician.* New York: Barnes & Noble.

Spong, John Shelby. 1996. *Liberating the Gospels: Reading the Bible with Jewish Eyes.* San Francisco: HarperSanFrancisco.

Steinsaltz, Adin. 1998. *Teshuveh: A Guide to the Newly Observant Jew.* Northvale, NJ: Jason Aronson.

Theissen, Gerd. 1991. *The Gospels in Context.* Minneapolis: Fortress.

Tillich, Paul. 1957. *Systematic Theology.* 2 vols. Chicago: University of Chicago Press.

Tribbe, Frank C. 1983. *Portrait of Jesus.* New York: Stein & Day.

_____. 2000. *I, Joseph of Arimathea: A Story of Jesus, His Resurrection, and the Aftermath: A Documented Historical Novel.* Nevada City, CA: Dolphin Publishing.

Vermes, Geza. 1981. *Jesus the Jew: A Historian's Reading of the Gospels.* Philadelphia: Fortress. First published in 1973.

_____. 1993. *The Religion of Jesus*. Minneapolis: Fortress.

Wilson, A. N. 1992. *Jesus: A Life*. New York: Fawcett Columbine.

Wilson, Ian. 1984. *Jesus: The Evidence*. San Francisco: Harper & Row.

_____. 1998. *The Blood and the Shroud*. New York: The Free Press.

Wink, Walter. 1984. *Naming the Powers: The Language of Power in the New Testament*. Philadelphia and Minneapolis: Fortress Press.

_____. 1986. *Unmasking the Powers: The Invisible Powers That Determine Human Existence*. Philadelphia and Minneapolis: Fortress Press.

_____. 1992. *Engaging the Powers: Discernment and Resistance in a World of Domination*. Philadelphia and Minneapolis: Fortress Press.

_____. 1998. *When the Powers Fall: Reconciliation in the Healing of Nations*. Philadelphia and Minneapolis: Fortress Press.

Winter, Paul. 1974. *On the Trial of Jesus*. 2nd. ed., ed. T.A. Burkill and Geza Vermes. Berlin and New York: Walter de Gruyter.

Wright, N. T. 1992. *The New Testament and the People of God*. Minneapolis: Fortress.

INDEX

Ancient Authors

Recent and Contemporary Authors